King Alfred's
Winchester

Martial Rose Library
Tel: 01962 827306

To be returned on or before the day marked above, subject to recall.

ROYAL HISTORICAL SOCIETY

STUDIES IN HISTORY

New Series

CONVERSATIONS IN COLD ROOMS

Woman at Black Gate, Castle Garth *c.* 1895

CONVERSATIONS IN COLD ROOMS

WOMEN, WORK AND POVERTY
IN NINETEENTH-CENTURY NORTHUMBERLAND

Jane Long

THE ROYAL HISTORICAL SOCIETY
THE BOYDELL PRESS

First published 1999

A Royal Historical Society publication
Published by The Boydell Press
an imprint of Boydell & Brewer Ltd
PO Box 9, Woodbridge, Suffolk IP12 3DF, UK
and of Boydell & Brewer Inc.
PO Box 41026, Rochester, NY 14604–4126, USA
website: http://www.boydell.co.uk

ISBN 0 86193 240 4

ISSN 0269-2244

A catalogue record for this book is available
from the British Library

Library of Congress Cataloging-in-Publication Data
Long, Jane, 1960–
    Conversations in cold rooms : women, work, and poverty in
nineteenth-century Northumberland / Jane Long.
        p.   cm. – (Royal Historical Society studies in history. New
series, ISSN 0269–2244)
    Includes bibliographical references and index.
    ISBN 0–86193–240–4 (hardcover : alk. paper)
    1. Poor women – England – Northumberland – History – 19th century.
2. Poor women – Employment – England – Northumberland – History –
19th century.   3. Poor women – Services for – England –
Northumberland – History – 19th century.   4. Charities – England –
Northumberland – History – 19th century.   I. Title.   II. Series.
HQ1599.E5L66   1999
305.48'96942'094288 – dc21   98–45076

This book is printed on acid-free paper

Printed in Great Britain by
St Edmundsbury Press, Bury St Edmunds, Suffolk

FOR VERITY

Contents

Illustrations

Frontispiece/Jacket illustration: Woman at Black Gate, Castle Garth *c.* 1895

Photographic Acknowledgements

Plates in this work are reproduced with the kind permission of the following individuals and organisations: plates 1, 3 and 6, Local History Division, Newcastle Central Library; plates 2, 5 and 7, the Gibson family, Northumberland; plate 8, Northumberland Record Office. Plate 4 and the frontispiece/jacket illustration are held by the author, but copies for further reference are also held at Tyne and Wear Archives Service. The dating of photographs from the Gibson collection is approximate, and here follow the dates suggested in R. Gard (ed.), *Northumberland memories*, Newcastle 1981.

Acknowledgments

Librarians and archivists in Western Australia, Newcastle and London, have been very helpful in the preparation of this work. In particular, I have appreciated the assistance of staff at the Public Record Office, Newcastle Central Library's Local History division, Tyne and Wear Archive Service, the Northumberland Record Office, the Wren Library at Trinity College, Cambridge, and the Salvation Army Heritage Centre Archives.

I am grateful for financial support from a number of sources, which allowed me to conduct archival research in England. These funds included an Australian Postgraduate Research Award, a travel grant from the History Department at the University of Western Australia, and awards from the Australian Federation of University Women (WA) and the Grace Vaughan Memorial Award Committee. While overseas, the hospitality of friends made that research a more manageable and enjoyable task. In particular I thank Bill Long for his continuing kindness and friendship.

This work is based upon my doctoral thesis which was undertaken in the Department of History at the University of Western Australia, and my most sincere thanks are due to the supervisors of that work, Iain Brash and Patricia Crawford. They have provided so many different forms of sustained intellectual support, guidance and friendship over an extended period that it is difficult to acknowledge them at all adequately. I am grateful for their abiding interest in my work both during and since that time. I would also thank the three examiners of that thesis for their generosity and encouragement. Friends and colleagues in Women's Studies and History at UWA – in particular, Patricia Crawford, Delys Bird and Philippa Maddern – have done much to create and maintain a viable institutional space in which feminist scholarship and attention to its continuing challenges may occur. That history has helped to make this history possible. More recently, I have appreciated the advice and interest of David Eastwood, Christine Linehan and the Royal Historical Society's Editorial Board, as this work emerged in its current form.

The consistent help and encouragement of my parents Liz and Ray and my family, has always been so generously given. In particular, my partner Matthew Allen has given me unparalleled professional and personal support. His intellectual engagement as well as his unflagging humour and optimism are things I cherish. Finally, my daughter was born at the time I was beginning this research. Whatever academic business is at hand she knows little yet of history – but she makes every day, in so many ways, a special kind of delight. This book is dedicated to my daughter Verity, with all my love.

Jane Long
April 1998

Abbreviations

BL	British Library
DU Archives	Durham University Archives
GLRO	Greater London Record Office
NCL	Newcastle Central Library, Local History Collection
NRO	Northumberland County Record Office
NU Archives	Newcastle University Archives
PRO	Public Record Office, Kew
PRO, Chancery	Public Record Office, Chancery Lane
RU Archives	Reading University Archives
SAA	Salvation Army Archives
TWAS	Tyne and Wear Archives Service

Introduction:
Conversations in Cold Rooms

'[T]here is a chill air surrounding those who are down in the world and people are glad to get away from them, as from a cold room: human beings, mere men and women, without furniture, without anything to offer you, have ceased to count as anybody, offer an embarrassing negation of reasons for wishing to see them, or of subjects on which to converse with them.'

George Eliot, *The Mill on the Floss*, 1860.

The comprehension of poverty in Victorian England was mediated by the creation of distance and of difference between those who experienced it and those who did not. Eliot's observations relate to the Tulliver family, an appreciation of whose circumstances by their neighbours was rendered painful for two reasons: first, it entailed a confrontation with their individual misfortune; second, the Tullivers' situation represented the more fearful possibility of downward mobility in economic and social terms for working people in general.

The phenomenon of recent and rapid impoverishment among those designated 'respectable' and 'independent' during the period, due to economic downturn or unforeseen personal crises, generated ideas whose specific meaning in relation to the wider subject of poverty in Victorian society is complex. The personal history of the Tullivers can be read specifically as one of the many contemporary literary representations of economic and social insecurity, and the potential dislocation which 'new' poverty could bring in its wake. This particular passage of Eliot's, however, can also be read in another way, as a comment upon one kind of response to deprivation in that society's midst. Introducing this dimension, the passage brings into focus an element with relevance, not simply to the specific case of the Tullivers, but, indeed, to the whole shape of the wider discourse on Victorian poverty.

The creation of difference and distance not only characterised discussions of poverty, however. Certainly, it is unquestionable that the Victorians perceived poverty as one of the central problems of the age. The dimensions, sources and perceived dangers of existing inequalities preoccupied a bewildering array of parliamentarians, social commentators, thinkers both radical and conservative, lay and clerical philanthropists, statisticians, literary women and men, local administrators, and an increasingly professionalised body of charity and 'welfare' workers. The sheer diversity of literature about the poor in the nineteenth century makes that literature impossible to characterise simply. Discussion of poverty did not occur in isolation: a focus upon the subject was intertwined with a considerable array of other concerns, as

1

Victorians attempted to make sense of the shape of their society and the course which they charted for its future. The nature of the working class, and the shape of the family and 'femininity', also figured prominently in discussions of social and moral reform. Yet, as was the case with poverty, discussions of the working class, and the nature of 'woman' both within and outside it were diverse in their nature. As Linda Shires has pointed out, perhaps one of the characteristics of 'Victorianism' was in fact the 'radical instability' of representation and ideology about all manner of social, economic and moral subjects.[1] Yet whatever the lines of dissent or agreement about the poor, and about working-class femininity, whether these subjects stimulated pity, revulsion, fear or sympathy, they were all usually dealt with by writers and observers at some distance, and with some ambivalence.

In some literature created by bourgeois observers, the very language used to describe poorer people and their relationship to the rest of society helped to foster and maintain such distance. While some historical research has emphasised the fluidity of the group designated as 'poor' in the nineteenth century, and the substantial proportion of working-class people who experienced poverty during their lifetimes, the image of the poor presented in contemporary social literature frequently implied a distinction between 'the poor' and the 'respectable' working class, as though considering two groups which were essentially separated, by habit and disposition as much as, if not more than, by income.[2] Sometimes seen as blending and overlapping with the 'respectable' working class at its shallowest point, the realm of the poorer working-class was portrayed as becoming gradually darker and more alien as poverty deepened, until it reached that level of destitution which was thought to be marked by a complete fracture from the social fabric. Here, in its extreme portrayal, the group was utterly separate: it was thought of as a different 'class of persons', argued Louisa Twining, adding that once utterly destitute and ensconced in the 'chilliest' of all rooms in the Victorian imagination, the workhouse, it was 'certainly "out of sight", and therefore "out of mind" '.[3] But never completely so.

Distance – social or geographical, real and imagined – and constructions of difference contributed to the marginalisation of poorer people in Victorian society. While the function and contour of such constructions varied, in broad terms difference and distance were mutually reinforcing notions: as the physical separation of the poor was further entrenched through urbanisation, the 'slum' areas of great cities demarcated with railway expansion and industrial agglomeration and defined through middle-class investigation, so

[1] Linda Shires, 'Afterword: ideology and the subject as agent', in Linda Shires (ed.), Rewriting the Victorians: theory, history and the politics of gender, London–New York 1992, 184–90 at p. 185.
[2] See, for example, Michael Rose, The relief of poverty, 1834–1914, 2nd edn, Basingstoke 1986, 16–17.
[3] Louisa Twining, Recollections of workhouse visiting and management during twenty-five years, London 1880, p. ix.

the idea of the poor as a 'race apart' was more easily sustained. In turn, a sense of moral, cultural and even biological difference served to justify the maintenance of distance, and perhaps heightened the ambivalence of those who were not poor.

While the 'problems' of the period – such as poverty and women's labour – may have seemed to cry out for 'solution', on what terms were solutions to be forged, and upon what understandings were they to be based? How could the poorer section of society be 'raised', taken out of 'cold rooms' where poverty and the tasks of 'making ends meet' confronted people on a day-to-day basis, and brought instead into the warmer, lighter, bustling world of Victorian productivity and 'progress'? Reformers may have recommended various solutions in the long-term; in the meantime, the 'problems' continued to exist and had to be conceptualised and accommodated somehow, however uncomfortably, in Victorian bourgeois consciousness.

Poorer people themselves were rarely heard in 'conversations' about their circumstances, and this silence finds its reflection in historical literature. Certainly, a growing number of social investigations by contemporaries such as Henry Mayhew, or later, Mary Higgs brought the life style of the poor sections of the working class into focus;[4] but generally, to linger too long in the shadows, to give a voice to those who had 'ceased to count' in any estimation of progress, detracted from the major task of transformation which was required. The silence imposed upon such people in much of the literature, moreover, was of a particular order. It was a silence predicated on the assumption made by observers that their situation, their daily lives, their views and their concerns, were self-evident. Contemporaries believed that these people either wished that they were better off, or were simply so ignorant that they were incapable of conceptualising a 'future' and their position within it. Georges Duby reminds us of the grave mistake of 'interpreting silence as absence' in historical discourse: attention must be given to such omissions, and 'their meaning must be analysed'.[5] As in other areas of contemporary discourse, the silence of women during the period was particularly marked, and historical interpretations of women's poverty and work have, indeed, at times exhibited the error against which Duby warns.

Robert Darnton has argued that for historians as well as anthropologists, useful 'points of entry' into a culture may be 'those where it seems to be most opaque':[6] the point is valid and useful, but the converse may also be argued. Those areas of the past, such as work and poverty, around which historical orthodoxies have grown and where the inter-relationships between these and other areas appear reasonably clear to contemporaries and later writers may

---

[4] M. Higgs, *How to deal with the unemployed*, London 1904, and *Glimpses into the abyss*, London 1906.

[5] Georges Duby, 'Ideologies in social history', in J. Le Goff and P. Nora (eds), *Constructing the past*, Cambridge 1985, 151–65 at p. 157.

[6] Robert Darnton, *The great cat massacre and other episodes in French cultural history*, London 1984, 78.

benefit from 're-entry'. To what extent does any apparent 'clarity' mask tensions and contradictions between discourses about women's work, and women's poverty? How have historians themselves served to further distance women from the realm of historical enquiry, and contribute to their discursively-constructed silence? While the emphasis upon progress, solutions to poverty and the 'problem' of female labour found in some Victorian literature has influenced historical conceptions of the subject, and has served at times to turn the focus away from working-class people as they lived and understood their lives, women have received less attention than other groups. Certainly, this lack of attention relates in part to the factors already outlined, which operated to silence voices from within the working class. Beyond this, however, the weight of assumptions held about the women of the labouring poor was made heavier and considerably more complex as specific meanings and characterisations were constructed around their gender.

To be a woman; to be a working woman; to be a poor woman: each of these categories carried particular, sometimes separate meanings in Victorian England. Views about poverty and work informed social and economic literature of the period, and the Victorians' vision of the future. Similarly, conceptions of 'woman' shifted across time and space. Discourses about working women and poor women, the comprehension of their daily life and prescriptions for 'improvement' within them, were not the result of any simple fusion of these varying discursive strands. Any focus upon women as workers and women as poor people entailed some reworking of general assumptions about labour and poverty, and, indeed, of generalised assumptions about the nature of femininity, to accommodate a more class-specific female identity. Butler maintains that gender 'is in no way a stable identity or locus of agency . . . it is . . . tenuously constituted in time':[7] just as prevailing views of women altered during the period, along with conceptions of progress, work and poverty, so too were the meanings attaching to poor women and working women subject to change.

The historical literature on working-class and poor women in Victorian society was for decades quite sparse. A number of historians in recent works have examined the processes by which women have been excluded from mainstream historical discourse, exclusion resulting both from deficiencies in the contemporary record, and the historians' approach to it. Working-class women, of course, bore a double burden of silence in their own society, and absence from the subsequent interpretation of it, as a result of both their gender and their class position. Surveying that historical record, the rooms of working women and poor women in nineteenth-century Northumberland seem cold indeed, rarely visited, distant, and quiet. My aim in this book is in part to 're-enter' those rooms, to consider the ways in which both the

7 Judith Butler, 'Performative acts and gender constitution: an essay in phenomenology and feminist theory', *Theatre Journal* xl (1988), 519–31 at p. 519.

Victorians and the historians have interpreted what was found there, and the scope of their 'conversations' about (but only rarely with), the women who lived and worked in them. The work is also concerned, however, with attempting to create new entrances, to better understand the meaning of poverty and work as it related to constructions of working-class femininity during the period.

I advance two main arguments. First, I argue that the dimensions of working-class women's lives in the Victorian north-east were materially and discursively linked. It is only by considering the two areas in conjunction that an appreciation of the ways in which women's dependence was constructed and maintained in those specific historical and regional conditions may be gained. Indeed, in broader methodological and theoretical terms, I argue that any tidy distinction between, or privileging of, the material or cultural aspects of women's experiences and constructions of femininity is to neglect the crucial and consistent inter-relationship between the two, and perpetuates a dualism which serves to erase the complexities of the Victorians' own gendered views and experiences of their society. Second, I argue that the categories of work and poverty in turn provide critical entry points for an examination of the construction of feminine working-class 'identities' during the period. The terms in which those identities were cast and experienced underwent shifts, and the book examines both middle-class discourses about the identity of poor and working women, as well as women's negotiations of prescriptions of 'feminine' identity.

I explore these themes in the specific regional context of nineteenth-century Newcastle upon Tyne and the surrounding rural areas of Northumberland. The focus upon one particular area was determined by a number of factors. First, many general assumptions and statements can be made concerning such subjects as bourgeois constructions of femininity, or the formulation of policies about work or poverty: in a narrower frame, the workings of these discourses in daily life can be more clearly traced. Further, it is within such a context that women's strategies and experiences which fell outside the orbit of direct dealing with bureaucrats, employers and a range of observers and 'experts' can best be traced. It is also important that at times the regional basis provides a useful context in which to consider the impact of other discourses which at times overlapped with those constructing gendered identities. How, for example, were discourses about women, and more particularly working-class women, positioned in relation to discourses about regional and national identity?

The choice of the region was made in part because of its diverse economy; a thriving port centre with a variety of industries operating close to the city itself, which acted as a magnet for migrant labourers, and which displayed many of the features and pressures associated with urban population growth in the industrial period, and a rural hinterland whose agricultural sector witnessed changes in its labour structure across the century. Further, while research to date concerned with women in particular has for some areas been sparse there has none the less been a good deal of work done about Newcastle and the poor law in the region which provides some historiographical back-drop for the current research.[8] In the contemporary literature about the region, there is little substantial, direct evidence from women themselves. None the less, given the proliferation of record-keeping charities in nineteenth-century Newcastle, a considerable amount of parliamentary and individual investigation, numerous regional newspapers and other sources, as well as evidence from the local guardians of the poor which may be critically analysed, a detailed focus upon the area allows a greater consideration of women's work and poverty in daily life across a longer period of change which a wider geographical focus would not achieve.

A regional evidential base is often perceived as carrying inevitable short-comings; but here I am not primarily concerned to gauge whether the Newcastle area was 'typical' of England as a whole, nor is the work situated primarily in the genre of local history. Certainly, the regional focus at times illustrates broader patterns, and at others exhibits regional differences, so that while some generalisations based upon Novocastrian experience may be drawn, in other respects the conclusions reached are necessarily specific. Patterns of female employment, labour structures, the demographic profile of the region, and local poor relief history displayed a particularity which, in a period of considerable social and economic variation, set it apart from other regions. These findings may suggest lines of inquiry for other regions, and an assessment of the interplay between work, poor law policy and practice, and women's strategies and life experiences elsewhere may well yield different results. While my research at times draws upon a local historiography, my aims here are situated within a different set of theoretical parameters. My work may illuminate certain largely unexplored areas of life for, and discourse about, women in the region which may contribute something to the local history of Northumberland, but I have been chiefly interested and motivated in my research to examine the ways in which 'feminine' identities have been constructed and interpreted in history. The north-east provides one rich site in which to explore the issue.

In the first chapter, I examine in greater detail some of the historiographical and theoretical issues which relate to the subject. In chapter 2, my focus shifts to examine the conditions and interpretation of life and work for women in nineteenth-century Newcastle, and in turn in chapter 3 I use the particular case study of women workers in the lead industry to consider the operation of discourses about women, and their impact upon women's material circumstances. Chapter 4 travels to the country, and it is here that

---

8 See, for example, Norman McCord, *North east England: an economic and social history*, London 1979, and Keith Gregson, 'Poor law and organized charity: the relief of exceptional distress in north-east England, 1870–1910', in Michael Rose (ed.), *The poor and the city: the English poor law in its urban context, 1834–1914*, New York 1985, 93–131 at p. 127.

I consider the ways in which some of the patterns and identifications of femininity with 'disorder' and women's work as an antithesis of 'progress' were played out. In this shift between Newcastle and its rural hinterland, I explore some of the links between the two areas suggested by gender analysis, which may be overlooked if operating within conventional divides between town and country. In the last two chapters of the book, I explore the connections between female work and poverty, the ways in which a poverty of dependence was constructed and experienced through formulations of poor law policy and within the regimes established by charitable organisations in the region. Finally, I consider women's negotiations of gendered identity within working-class culture itself.

While the women I discuss are for the most part working-class and poor, and their class position constantly intersected with both material and cultural elaborations of their gender, less attention is given here to the complex contemporary and historical debates about processes of class formation and their political manifestations. Similarly, factors of ethnicity came into play in a region where Irish and Scots women and men in particular travelled and worked in both the urban and rural contexts, but while some broad investigation of the connections between 'foreignness', national and regional identity, and discourses about femininity are made, these are not explored in consistent detail. The treatment of work and poverty here is selective within the region; and the complex processes contributing to the formations of masculinity do not provide a focus. Joan Scott once wrote of labour historians' acknowledgment of the significance of women as an historical subject in their works, only to move rapidly to explain their non-inclusion, due to reasons of time and space.[9] I may cite the same *technical* reason for the exclusion of masculinity, but I do not operate with a simplified view of masculinity in history. Certainly, the meanings of 'masculinity' here and in general during the period are subjects which, like 'femininity', I see as shifting, complicated and problematic: the necessary exclusion of more detailed treatment of masculinity within the work is certainly not designed to naturalise Victorian Man.

Overall then, the study seeks to illuminate the construction and contestations of feminine working-class identities in the north-east, through the subjects of poverty and work: it is concerned with the way in which discourses on work and poverty intertwined, and the way women became poor and often remained so. It is also fundamentally concerned with illustrating the importance of gender in historical analysis, and specifically with its comprehension within Victorian society. In the process, the comparative neglect of working-class women in north-eastern historical literature may be partly redressed. George Eliot's contentions may have rung true for her contemporaries, the rooms of the poorer sections of society appearing distant

---

[9] Joan Scott, 'On language, gender and working-class history', *International Labor and Working-Class History* xxxi (1987), 1–13 at p. 2.

and uninviting, the people themselves offering that 'embarrassing negation of reasons' for talking with them or contemplating their situation. For historians, however, as well as for those concerned with constructions of gendered identity in contemporary societies, a larger problem remains. Upon what terms may we approach those 'cold' rooms, what 'conversational' parameters can historians construct which better elucidate the experiences and strategies of women in the past, and the shifting discourses of femininity within which these experiences were interpreted?

1

Constructing Femininity: Women, Work and Poverty

From the 1860s in Britain, there appeared a flurry of specific reporting about poverty and the conditions of the poor. Prominent within this literature were the investigative exposés of reformers such as Mary Higgs and Dr J. H. Stallard. They employed the use of disguises to gather 'first-hand' experience of the life of poor people, as they tramped through the country in search of work, or sought assistance from local authorities.[1] Stallard's approach was particularly interesting: he employed a woman he called 'Ellen Stanley', 'a pauper widow, who, having received some slight assistance in a period of great distress', volunteered gratefully to visit workhouses for Stallard 'for the express purpose of describing them'. Later in the book, he recounts Ellen's own description of her admission to Newington workhouse:

> [The workhouse inspector] scrutinized me very fiercely, and wanted to know why I came there. . . . Whilst this was going on, several men of the [police] force stood by, and one in particular stared very closely at me, and they laughed and jeered at me as if it was fine fun; one was different, and seemed to pity me. . . . I waited ten minutes [at the workhouse door] and a lot of people came out of the neighbouring cottages to stare at me, which they did until the porter let me in.[2]

This example of nineteenth-century imposture in the cause of capturing 'authentic' experience is more grimly ironic than most. Ellen's own circumstances saw her 'performing' a role which in many ways may have been close to her own already, starring in some strange Victorian semi-autobiographical melodrama. Ellen's observations about this experience were preserved in some manner through Stallard, while the reader learns nothing about her 'real' experiences as a pauper widow and is left to wonder how far the role she played for Stallard accorded with her broader situation and impressions of life. But when the workhouse inspector, the police and the neighbours stared at Ellen, what did they see? What did they expect to see? What did being a woman, a working woman, a poor woman, mean in Victorian society? How did such meanings interact with the gender-based and class-based conceptions of identity, progress and social order? And what did it mean to women

---

[1] Rachel Vorspan, 'Vagrancy and the new poor law in late-Victorian and Edwardian England', *English Historical Review* xcii (1977), 59–81 at pp. 66–8.
[2] J. H. Stallard, *The female casual and her lodging*, London 1866, 4, 7–8.

themselves as they negotiated the terms of their economic and social existence?

This first chapter considers some of the historiographical and theoretical issues which inform my overall approach. The chapter is not an exhaustive historiographical study. Rather, my purpose is to explore the potential of some scholarly discourses (and the limitations of others) in producing better understandings of gendered identities in nineteenth-century Britain.

Women, poverty and work in Victorian society

The Royal Commission for Inquiry into the Poor Laws was established in February 1832. Its report was presented in June 1834 and the commission's recommendations, with some important amendments, passed into law two months later.[3] There was perhaps a certain weariness over the poor laws even before the report had been presented. As A. W. Coats notes, a *Westminster Review* writer some decades later reflected on the terrain of debate about poverty since 1834, and remarked that the issue appeared to have been 'worn threadbare. It has been treated so often, by so many able men, and in such a variety of aspects, as to leave little more to be said.'[4] However, many who participated in debates on poverty and the poor laws both before and after 1834 clearly did not share this writer's assumption. The debates on poverty and relief in turn receded and gained renewed prominence in the political and economic life of nineteenth- and twentieth-century Britain, with the 1834 Poor Law Amendment Act usually cited as a benchmark. But while the terms of the debates and the definitions of poverty themselves shifted over time, the issue never disappeared entirely. In parallel with this focus, both the 1834 act and related policy discussions of poverty have 'come to assume a dominant role in British historiography'.[5] David Thomson describes this historiography as a captive of 'the rise of the Welfare State', since many historians have employed chronologies and definitions which naturalised poverty as a standard theme within a 'familiar narrative of progress and achievement'.[6] Poor people were written about merely as the reactive objects of scrutiny from above, their inclusion determined purely by the conjunction of their experience with administrative and policy evolution, and their poverty reduced thereby to a fixed, 'snapshot' image rather than as a more fluid state whose meanings intersected with a broad range of analytic

---

3 S. G. Checkland and E. O. A. Checkland (eds), *The poor law report of 1834*, Harmondsworth 1974, 29–30.

4 'The philanthropy of the age and its social evils', *Westminster Review* xxv (1869), cited in A. W. Coats (ed.), *Poverty in the Victorian age: debates on the issue from nineteenth-century critical journals*, II: *The English poor laws, 1834–1870*, Westmead 1973, p. ii.

5 John Knott, *Popular opposition to the poor law*, London 1986, preface.

6 D. Thomson, 'Welfare in the past: a family or community responsibility?', unpubl. paper, 5th AMBHA Conference, Nov. 1987, 1.

variables. Further, whether proceeding from the traditions of liberal historiography, or socialist critiques of the dominant Whiggish orthodoxy, analyses of poverty which naturalised and centralised the poverty of adult males within historical discussion militated against consideration of different gendered experience.

Joan Scott wrote in 1987 that 'if women have increased in visibility, the questions raised by women's history remain awkwardly connected to the central concerns of the field'.[7] The claim is relevant to the historiography of poverty up to the 1980s. Indeed, surveying that literature to assess the degree to which gender was considered can be a brief and unrewarding experience. With some notable exceptions,[8] the relationship between gender and poverty and the structures of gender through which poverty was experienced in Victorian England were ignored or treated incidentally. Where women figured, it was usually in a descriptive context: gender distinctions made in legislation and social commentaries were sometimes noted, but the frameworks which most historians used did not accommodate or even suggest the step of engaging in further analysis of the gendered discourses of the Victorians. Such absences in individual historical studies provide some insight into the ways in which the historiography of poverty has replicated the omissions and assumptions of the past discourses. Michael Rose made this sort of uncritical replication when he referred to the 'wives and children of the poor'.[9] Perhaps this move seemed unproblematic to him, but as Gerda Lerner states, 'the terms we use define the questions we can ask of historical material'.[10] When the working class and the poor were defined as male, or were portrayed as functioning within a predominantly masculine labour market and living within the setting of the 'private' patriarchal family, women's

7 Scott, 'On language, gender and working-class history', 1.
8 Those exceptions include Ursula Henriques, 'Bastardy and the new poor law', *Past and Present* xxxvii (1967), 103–29, and P. Thane, 'Women and the poor law in Victorian and Edwardian England', *History Workshop* vi (1978), 29–51. On poverty see Laura Oren, 'The welfare of women in laboring families: England, 1860–1950', in M. Hartmann and L. W. Banner (eds), *Clio's consciousness raised*, New York 1974, 226–44, and Elizabeth Roberts, *A woman's place: an oral history of working-class women, 1890–1940*, Oxford 1986. The important contributions of Ellen Ross are discussed below.
9 Rose, *Relief of poverty*, 48. Historians working within alternative paradigms of course challenged the mainstream interpretations of poverty and poor law formulation in important ways, most notably through works such as Gareth Stedman Jones's *Outcast London*, Oxford 1971, which attempted to restore agency, drawing intellectually upon the traditions and foci established by the Hammonds, Hobsbawm, Hoskins and E. P. Thompson. While Stedman Jones's early work includes women as workers, it is primarily in the context of a family economy where they are defined according to their relationship to the male 'breadwinner': ibid. pt i and chs xv–xvi.
10 E. DuBois and others, 'Politics and culture in women's history: a symposium', *Feminist Studies* vi (1980), 26–64 (Gerda Lerner at p. 49).

presence was obscured and their experiences of poverty remained at best a subject of 'only tangential concern'.[11]

The historiographical impetus to redress these omissions and to analyse critically the terrain of poverty for women derived from a conglomeration of factors both within academic scholarship and beyond. As discussed below, there were crucial developments within feminist theory. Moreover, the 'soft-focus nostalgia'[12] and golden-age myth-making about 'Victorian values', which were exploited aggressively by conservatives in Britain in the 1980s, fuelled concern about the limitations of existing histories of poverty with their persistent exclusion of women, at a time when poverty itself, according to some theorists, was becoming increasingly 'feminised'.[13] As well as highlighting gender differences in the treatment and experiences of the poor, feminisation theorists reiterated a theme which had already developed in some historical literature: that it was a fallacy to assume that 'poverty' was spread evenly and experienced equally by all members of a family.[14] However, while such work had specific political utility and, very importantly, highlighted gender as a variable in analysis of the experiences and meanings of poverty, its elaboration was at times problematic.[15] Advocates of this approach described in detail the particular contours of poverty experienced by women and the economic and political structures which compounded their poverty of dependence. However, in broad terms, the vocabulary of 'feminisation' itself suggested that poverty was a discrete entity, a 'transferable burden' of which women were bearing proportionately more. Yet in the nineteenth century, women already constituted the 'majority of adult recipients of Poor Law relief'.[16] In the previous century as well, 'conditions [of poverty] bore more heavily upon women than upon men'.[17]

Historians and social scientists have argued at great length about ways to measure poverty, and how it may be conceptualised.[18] In doing so at times they replayed old debates, for, in Victorian England, there was no shortage of

---

[11] J. Lewis and D. Piachaud, 'Women and poverty in the twentieth century', in C. Glendinning and J. Millar (eds), *Women and poverty in Britain*, Brighton 1987, 28–52 at p. 51.

[12] Raphael Samuel, 'Soft-focus nostalgia', *New Statesman*, 27 May 1983, special supplement, p. ii.

[13] See Hilda Scott, *Working your way to the bottom: the feminization of poverty*, London 1984.

[14] Oren, 'Welfare of women', 240.

[15] Stated generally, the thesis argued that a trend was being revealed in which both the proportion of women experiencing poverty was increasing, and the risk of women becoming and remaining poor in future was rising in association. Bettina Cass cautioned, however, that feminisation should not be seen as a recent phenomenon, but as 'a *recently recognised* phenomenon': 'The changing face of poverty in Australia, 1972–1982', *Australian Feminist Studies* i (1985), 67–89.

[16] Thane, 'Women and the poor law', 29.

[17] Bridget Hill, *Eighteenth-century women: an anthology*, 2nd edn, London 1987, 156.

[18] The most notable debates in the twentieth century have been around the work of Peter Townsend and the concept of 'relative deprivation': 'Measuring poverty', *British Journal of Sociology* v (1954), 130–7, and *Poverty in the United Kingdom*, Harmondsworth 1979.

'able men' who attempted to determine appropriate indices of want,[19] or who developed social and moral arguments to aid in a more accurate differentiation of the 'deserving' and 'undeserving' poor. At base, poverty may be conceived in terms of economic/bodily need. Victorians sought to narrow and contain their measurements of poverty in various ways, yet for the historian more fruitful work can be done in expanding the definitions. Poverty was need, but as the Victorians themselves at times recognised, it was also much more. As a state of existence, the impact and meanings of 'being poor' were constantly filtered through the spectra of gender, age, ethnicity, class and regional representations and conditions. In turn, the development of 'appropriate' categorisations of the poor in society and the way that poverty was viewed and understood by the non-poor always took place within a broader grid of cultural and economic references. That grid itself was subject to change over time and in accord with the position of the observer. To define poverty as a fixed category of existence which men, women and children variously slipped into and out of neglects these critical interactive discursive dimensions and renders invisible the negotiations of gendered identities involved in 'being poor'. The argument here is that conceptions and experiences of poverty in the Victorian period were so intertwined with gender and class identity, gendered life cycles, and a constellation of (insistently gendered) discourses on the meanings of Victorian progress and social order, that poverty was much more than a transferable burden of quantifiable economic need.

There are two necessary consequences arising from this position. First, we must consider how the experience and treatment of that female majority of the poor was culturally constructed so as to enable its occlusion, to allow it to fade off the edges of the pages of parliamentary reports and certain other types of contemporary sources. Second, if women's poverty was usually marginalised, we must closely scrutinise those frames in which it *did* appear. How was being poor understood by women themselves? What alternative discourses were mobilised around poor women to explicate their position, and with what purposes and effects? How did the codes and meanings constructed around poor women and by poor women themselves intersect with broader codes and meanings of femininity and class in that society? Consideration of these questions is important, if we are to move beyond replicating contemporary discourse.

Women's marginalisation in the poor law debates and in economic commentaries was not simply due to a dogged refusal of contemporary observers to see poor women before their very eyes: Robert Pashley, for example, referred to the preponderance of women who were adult paupers as a standard 'law of pauperism' which could be seen not merely in Britain, but

---

[19] Chief among these were the 1834 Poor Law Commissioners and, for the later period, Charles Booth and Seebohm Rowntree: Charles Booth, *Life and labour of the people in London*, 2nd edn, London 1892; B. S. Rowntree, *Poverty: a study of town life*, London 1901.

in France and Belgium as well.[20] Victorian novels of social criticism were littered with images of poor women; and art contained many representations of poverty with a female face depicted in sentimentalised form. In some respects, the phenomenon of female poverty was viewed as an entrenched feature of the social landscape, part of the 'natural' order (or rather, disorder) of things. So how might the relatively consistent marginalisation of women in mainstream contemporary debates on poverty and its solutions be explained? Put simply, *female* poverty was a 'different' category of problem. It was an unfortunate symptom of disorder which, although seen as attaching to the principal problem (the poverty of men), could not be scrutinised or accommodated within an overarching discourse about poverty, because despite its apparent gender-neutrality, this discourse itself was persistently and fundamentally gendered.[21] Hence, not only was female poverty 'disorderly' in the social world, it also disordered the Victorian desire for an inclusive explanatory scheme through which to describe and contain this world.

To address the questions outlined above, I work with a fluid definition of 'the poor', and utilise the general category of 'poor women' in two ways. First of all, this category is taken in its material context, relating to the economic circumstances of Victorian women. Through contemporary sources, such as poor relief records and the sources from charitable institutions, the material facts of women's poverty become clear: they were recognised by both women themselves and other contemporaries. No easy generalisations can be made about women who fell into this group: certainly some had in their lives experienced more prosperous circumstances, but had become impoverished through old age or illness. Many others had lived for much longer periods on the margins of economic sufficiency, engaging in casual work, experiencing chronic underemployment, and for years coping with the endless demand to 'make ends meet' for themselves and their families. Of the women represented in the records, many were on their own or were the heads of families, rather than appearing as wives within the orbit of a patriarchal family structure. In some respects, while it is recognised here that women with husbands or male partners experienced poverty as well, such women were less likely to have their individual details and circumstances recorded when families presented themselves for relief, and were statistically less likely to resort to relief than were widows and single mothers. It was upon the death or desertion of spouses that married women were most likely to seek relief and thus find their way into the historical record.

The second element of definition of 'poor women' focused upon here is at once more slippery and more generalised, and very important in an exploration of poverty and the meanings attached to it in discourses about working-

---

[20] Robert Pashley, *Pauperism and the poor laws*, London 1852, 19.
[21] Although I would agree with Linda Shires, that the pervasiveness of gender as a discursive reference was by no means stable: 'Afterword', 185.

class femininity. These definitions are the ones forged in the realm of the cultural and the symbolic, that repertoire of representation and imagery which was drawn upon consistently by contemporary reformers and philanthropists in Victorian society as well as working-class people, in discursive constructions of poor women. The relationship between the material experiences of poverty, of poor women in receipt of relief, and wider cultural conceptions of poor women, is neither intended to construct some dialogue between 'image' and 'reality', nor to subordinate what were often (even by nineteenth-century standards) appalling individual circumstances, to the immateriality of language and representation. On the contrary, a key position within this study is that the material and the cultural, the individual experiences and the collective representations of female poverty, were two aspects of the same whole. It is the dimensions and changing course of discourses of female poverty; the contradictions and tensions, the consistencies and inconsistencies within it – which are charted here in the context of the Victorian north-east.

It is the inter-relatedness of material and cultural factors in the construction of gender identity for working-class women that leads to consideration of work for women in that same period and location. Again, in some instances there are direct and obvious material links between women's work and women's poverty. The exclusion of women from coalmining in the late eighteenth century and from the lead works in the late nineteenth century, for example, contributed directly to women's unemployment or to a reliance upon more precarious forms of self-employment on the margins of the commanding sectors of the Northumbrian economy. However, even material relating to a group of comparatively well-paid women workers such as the agricultural bondagers in the region illustrates that, for these women, the particular requirements of the job – youth, strength, mobility and single status – meant that their days of adequate self-sufficiency were none the less numbered. Along with increasingly entrenched assumptions on the part of village clergy and other social reformers about the undesirability of their 'unfeminine' labour, even for a group with comparatively privileged economic circumstances, privilege could prove transitory. Older women in rural areas faced uncertain futures, while all working women in the region negotiated their existence and identity in relation to broader discourses about femininity and dependence. Thus, if the processes through which some women experienced a 'poverty of dependence' are to be understood, the ways in which that dependence was constructed require attention. Consideration of the conditions of work for women provides some important insights into the ways in which female dependence was sustained and reshaped in changing economic and social conditions, and the ways in which the identities and experiences of working women and poor women at times overlapped. More important, the discussion highlights the ways in which 'work' and 'not-work' were not opposite states. Not only were there numerous points in between these clear-cut categories which at times elided material distinctions between 'poor' women and 'working' women, but both groups functioned culturally within similar modalities of gendered identity.

In the historiography of work, the tendency to exclude women and make them invisible is similar to that observed in the historiography of poverty. Until relatively recently, as Shirley Dex has pointed out, 'everything that needed to be known about women workers could be captured in a few stereotypes'.[22] Indeed, the historiography of the north-east generally exhibits a traditional focus upon those expanding trades in the region which were themselves overwhelmingly dominated by male labour.[23] In the past two decades, however, historians have traced the mechanisms of exclusion from the historical record, looking at the ways in which both the limitations of contemporary sources, and the definitions and assumptions of historical interpretation of them, have underpinned women's erasure from labour histories. Historians such as Sonya Rose and Catherine Hall[24] have shown how analysis of work can provide a way of exploring gender meanings and experiences in the context of capitalist development in the nineteenth century. In particular (and as I examine below in the ways in which 'custom' and 'natural' difference were called upon to underpin discourses calling for the exclusion of women from the workplace, and how these notions operated in the face of considerable contradiction and contestation), such studies further highlight the difficulty of maintaining clear distinctions between 'work' and 'not-work', once 'work' itself is refigured through gender. Such preoccupation with workplace as one important site where gender was elaborated, and with the relationships between changing work processes and the historical instability of gender and class identities, has appeared as part of a broader trend of examining, challenging and redefining theoretical and methodological approaches so that gender perspectives may not simply be added to historical discourse, but change its very shape.

This study contributes, then, to the continuing process of defining the dimensions of gender. Gender has been defined in various ways: as a variable influencing individual life experience in specific historical circumstances; as a system of ideas determining social roles and cultural constructions; as an analytical category alongside class and ethnicity; and more recently as a

[22] Shirley Dex, 'Issues of gender and employment', *Social History* xiii (1988), 141–50 at p. 143. For recent overviews and reassessments of women's work in the nineteenth century see also Judith Bennett, ' "History that stands still": women's work in the European past', *Feminist Studies* xiv (1988), 269–83, and Maxine Berg, 'What difference did women's work make to the industrial revolution?', *History Workshop* xxxv (1993), 22–44.

[23] The contribution of scholars such as Eve Hostettler in the north-east redressed some of these imbalances: E. Hostettler, 'Women farm workers in eighteenth- and nineteenth-century Northumberland', *North East Labour History* xvi (1982), 40–2, and 'Gourlay Steell and the sexual division of labour', *History Workshop* iv (1977), 95–100.

[24] Sonya Rose, *Limited livelihoods: gender and class in nineteenth-century England*, London 1992, and Catherine Hall, *White, male and middle class: explorations in feminism and history*, London 1992.

language system structuring the 'organisation of all social life'.[25] These different, but inter-related levels of gender definition and their reframing of historiography inevitably lead to important theoretical reconsiderations.

Gender, discourse and experience

Here, gender is conceptualised, following Sonya Rose, as both 'a system of meanings articulated in practices that position men and women differently and structure their lived experience in different ways', and as a 'symbolic system for representing difference'.[26] Within this formulation, distinctions between 'image' and 'reality' or cultural processes and materiality are revealed as problematic. These dualisms are usually presented in a foundationalist sequence which appear to 'make it difficult to discuss the relevance of cultural forms for social life'.[27] Some recognition of the consistent interplay between the two areas is required to explore the meanings of gender in the past, and to establish it more firmly as an analytical, rather than merely descriptive, category.

The challenges involved in gender definition have encouraged scholars to move beyond those traditional disciplinary practices and scholarship which have occluded gender, to engage instead in a more fluid yet critical interdisciplinary tourism. Moreover, the very 'rigour' of methodologies and approaches which have in the past been constructed upon foundations of scholarly 'distance' and 'separation'; of object from subject, of observer from observed, of past from present – have been critically scrutinised.[28] This cross-disciplinary trend has challenged traditional approaches: to move beyond the epistemological assumptions of any one discipline tends to reveal that those assumptions, especially where they are of an empiricist character, are not unproblematic 'givens' but contribute significantly to the production of knowledges particular to that discipline.[29] Gender scholarship has contributed significantly to theorising across disciplines, and establishing a more critical self-reflexive position within disciplinary boundaries, the results of which are clearly discernible within historical and other research.[30]

---

[25] Joan Scott, 'Gender: a useful category of historical analysis', *American Historical Review* xci (1986), 1059–75 at p. 1069.
[26] Rose, *Limited livelihoods*, 13, 16.
[27] Ibid. 11.
[28] See, for example, Sneja Gunew, 'Feminist knowledge: critique and construct', in S. Gunew (ed.), *Feminist knowledge: critique and construct*, London 1990, 13–35 .
[29] For a critique both of the strategies of empirical history and the 'postmodern interdiscourse' see R. Hennessy, *Materialist feminism and the politics of discourse*, New York 1993, ch. iv.
[30] Cora Kaplan, ' "Like a housemaid's fancies": the representation of working-class women in nineteenth-century writing', in Susan Sheridan (ed.), *Grafts: feminist cultural criticism*, London–New York 1988, 55–75 at p. 56.

Some useful critical approaches which have developed in recent years centre around the notion of discourse. By utilising theories of discourse which seek to articulate material conditions and textual inscriptions, these approaches have not – as some may have feared – led to a collapse of historical research into the void of textualism. Rather, methods of analysis which emphasise the construction of historical subjects through discourses operating at particular times, contribute significantly to a discipline which is concerned to emphasise the importance of *historicised* specificity. 'History', as Joan Scott has written, 'is a chronology that makes experience visible, but in which categories appear as nonetheless ahistorical': in traditional chronological formulations, categories such as 'femininity' become 'fixed entities being played out over time, but not themselves historicized'.[31] This study is fundamentally concerned to disrupt such notions of a 'fixed' femininity and I look closely at how discursive constructions and representations variously fostered and undercut the possibility of a stable female identity.

Using the term 'discourse' immediately leads historians into the complex debates of semiotics and linguistics. Traditionally, 'discourse' has been used as a collective noun to describe the sum of individual utterances on a particular issue. In this sense, the term discourse has no critical function: it simply delimits particular areas of a society's conversations which might then be studied for the 'facts' which they reveal.[32] Such uses assume that language is a transparent medium through which some pre-existing reality is made available for thought and discussion: that true statements are those which accurately reflect this reality and that false statements are those which do not. It is the rejection of this assumption which leads theorists such as Foucault to offer a new meaning for 'discourse'. In this conceptualisation, discourse operates between 'words and things',[33] providing (through a network of assumptions about, or rules of knowledge for, what is or is not 'true', what can and cannot be said) definitive meanings for real 'things' which do not, of themselves, *mean* anything until they are translated from material reality into language. A discourse is like a set of unspoken criteria for specifying what things mean. Since reality does not of itself provide these meanings, but simply a set of indeterminate signifiers which may mean many things, discourses necessarily emerge to organise language use in ways that enable meaningful statements to be made.

This theoretical position has dramatic implications for the writing of history. As McHoul and Grace conclude:

---

31 Joan W. Scott, 'The evidence of experience', *Critical Inquiry* xvii (1991), 773–97 at p. 778.
32 A. McHoul and W. Grace, *A Foucault primer: discourse, power and the subject*, Carlton 1993, 29.
33 M. Foucault, *The archaeology of knowledge*, Paris 1969, trans. A. M. Sheridan-Smith, New York 1971, 48.

in any given historical period we can write, speak or think about a given social object or practice . . . only in certain specific ways and not others. 'A discourse' would then be *whatever* constrains – but also enables – writing, speaking and thinking within such specific historical limits.[34]

If historians do not attend to the discursive nature of their 'objects' of study, then they simply capture and reproduce the dominant texture of discussions and practices about those objects from the past. Such reproduction may be no bad thing, but it fails to attend to the most important aspect of recent theorising: discourses are never neutral in their effects, but are intimately connected with the emergence, maintenance and extension of unequal social relations. Discourses might, at one level, be a function of language (in constituting 'knowledges' and 'truths' about the world) but they also operate socially through institutions and practices which are organised around specific modalities of power.

While discourses of poverty are textual in that they provide codes by which to organise meaningful representations, they are also material in the practices which flow from and maintain these codes. At the same time, physical signs of poverty provide the 'raw' material from which these codes are constructed. Text and material blur. Similar processes operate in relation to work. My discussion of women's work in both urban and rural contexts in the north-east for example, reveals that changing economic and social conditions and shifting cultural interpretations of femininity were dynamically interwoven, supporting John Fiske's contention that '[m]aterial conditions are inescapably saturated with culture and, equally, cultural conditions are inescapably experienced as material'.[35] The work of deconstructing[36] this relationship through historical sources reveals the different and overlapping strands of discourse whose material and cultural impact was experienced by poor women and working women both individually and collectively.

Contrary to some undifferentiated critiques of poststructuralist perspectives such as that offered by political theorist Somer Brodribb (who argues that adoption of such perspectives duplicates theory which so neutralises women's experience and endlessly defers consideration of power relations that, within its own logic, 'nothing matters'[37]), the work of Linda Nicholson, Nancy Fraser and Joan Scott has contained persuasive arguments for the selective appropriation of perspectives which can be used to expose the unequal weight of authority in societies, and the ways in which that authority is contested.[38] Discourses and their effects are, theoretically speaking,

34 McHoul and Grace, *A Foucault primer*, 31.

35 John Fiske, *Power plays, power works*, London 1993, 13.

36 Deconstruction is used here in a general rather than in any strictly Derridean sense.

37 Somer Brodribb, *Nothing mat(t)ters: a feminist critique of postmodernism*, North Melbourne 1992, passim.

38 Nancy Fraser and Linda Nicholson, 'Social criticism without philosophy: an encounter between feminism and postmodernism', *Theory, Culture and Society* v (1988), 373–94 at pp. 390–1. See also Linda Nicholson (ed.), *Feminism/postmodernism*, New York 1990; Nancy

inescapable in considering women's work and poverty. Yet in the nineteenth-century Northumbrian context, one is immediately confronted with the conceptual debates which have emerged around the use of discourse in feminist analyses. If discourse is whatever constrains and enables writing and speaking within specific historical limits, then in relation to Victorian working-class women the historian is dealing overwhelmingly with 'constraint' and silence. Yet while recognising that at nearly every turn, women's voices were interpreted and embedded in middle-class writing, a critical reading of extant sources may none the less reveal those points at which women's own understandings of their cultural and economic position diverged from the generalised constructions of others as well as reveal something of the range of strategies and tactics women adopted in different situations.

If discourse can be seen as a generalised moment when representation and 'reality' flow together, then the corresponding moment for specific individuals is in processes of identity formation. In discussing the ways in which the identities of different women were constructed in this particular historical context, the concept of 'identity' itself is based always in a notion of its historical instability, and is viewed as a *process* which is many-stranded, incomplete, and the subject of constant negotiation. Identities were formed through transactions between working-class women and men, between working-class women and middle-class reformers, and between dominant discourses of femininity which posited 'Woman' as an identity fixed in biology and those which argued for a more fluid identity springing from changing economic and social conditions. In examining the meanings of feminine identity in past societies, scholars such as Mary Poovey and Leonore Davidoff have sought to elaborate the binary oppositions which underpinned Victorian discourses.[39] These oppositions were the points of reference in this process of identity formation through transaction; they can be seen as the opening balances of the bank accounts of cultural sensibility which provided a source of funds and a place for deposits in this 'economy of representation'.

A focus upon the fluidity of identities in life and instability in Victorian representation is both a challenging and problematic perspective. Some feminist scholarship has explored the ways in which 'gender never exhibits itself in pure form but in the context of lives that are shaped by a multiplicity of influences, which cannot be neatly sorted out'.[40] Multiple factors, shifting subjectivities, and the important recognition of the differences as well as points of unity between women: all these make the inevitable generalising

---

Fraser, 'The uses and abuses of French discourse theory for feminist politics', *boundary 2* xvii (1990), 82–101; Scott, 'Evidence of experience', and 'Gender: a useful category'.

[39] Mary Poovey, *Uneven developments: the ideological work of gender in mid-Victorian England*, Chicago 1988; Leonore Davidoff, 'Class and gender in Victorian England', in J. L. Newton and others (eds), *Sex and class in women's history*, London 1983, 17–71 at pp. 41–4.

[40] Susan Bordo, 'Feminism, postmodernism, and gender-scepticism', in Nicholson, *Feminism/postmodernism*, 133–56 at p. 150.

tendencies of historical writing appear awkward and insufficiently nuanced. Yet as Bordo maintains, the ideal of a scholarship which meticulously elaborates all analytical categories to secure an appropriate recognition of difference is methodologically and theoretically mind-boggling, and could perhaps only be attempted at the cost of meaningful analytical focus: the ideal view from everywhere, Bordo says, may in practice collapse into 'the view from nowhere'.[41]

This book does not take the view from nowhere. It seeks to explore the shape and function of discourses and processes of identity formation in specific settings. I attempt to provide a sense of the ways in which generalised views of femininity were deployed in everyday life to argue a particular case, but also to illustrate how these deployments varied, were contested, and contradicted one another. Although historians, inevitably, generalise about the meanings of femininity in the Victorian period, there was nothing straightforward or simple about the ways these meanings were forged in 'real' time and space. I locate gender here as just one aspect in the process of identity formation,[42] indicating how the male/female dichotomy was just one of a number of oppositional codes of meaning formed around the central idea that the drive to create a subject position relies always upon the construction of the 'other' against whom one's dominant subjectivity may be affirmed and shaped.[43]

I am fascinated by the ways in which symbolic 'others' figured within the imaginary, and how such 'otherness' was played out in the realm of materiality, how material signs were constituted as meaningful through discourse. In the discourses which positioned the working-class, women, and working-class women as 'other' in the period, scholars have also turned increasingly to the material environment and its interpretation as a manifestation of 'otherness'. This environment included the physical separation and designation of 'slums', and practices of Victorian institutional regulation and of bodily discipline. Identities are never forged independently of spaces, for identity formation is in part a process of bodily inscription and bodies are always located in and delimited by space. In the nineteenth century, women's bodies were inscribed as 'appropriate or, as the case may be, inappropriate'[44] for Victorian cultural requirements. A focus on the body can illuminate the connections between imagination, metaphor and specific conditions.

---

41 Ibid. 139–40.

42 I use 'identity' here, but in ways which emphasise its historical instability and incomplete nature, rather than to posit any fixed notion of 'self'. To the extent that Victorians themselves conceptualised identity around the axes of gender and class, moreover, the concept seems historically relevant, although of course intensely problematic within current feminist philosophy.

43 Rosemarie Tong, Feminist thought: a comprehensive introduction, 2nd edn, London 1992, 217–22.

44 Elizabeth Grosz, Volatile bodies: towards a corporeal feminism, St Leonards 1994, 142; see also pp. 208–10.

From this theoretical position, the 'place' in which 'woman' was inscribed and located becomes crucial, as does a general notion that Victorian culture was anxious about 'proper' places for women. As Lisa Tickner contends, at the end of the nineteenth century and beyond, 'Woman, or rather "womanliness", was the lynchpin in bourgeois ideology and a structuring category in the principal discourses of civil society. . . . If woman was out of place everything was out of place.'[45] Being out of place or making existing places 'improper' relates closely to the idea of disorderly and disordering female presence. In nineteenth-century Northumberland, the rhetoric of disorderliness attaching to visions of 'uncontrolled' femininity was clearly in evidence by mid century, and critically influenced views about women's work and women's poverty, and women's experiences of both. Constructions of disorderliness were sustained and shaped by historically-specific developments, which at times were particular to the region, and at others operated to situate the region within the imagined community of the 'nation'. In the Northumbrian context, the key role of the family and women's role within it loomed large in the conception of an orderly social and economic life contributing to progress. The stability and security of the family, the region, the nation, was positioned as relying fundamentally upon a fixed and ordered femininity, which the presumed instability and excess of working-class femininity, and especially of feminine sexuality, threatened to unravel. A generalised iconography of feminine disorder was, of course, not peculiar to the Victorian period. Yet, in the nineteenth century, when feminine 'disorder' is set alongside other categories of difference and otherness and tied to the particular logics of spatial progress and cultural order of the bourgeoisie, it becomes a crucial aspect of the dominant cultural formations of the time.

These formations of femininity, and bourgeois imaginings of the cultural meaning of 'woman', were underpinned by a proliferation of specialist and 'expert' discourses, which sought to secure 'knowledge' that, through rational scientific planning, might provide a way to reform society and secure the path of progress. Regimes of surveillance, necessary to produce this knowledge, were increasingly influential: investigative newspaper journalism, artistic and photographic representation produced for mass consumption, the growth of local and national bodies charged with the task of measuring, containing, reporting on, and remedying social and economic malaise, led to a substantial shift in both the qualitative and quantitative sources through which society reflected upon and defined its problems. At the same time, as Foucault has indicated,[46] regimes of surveillance were readily and easily extended into institutional forms of regulation and control that might produce self-disciplined social subjects, as in the way that workhouses and 'rescue' homes

45 Lisa Tickner, *The spectacle of women: imagery of the suffrage campaign 1907–1914*, London 1987, 170.
46 M. Foucault, *Discipline and punish: the birth of the prison*, Paris 1975, trans. A. Sheridan, Harmondsworth 1977, 201.

provided significant places in which to police the 'disorderly' femininity of poor women. This ordering of individal subjects, it was claimed by experts made knowledgeable through medical, criminal and other discourses, was a primary goal within social life since it would ensure the maintenance of order and progress. Once again, the body – that most tangible and observable locus of disorder – became a primary site for the realisation of these discursive imaginings. The body, especially of poor working-class women, was both the root of the problem and the place where it might be addressed.

While some debt to Foucauldian interpretation is due in developing the study, it is a critical debt in two respects in particular. First, following Bartky, I would argue that while the regimes of surveillance and regulation clearly operated in relation to femininity in nineteenth-century Northumberland, these regimes were not solely bounded by institutions. In many contexts, as Bartky contends, regimes of femininity operate in more complex and diffuse ways throughout culture, and involve women in their production. It is not just 'total' institutions to which one must look to appreciate the forms which, for example, feminine bodily discipline as an expression of orderliness has taken: as Bartky states in relation to the late twentieth century, 'no one is marched off for electrolysis at gunpoint'.[47] In the nineteenth-century context similarly, women working as bondagers in rural Northumberland were not marched off the fields to their 'proper' place in domestic service or the family hearth, nor overtly 'coerced' into exchanging their functional, standard uniforms for frills and flounces towards the end of the period. Yet such occurrences serve as reminders that outside institutions as well – at the workplace, in the community, in the home – women were subject to the impact of, and interacted with, the more subtle regulatory imperatives established around 'femininity'.

The second departure, leading from the first, resides more in a matter of emphasis. While Foucault's own conception of power clearly designates a space for the operation of agency, the effect of his work overall in a close application to femininity[48] would be more reiterative of the themes of subordination and the production of women's 'object status', than of women's resistance to dominant conceptions of femininity and the practices which seek to maintain them.[49] There is of course an overwhelming bias in the extant source material for the nineteenth-century north-east which could be interpreted as constituting a cultural hegemony of the bourgeoisie. In many ways I would argue that indeed, in cultural, social and economic life, the middle-class reformers, commentators and critics of working-class life in Newcastle and the countryside exercised both practical authority and discursive clout in

---

[47] S. Bartky, 'Foucault, femininity and the modernisation of patriarchal power', in I. Diamond and L. Quinby (eds), *Feminism and Foucault: reflections on resistance*, Boston 1988, 61–86 at p. 75.
[48] See L. McNay, *Foucault and feminism: power, gender and the self*, Cambridge 1992.
[49] Ibid. 41–3.

everyday life. Yet what is also evident from the north-eastern records is that such power did not 'comprise a monolithic and seamless web . . . an absolute top-down control of meaning': as Nancy Fraser argues, the notion of hegemony can also designate 'a process wherein cultural authority is negotiated and contested'.[50] Contradictions and tensions *between* contemporary middle-class interpretations in the nineteenth century abounded, and it is only by recognising these contradictions that the urgency which at times arose around the attempt to 'fix' the meaning of working-class femininity may be understood.[51] Further, while the economic and political authority of the Novocastrian middle class was evident, in the hierarchies of power and subordination within Victorian society the axes of domination ran beyond class lines, so the work at times is concerned to chart the ways in which working women and poor women negotiated their identities as women within the working class as well, with (or against) male partners, co-workers, fathers and other women.

Discussion of women's agency has long been problematic in feminist scholarship,[52] and certainly within a work which considers constructions of femininity while utilising an overwhelmingly middle-class source base, the perceptions and actions of women themselves appear so refracted and so mediated that the women may seem, as Carol Smart maintains, 'mere plastic, the quintessential cultural dupes of history'.[53] But, following Smart, I would argue that within a study which highlights the ways in which discourses 'bring into being the problematic feminine subject', that subject 'is not merely subjugated; she has practised the agency of constructing her subjectivity as well. . . . Woman is not merely a category, she is also a subjective positioning within which there is room for manouevre.'[54] The strands of resistance, the subversion of bourgeois ideals, the explicit and covert transgression of boundaries of 'appropriate' behaviour set within working-class culture as well as by middle-class women and men, appear as dynamic and important ingredients in the history of working-class women in the region.

---

50 Fraser, 'The uses and abuses of French discourse theories', 85.

51 In using the terms 'bourgeoisie' and 'middle class' I am not suggesting that the group was undifferentiated. Such generalised class designations also prove problematic in respect of the working class. None the less, again while I seek to explore the ways in which women's outlook and position varied within the working class, I use more generalised designations both to reflect the lack of 'voice' women had in relation to their own representation, and to capture the sense of 'otherness' of poor working-class women as it was constructed in contemporary discourses.

52 Louise Tilly, 'Gender, women's history and social history', and replies, *Social Science History* xiii (1989), 439–77 at p. 452. See also the further discussion in E. Varikas, 'Gender, experience and subjectivity: the Tilly–Scott disagreement', *New Left Review* ccxi (1995), 89–101.

53 Carol Smart, 'Disruptive bodies and unruly sex: the regulation of reproduction and sexuality in the nineteenth century', in Carol Smart (ed.), *Regulating womanhood: historical essays on marriage, motherhood and sexuality*, London 1992, 7–32 at pp. 7–8

54 Ibid. 8.

Overall then, the theoretical and methodological underpinnings of the work are situated loosely between 'things' and 'words', between the recuperative, gap-filling strategies of earlier social history (a necessary precursor to any cultural reading), and a reading of what is discovered in those gaps which is based upon some insights afforded by cultural analysis. It is from this vantage point that I explore women's work, women's poverty, the relationship of each to shifting formations of feminine identity, and the relationship of all three subjects in turn to broader narratives of Victorian progress. Some of these broad themes are introduced in the particular space of nineteenth-century Newcastle upon Tyne, in the following chapter.

2

Invading Bodies:
Gender and Danger in Newcastle

In 1905, the year in which the Royal Commission on the Poor Laws was established, photographer Edgar G. Lee moved through the slums of Newcastle, camera in hand, to record the street life he found there. Other photographs from the period capture the buildings, work sites, leisure activities and 'occasions' within the city. These images range from predictable formal poses of workers in factories and shop doorways, to opulently-dressed riders astride elephants draped in 'oriental' cloth parading outside the Theatre Royal in Newcastle to advertise the circus, an exotic display whose hints of the grandeur of empire appear so incongruous to a late twentieth-century eye.[1] Lee and other photographers, who remain anonymous to the historian, were part of a growing tradition of documentary photography[2] actively contributing to the construction of the area as an undifferentiated zone of social problems and material impoverishment. Such photographers built upon earlier investigative activities, becoming 'an extension of the anthropologist',[3] 'showing us places we never hope to go'.[4]

Rachel Bowlby argues that the spreading interest in the photographic medium around the turn of the century 'both indicated and helped to promote a willingness on the part of society to look at images of itself, collectively and individually – to see its own image reflected or refracted back through the technological medium'.[5] It was perhaps the perfect medium for those members of society who for long had been intensely preoccupied with social questions. Yet the notion of a 'self' looking at its own image is intensely problematic, suggesting that there existed some broad, cohesive identity which constituted 'Victorian society'. An alternative reading would suggest that the fascination with such images lay not in the bourgeois pursuit to identify readily with some ultimate unifying likeness which stood beyond differences of class, gender and culture, but rather in the possibility presented of pondering the curious and alien 'other' within that society. Photographers like Lee, following in the path of earlier bourgeois observers, negotiated the

---

1   See plate 1.
2   Margaret F. Harker, *Victorian and Edwardian photographs*, London 1982, 63.
3   Susan Sontag, *On photography*, New York 1977, 42.
4   Martha Rosler, *3 works*, Halifax 1981, 73.
5   Rachel Bowlby, *Just looking: consumer culture in Dreiser, Gissing and Zola*, New York 1985, 29.

Plate 1. Circus Parade in Grey Street,
Newcastle c. 1905

Plate 2. 'Hand Camera in the Slums',
Sandgate c. 1905

Plate 3. Women on the doorstep, Sandgate c. 1890

Plate 4. Marketplace, Sandgate c. 1895

Plate 5. Fish stall, Sandgate *c.* 1905

Plate 6. Organ grinder and children, Quayside *c.* 1905

Plate 7. Sandgate *c.* 1905

Plate 8. Bondagers and male fieldworkers, near Wooler *c.* 1900

space which marked out the imagined geography of social difference. Through the genre of documentary photography – attempting as it did some 'realistic' representation – decadence, decay and squalor could later be viewed at some safe distance by consumers of the form.

The 1905 slum photographs[6] combine many of the symbols which were clear markers of impoverished circumstances in conventions of Victorian representation: tatty shawls, scarves and barefooted people; a small table perched on the cobblestones of the gutter, bearing a scanty offering of fish for sale; spontaneous entertainment from an organ grinder who has set up trade amidst grubby, nondescript buildings for the fascination of tiny onlookers; and perhaps reflecting the more particular preoccupations of *fin-de-siècle* reformers, the ubiquitous children of the poor. In Lee's photograph, 'Hand Camera in the Slums',[7] seven children congregate in the middle of the street around a barrow pushed by a boy. Some are without shoes. Two or three are very young children, perhaps in the care of the eldest child who, with a bemused look, returns the gaze of the photographer. In the background, a bearded onlooker surveys the proceedings, a rickety stall flanks a building, and in the more crowded section at the very end of the street, adults are milling about. But Lee's focus is upon the children, apparently unattended, captured in a moment of discussion or play. Most unusually, and perhaps attesting to the relative novelty of the art and its technology, Lee includes another photographer in bowler hat, tie and winged collar in his own picture, frozen in the same act of pictorial surveillance which engaged Lee, and which was so growing in popularity. Such an inclusion along with the returned gaze of the child undermines the naturalism which documentary photographers usually sought to achieve as invisible Victorian 'supertourists'[8] who visited, recorded, but did not 'intervene' in the life around them.

Consideration of Lee's photograph is an appropriate point of entry for examination of Newcastle in the nineteenth and early twentieth centuries, to the experiences of the poor within that city and to the cultural meanings which were forged around them. It alerts us at the outset to some important and recurring themes in this interpretation of Victorian poverty which inform the structure of this chapter. A general trend to naturalism notwithstanding, Lee's particular study contains visual evidence which directs us towards the complex theoretical positions and insights developed by Foucault and others in relation to surveillance, be it photographic or written, overt or covert.[9] Surveillance never involves mere passive recording, but is linked instead to processes of interpretation which render a particular scene

---

6 See plates 5–7. Plates 3, 4 and frontispiece, also depicting Sandgate and the slum areas around the Castle, were taken about ten years earlier by unknown photographers.
7 Plate 2.
8 Sontag, *On photography*, 42.
9 On Foucault, and the investigative preoccupations of the Victorians, see Andrew Tolson, 'Social surveillance and subjectification: the emergence of "subculture" in the work of Henry Mayhew', *Cultural Studies* iv (1990), 113–27 at pp. 124–5.

comprehensible to a particular audience. Such images are never read in an unmediated fashion, nor are they captured by the photographer initially as spontaneous; photographs, even when 'snapped' and not posed, are always already orchestrated, revealing the pre-existing ensemble of images and symbols in the photographer's mind. 'Realistic' photography drew upon those repertoires which bore meaning within a culture, its naturalistic effects relying upon the minimisation of interpretive gaps which lay between construction and consumption of the image. Each blink of the camera's eye as it revealed a corner of working-class life could perpetuate stereotypes and ironically, like other slum studies, act 'as a shutter closing the minds of contemporaries to the inner life and outlook of the poor'.[10]

Pictures never speak for themselves; they 'bear the traces of the capitalist and patriarchal social relations in which they are produced, exchanged and consumed'.[11] Such evidence raises general questions about the ways in which relations of class and gender are actively constructed in other sources used by the historian. This focus upon construction involves not merely the consideration of the agendas, priorities and presuppositions of historically-defined investigating subjects and objects of investigation, but also those which the historian brings to the act of interpretation. As discussed in the previous chapter, developments within gender analysis have challenged historians to consider the ways in which the meanings of gender were articulated and contested in specific historical contexts. The historical instability of gender definitions and representations demands some focus upon the ways in which gender was shaped and reshaped within the dominant discourses of the period. Further, the debate about poverty and its meanings in Newcastle, and the constructions of poor women in the sources, saw no single overarching 'truth' emerge about those subjects.

Edgar G. Lee provides one image of poverty in the moment frozen in 1905. Whether viewed from the position adopted by Lee, who stood within the landscape of the slums, or from a multitude of other vantage points provided by the sources, urban Newcastle affords rich evidence that the terrain of poverty, its meanings and avenues of negotiation, was shifting and contested ground across the century. This chapter moves through working-class and 'slum' areas of Newcastle, to examine the ways in which constructions of gender and meanings of poverty were elaborated. It charts the responses of bourgeois observers to explore the relationship between the representation of poor women, and the wider rhetoric of disorder in the midst of progress which increasingly informed discussion of social problems. Notions of the poor as a

---

10 G. Davison, 'Introduction', in G. Davison and others (eds), *The outcasts of Melbourne*, Sydney 1985, 3, cited in A. Mayne, *The imagined slum: newspaper representation in three cities 1870–1914*, Leicester 1993, 3.
11 F. Borzello, A. Kuhn, J. Pack and C. Wedd, 'Living dolls and "real women"', in A. Kuhn (ed.), *The power of the image: essays on representation and sexuality*, London 1985, 9–18 at p. 10.

'race apart', the intense focus upon the morality of the poor woman, the urgency with which views about the need to check the spread of vice and squalor were at times expressed – the generation and maintenance of such rhetoric can best be examined by locating the poor woman in the broader landscape of 'disorder', represented most powerfully in the imagination of the bourgeoisie by the city's slum areas.

Conventionally, such analyses situate prostitution as their centrepiece. Often the resort of poor women faced with hardship, prostitution appears as the activity around which so much reforming zeal clustered. Here, too, prostitution in Newcastle is examined in this context. In Philippa Levine's recent appraisal of the treatment of prostitution within social history, however, she argues persuasively that historians should avoid perpetuating that 'pathology of victimisation' constructed around the prostitute by contemporaries: 'we may just as usefully ask why [women] should become coal-drawers in the mines or factory hands in the mills'.[12] Bearing in mind such caveats, my emphasis upon a wider discourse of disorder is designed to position prostitution here as part of a social, economic and metaphoric continuum which also extended to other areas of working women's lives. Women's work in the increasingly controversial white-lead industry in the 1890s for example, examined here and in the following chapter, illustrates the links between women's work, women's poverty, and the impact of assumptions about morality and female sexuality.

Finally, the photographic evidence from Lee includes a reference to relatively new technology, which serves as a small but appropriate reminder that the period is one which had witnessed vast economic and social changes which were by no means confined to the earlier nineteenth century. While the explosion in industrial production and population growth to mid century dominates some historical interpretations of rapid change and its attendant social problems,[13] the fluctuations in material conditions continued throughout the period, crucially shaping the patterns of constraint and opportunity within which poor women existed. The relationship between cultural meanings and material conditions has been a tense yet fruitful source of debate among historians; as Sonya Rose and Judith Walkowitz have argued in their recent works, however, these focal points are not mutually exclusive. The privileging of any view alone carries with it the risk, on the one hand, of excluding 'the material context of discursive struggle and . . . the specificity of women's experiences in these struggles',[14] and on the other, neglecting to appreciate the extent to which 'economic relations were shaped by culture'.[15]

---

[12] Philippa Levine, 'Rough usage: prostitution, law and the social historian', in A. Wilson (ed.), *Rethinking social history*, Manchester 1991, 266–92 at pp. 269, 283.
[13] For an overview see Pat Hudson, *The industrial revolution*, London 1992.
[14] Judith Walkowitz, *City of dreadful delight: narratives of sexual danger in late-Victorian London*, Chicago 1992, 9.
[15] Rose, *Limited livelihoods*, 11.

Material existence and cultural representation were inextricably linked, conditioning what was possible, and how those possibilities were perceived, not only by bourgeois observers but by poor women themselves. Attention to this nexus is of central significance when exploring the ways in which poverty itself was a deeply gendered and fluid category of experience and meaning in nineteenth-century Newcastle. It is the broad material parameters within which women operated – the changing economic, social and spatial environment for women, the work which they performed, and the factors contributing to female poverty in the urban context – which I sketch in the first section of this chapter.

Urban growth, women's work and patterns of poverty

Historians have long recognised the multiplicity of identities and variations within the vast metropolis of London. Less apparent, however, has been the historical recognition of such diversity in the provincial centres of the period, where industrial growth and the attendant proliferation of civic monuments have appeared so emblematic to writers concerned with the development of the 'great' Victorian city.[16] Yet few historians who go beyond the standard celebratory literature could help but be struck by the divergent views which have emerged about the character of Newcastle. The divergences, indeed, have been extreme. Reconciling the laudatory writings of architectural historians who focus on the majesty of the work carried out by the nineteenth-century 'improving' triumvirate of Richard Grainger, John Dobson and John Clayton with the plain disgust of some contemporaries suggests that the divergence went beyond mere aesthetics. Where one's focus lay, or even the approach which one took into the city, could determine such appraisals. For a carriage visitor travelling along the main thoroughfares, theirs would have been the Newcastle of Grey's monument, the domed Central Exchange and the grand pillars of the Theatre Royal. Looking into the city from the vantage point of the High Level Bridge connecting Newcastle and Gateshead, which itself stood as a monument to the technical ingenuity of Robert Stephenson, the outline of the city's more splendid buildings, such as St Nicholas and All Saints' church, was clearly visible.

Perhaps less immediately apparent, but in close proximity none the less, were the districts increasingly referred to as slums, the overcrowding in which reflected the unprecedented population growth which the city had witnessed in the first half of the century. Between 1801 and 1851 the number of people living in Newcastle had almost trebled. While this growth slowed slightly to 1901, by that time the population was more than twice its 1851 size, and six and a half times greater than it had been one hundred years

16 Asa Briggs, *Victorian cities*, 2nd edn, Harmondsworth 1968, 51–2.

earlier.[17] Particular districts within the urban area, such as Wallsend, or Elswick to the west, the site of major expansion of industry on Tyneside, had grown at even faster rates. Demand for housing and transport improvements led eventually to suburbanisation, with its familiar pattern of spatial segregation along class lines. Until the third quarter of the century, however, the mushrooming population remained concentrated mainly in the heart of the 'walking' city, and increasingly inadequate sanitary systems and other amenities were the source of ongoing concern to reformers.[18]

The proliferation of crowded dwellings in the lowest-lying sections of the city around the quayside drew particular focus. The conditions which typified lower working-class areas of Victorian cities were here especially acute. In the shadow of the Castle stood the buildings which had once housed Newcastle's upper classes, now 'parcelled into tenements [and] turned into the foulest shelters of the poor'.[19] Such squalor gave way further east to a poorly ventilated and filthy warren of entries and 'chares' around Sandgate, the location commonly associated in the bourgeois imagination with prostitution, crime and poverty. While Sandgate proper was only one street, in common parlance it had come to designate an entire area,[20] an area in which '[n]ot even a De Quincey', claimed William Tomlinson in 1888, 'through the midst of an opium dream, could find a picturesque feature'.[21] Bounded on the one side by the Tyne and its wharves, the geographic and social separation of the area was further entrenched by the construction of the railway through the city in the 1840s. By 1850, it was claimed, 'respectable people, having no occasion to visit [the area] scarcely know anything about it'.[22] 'Respectable' Newcastle could, and did, construct the poor at a distance from the everyday life of working people.

In short, Newcastle in the nineteenth century appeared to some as a city in contention with itself. A city at once both ugly and beautiful, Newcastle contained impressive and arresting monuments to the area's expansion and provincial status, as well as hideous overcrowding and urban degeneration which attested to the problems of poverty in the same domain. That these features existed alongside each other is easily explicable in geographical and economic terms: they were a direct result of rapid urban growth, shaped and constrained by local features which prevented building expansion in the

---

17 N. McCord and D. J. Rowe, 'Industrialisation and urban growth in north-east England', *International Review of Social History* xxii (1977), 30–64 at p. 42 n. 1.
18 For example, see *Report of the commissioners for inquiring into the state of large towns and populous districts, second report,* 1845 [610] xvii, pt ii, appendix 'Report by D. B. Reid on the sanatory [sic] condition of Newcastle', 157–74.
19 Ibid. 89.
20 J. R. Boyle, *Vestiges of old Newcastle and Gateshead,* Newcastle upon Tyne 1890, 86.
21 W. W. Tomlinson, *A comprehensive guide to the county of Northumberland,* London 1888, repr. Newcastle upon Tyne 1985, 23.
22 Anon., *Inquiry into the condition of the poor in Newcastle upon Tyne,* Newcastle upon Tyne 1850, 1st ser., letter iii, 22.

city's core.[23] That they were increasingly interpreted as a contradiction, however, can only be understood with reference to the broader and distinctively Victorian discursive framework of 'progress', whose meaning was inscribed upon, and whose advance was measured with reference to, the very buildings, places and spaces within the city itself. The image of a 'city within a city' was strongly expressed in the nineteenth century. As Elizabeth Wilson has contended, the city was a place of 'triumphal scale . . . [and] routinised order', yet also, disquietingly, contained spaces of 'deviation, disruption . . . [and] labyrinthine uncentredness'.[24] Newcastle shared in this pattern.

Such population growth was fuelled by regional economic development.[25] Newcastle's own industries and the transport functions centred around its Tyneside harbours increased spectacularly in size and scope. Moreover, the city's role at the heart of commerce and as the chief centre for the provision of goods and services to adjacent areas flourished in line with the broader economic expansion of the north-east region it served. The patterns of economic growth and employment in Newcastle in the nineteenth century bore some of the hallmarks associated with industrialisation generally during the period. As well as some major 'success' stories of locally-celebrated industrial concerns, much production remained concentrated in smaller, scattered workshops. While the commanding economic interests of coalmining, shipbuilding, and their associated industries dominated, the area's economy was also structured around a wide range of other activities including iron and lead smelting, glass-making, and the production of soap, pottery, rope, paint, alkali and other chemicals.

The nineteenth-century economy in the region was no simple story of unbroken expansion and development. Sectors within the economy were subject to seasonal decline, downturn in demand as a result of national or international competition, or more serious long-term reversal as a consequence of outdated technology. Despite an overall profile of industrial growth which situated Newcastle squarely within an optimistic rhetoric of economic 'progress', development was not without costs to sections of its workforce, which struggled at times to survive and adapt to changing market conditions.[26]

The economic structures which underpinned Newcastle's growth had a marked impact upon female employment patterns. Throughout the century and up to the First World War, observers remarked consistently that there was in Newcastle 'no large number of women's industries', that 'the extreme north is not an area in which the woman worker is in great request'.[27]

---

23 McCord and Rowe, 'Industrialisation and urban growth', 42.
24 Elizabeth Wilson, *The sphinx in the city*, London 1991, 46, 47.
25 See Norman McCord, 'The making of modern Newcastle', *Archaeologia Aeliana* 5th ser. ix (1981), 333–46 at pp. 333–4.
26 L. W. Hepple, *A history of Northumberland and Newcastle upon Tyne*, Cicester 1976, 126.
27 R. Sherard, *The cry of the poor*, London 1901, 149, and Charles E. Russell, *Social problems of the north*, London 1913, repr. London 1980, 149.

Women's work opportunities in Newcastle were fragmented. Only relatively patchy employment opportunities for women existed in the city. Absent was any dominant 'logical' choice for wage earning which occurred in other areas, around industries such as cotton spinning which relied so heavily upon the labour of young single women and outwork systems. Compared with regions of textile production, the formal larger-scale industrial economy of the north-east, centred around Newcastle, was overwhelmingly masculine in its worker profile. Textile work in the region was small scale, and decentralised. Certainly, women contributed to local production and were found in greatest number in the pottery, rope-making, glass-making and lead industries. Sections of trades continued throughout to rely heavily upon the recruitment of women as unskilled labour, but in relatively small numbers in relation to the overall workforce.[28]

Whether in the lead industry, dye works or other manufacturing sites, women were to be found in jobs which were often casual, and invariably poorly paid. Weekly earnings of women workers were estimated by Emily Davies in 1861 at anything from 4s. to 12s. per week.[29] These estimates, however, were extrapolations based upon payments for the day or by the piece, and are problematic: as Maxine Berg has pointed out, 'wages were not earnings', and the latter were calculated on the (often erroneous) assumption of steady employment 'over the week, the seasons, and the economic cycle'.[30] Piece rates for scraping rabbit skins for example – 'very unpleasant work, for the smell of the skins is most disagreeable and performed exclusively by women' – could result in a week's wage of 12s. in 1899, but this rate was calculated upon labour which was both quick and constant.[31] A female 'general hand' in the lead industry in the 1890s could earn 10s. to 12s. per week, although critics of the industry argued that averaged over a year, weekly earnings were closer to 7s.[32]

Throughout the period in numerous industries, it is clear that wage differentials between men and women were considerable. Men in the lead industry earned amounts which were double that of women, 'for the same quality and quantity of work'.[33] Even in the relatively new areas of office work which

---

[28] See *Census of England and Wales, 1891, 1892–3* [c. 7058] cvi, 'Northern counties, table 7, occupations of males and females'.
[29] 'Northumberland and Durham branch of the society for promoting the employment of women, 1861', in Emily Davies, *Thoughts on some questions relating to women, 1860–1908*, Cambridge 1910, 30.
[30] Berg, 'What difference did women's work make?', 31.
[31] Sherard, *Cry of the poor*, 149.
[32] Idem, 'The white slaves of England, V: the white-lead workers of Newcastle', *Pearson's Magazine* ii (1896), 523–30 at p. 525.
[33] Helen Dendy, 'The position of women in industry', in Bernard Bosanquet (ed.), *Aspects of the social problem*, London 1895, 63–74 at p. 66.

were becoming increasingly feminised after the turn of the century, most women worked for 10s. a week, while during about the same period unskilled male labourers in engineering works and shipyards earned from 21s. to 23s. per week. Of course, the 'aristocrats' of the Newcastle industries, such as platers, riveters and boilermakers, could earn considerably more.[34] Payments for overtime and night-work further contributed to men's earnings, but these same options were increasingly closed to women as a result of legislative enactments.

In most of these industries, the complex relationship of gender to attributions of occupational 'skill' and designations of technical expertise examined by Sonya Rose in relation to the Kidderminster carpet industry[35] were broadly replicated. Where women participated in industries with a 'mixed' labour force, specific activities within them were earmarked as predominantly or exclusively 'female' occupations. A few women rose by virtue of their long service and experience to fill a position as a forewoman in the lead industry, for example, supervising groups of three or four other women.[36] But in general, as one employer wrote to Davies, men usually supervised work in industry: 'as it "is not the custom" to apprentice girls, there are no women competent to overlook'.[37] Formal avenues of training and advancement were blocked by such custom, by assumptions about women's domestic roles, and by the entrenchment of these factors in the policies of trade unions which sought to protect the 'skill' designations and apprenticeship privileges of their male members.[38]

While women's employment opportunities in some dominant local industries were very limited, in other cases they were simply non-existent. Women did not participate, for example, in the coalmining industry, one of the foundations of the regional economy. While women elsewhere continued to work in this sphere up to and beyond the introduction of 'protective' legislation in the 1840s, the labour force of the Northumbrian collieries had been exclusively male from about 1780.[39] The reasons for this wholesale early exclusion of women are very obscure, and do not receive treatment in contemporary sources. Ivy Pinchbeck suggests that exclusion came about as a result either of an increased pool of male labourers displaced through restructuring in the agricultural sector, or because 'innovative' northern mine owners had begun

---

[34] Russell, *Social problems of the north*, 148.

[35] Rose, *Limited livelihoods*, 28–9.

[36] *Report from the departmental committee on the various lead industries*, PP 1893–4, [c. 7239–1] xvii (cited hereafter as 1893 Report), appendix 'White lead committee minutes of evidence before the departmental committee', 55.

[37] Davies, *Thoughts on some questions*, 30.

[38] At national level, women had no formal representation from unions in metals, chemicals or distributive trades until at least the end of the century: Barbara Drake, *Women in trade unions*, London 1920, repr. London 1984, appendix, tables 1, 2.

[39] Angela John, *By the sweat of their brow: women workers at Victorian coalmines*, London 1980, 21, 73.

at an earlier stage than elsewhere to introduce more efficient techniques in and above their mines, obviating the necessity of employing cheaper female labour.[40] While Pinchbeck favours the latter explanation, the deeper structures of capitalism and patriarchy which underpinned such exclusion remain unaddressed. Sylvia Walby rightly contends that it explains little to say that regional variations in female activity rates are accounted for by the industrial structure of that region, and Pinchbeck's work inevitably raises questions about the older 'sedimented forms'[41] of the sexual division of labour underlying such later exclusions. None the less, as is clear from Pinchbeck's survey of women's wages in other mining areas in the mid nineteenth century, the Northumbrian pattern removed one significant and relatively well-paid source of employment for women in the region.[42]

Although the coalfields were 'clear of [the] blot' of female labour,[43] some consternation was voiced about other peculiarities in local employment practices. The 'singular' custom of employing women as labourers to bricklayers and roof slaters earlier in the nineteenth century was condemned as 'disgraceful to the town' by local commentator, Eneas Mackenzie. 'We hope', he wrote, 'that the ladies will exert themselves successfully in abolishing [the] custom . . . and in providing employments more suitable and becoming for those poor girls than that of mounting high ladders, and crawling over the tops of houses.'[44] Certainly, this field of employment for women too, was declining. More satisfying to middle-class observers than women working on rooftops was the custom of women working under them in the traditional work of domestic service, training for which provided the major focus of schemes in Newcastle's charitable institutions throughout the period. Domestic service remained the single largest occupational group for women in Newcastle throughout the century.[45] Approval was also given by Mackenzie to other traditional areas of local employment, where women worked as family members in a subsidiary role, their work opportunities created by the primary economic function of males. The keel workers of Sandgate and Quayside, loading and transporting coal in their distinctive blue garb, were all men and boys. The wives and daughters of the keelmen contributed to the industry as 'keeldeeters', cleaning the keels and 'receiv[ing] the sweepings for

---

[40] Ivy Pinchbeck, *Women workers and the industrial revolution 1750–1850*, London 1930, repr. London 1969, 241.

[41] S. Walby, *Patriarchy at work: patriarchal and capitalist relations of production*, Minneapolis 1986, 87.

[42] Ibid. 257.

[43] J. Wilson, *Memories of a labour leader*, London 1910, 35.

[44] E. Mackenzie, *A descriptive and historical account of the town and county of Newcastle upon Tyne, including the borough of Gateshead*, Newcastle 1827, ii. 730.

[45] *Census of Great Britain 1851*, 1852–3, [1691–11] lxxxviii, pt ii, 'Occupations of females in principal towns', 795–7; *Census England and Wales 1891*, 1893–4 [c. 7058] cvi, 'Occupations of males and females aged 10 years and upwards', 464–79.

their pains'.[46] The sale or private use of the sweepings in turn contributed to the family economy, but the women's role was contingent upon the continuation of the chief male breadwinner's employment.

The diverse and fragmented nature of women's work in the city was, indirectly, a source of delight to contemporaries like Eneas Mackenzie, who believed that 'the general steadiness of trade', and the absence of major industries dependent upon women's work in factories, 'conduce so much to the production of virtue and happiness'. Even the poorest members of the population were thought to benefit from existing economic arrangements: 'The sober and industrious may always obtain employment.'[47] Yet Mackenzie's idealisation of the Novocastrian poor, and his assumptions about the utility of patriarchal family structures which drew women into a 'safe' orbit of economic and social existence, stands in stark contrast to evidence from other sources which highlight many women's dependence upon a hidden economy of haphazard, ill-paid employment, and the structural disadvantages which assumptions about the ubiquity of male breadwinners served to entrench.

While census material from the period provides some useful indicators of women's participation rates in the formally-defined Victorian economy, the scope for under-estimation of women's participation structured into the census classifications is now well recognised.[48] The complex patterns of unemployment and under-employment for women in Newcastle which made them, along with women in other cities during the period, the chief recipients of poor relief throughout the century,[49] found no reflection in this material. Yet beyond clearly defined work roles which were recognised by contemporary statisticians, large numbers of women participated in a hidden economy, feeding off the scraps of progress, and cleaning up its refuse. Scavenging, bartering, street-selling and pawning – activities in this sphere underscored women's marginal economic status. Poor women attempted to sell all manner of goods – matches, herrings, rags, china – in the streets and at local markets, both during the day and at night. Transport of goods was also a task women performed, even into old age. Sarah Nichols at sixty-nine was a flesh-carrier when she applied for poor relief, while Elizabeth Weallans at sixty-eight had worked as a water-carrier for twenty-seven years to earn her living.[50] Such poor relief records also indicate the extent of women's reliance

46 W. Whellan, History, topography, and directory of Newcastle upon Tyne, London 1855, 139.
47 Mackenzie, Descriptive and historical account, ii. 731.
48 See Edward Higgs, 'Women, occupations and work in the nineteenth-century censuses', History Workshop xxiii (1987), 59–80.
49 Thane, 'Women and the poor law', 29.
50 Sarah Nichols, Elizabeth Weallans, applications for parochial relief, parish of All Saints, TWAS, T241/2.

upon income earned through the provision of casual domestic-style services, taking in sewing, accommodating lodgers, charring or 'keeping a mangle'.

It would be wrong to suggest that any strict division existed between women in recognised areas of employment, and poor women who survived on the margins of economic life. Movement between the groups is clear from poor relief and other records from the period. Factors such as casuality and seasonality and the risks associated with heavy manual labour and occupational hazards such as lead poisoning were not peculiar to women workers. Yet these factors were accompanied by others more specific to 'women's employment', such as lower status, unskilled designations, and low pay relative to men in the same trade. They increased women's vulnerability, and the consequent danger they faced of slipping from one 'group' to another.

While a few sources document the success of individual working women in business and trade in the area,[51] for the majority of female workers the reality remained low paid labour where access to well-defined occupational status through training was extremely unlikely. Many women at some stage of their working lives would experience considerable hardship and economic insecurity, sometimes sufficient to see them officially cast as part of the 'poor'. The uncertainty faced by many self-supporting working-class women in Newcastle was summed up by Clementina Carr, an applicant for poor relief who found it difficult to estimate her 'usual' earnings from her previous employment, since 'sometimes [I have] more and sometimes less I can't exactly tell you for sometimes I have nothing'.[52]

Even a partial account of women's employment in the city, however, illustrates that the situation of women was not based simply upon material conditions. The more complex inter-relationship between their economic position in an expanding capitalist economy and cultural frames of reference which mediated the meanings of gender and work is highlighted in the Newcastle records: the exclusion of women from coalmining, and the sanctioning of domestic service as the most appropriate women's work activity illustrated the importance of this inter-relationship in conditioning women's experiences in the city.

The example of prostitution provides further important evidence of this link. In terms of its structure and economic basis, prostitution bore many of the same hallmarks as other marginal employment in which women engaged: unrecognised in employment statistics, prostitution provided a means to supplement inadequate wages derived from other employment, or was a principal occupation for women who were unemployed, or unimpressed with the limited alternatives. While it would be simply wrong to argue that participation in prostitution can be taken as evidence of untrammelled 'female agency', later discussion will show that some women did opt for prostitution in preference to that range of other haphazard, constraining, or ill-paid activities

---

[51] Whellan, *History, topography, and directory*, 312–65.
[52] Clementina Carr, applications for parochial relief, parish of All Saints, T241/1.

which confronted those on the margins of Victorian economic life. As well as considering the economic context of prostitution and its possible adoption as a strategy by women seeking to earn a living and avoid destitution, the subject warrants attention for other reasons. First, at a time when women's activities generally find little reflection in the sources, prostitution provides the exception. Although the volume of discussion and characterisations of prostitution varied throughout the period, it was the single activity which in one way or another commanded the virtually unbroken attention of commentators. In her discussion of prostitution in London, Judith Walkowitz draws on the perspective of Stallybrass and White, who argue that 'what is *socially* peripheral is so frequently *symbolically* central'.[53] The prostitute in London (and, I would add, Newcastle), was for some commentators 'the quintessential female figure of the urban scene',[54] a potent sign of sexual disorder. Views about prostitution can illuminate some important features of the cultural framework of those bourgeois observers of 'low' working-class life and the meanings constructed around it.

However, I would argue further that echoes of 'disordering' female sexuality, while appearing most strongly in the records in relation to prostitution as may be expected, can be detected too in discussions of women's other work, and in discussion of more general social problems and crises in Newcastle. Focusing upon the discourses around the body of the poor woman in particular urban spaces, the discussion of disordering femininity which follows is not, therefore, an abandonment of materialist analysis in favour of symbol, metaphor and construction. Rather, examination of the meanings attached to gender, sexuality and women's work in this very specific context is intended to reiterate the constant interaction between the constructed identity, and the experiences, of poor women.

Working-class women, urban space and the disorder of 'otherness'

In her work *Volatile bodies*, Elizabeth Grosz poses a question:

> Can it be that in the West, in our time, the female body has been constructed not only as a lack or absence but with more complexity, as a leaking, uncontrollable, seeping liquid . . . not a cracked or porous vessel, like a leaking ship, but a formlessness that engulfs all form, a disorder that threatens all order? . . . The metaphorics of uncontrollability, . . . the association of femininity with contagion and disorder, the undecidability of the limits of the female body[,] . . . its powers of cynical seduction and allure are all common themes in literary and cultural projections of women.[55]

---

[53] Peter Stallybrass and Allon White, *The politics and poetics of transgression*, Ithaca, NY 1986, cited in Walkowitz, *City of dreadful delight*, 20.
[54] Ibid. 21.
[55] Grosz, *Volatile bodies*, 203.

How was female working-class identity constituted in nineteenth-century Newcastle upon Tyne? The particular focus of this section is the body and its meanings in the poor working-class area of Sandgate and neighbouring Quayside. I am interested to track the female body through the home, workplaces, institutions and streets of that district, to examine how the 'metaphorics of uncontrollability', the dangerous 'formlessness' of femininity, can be traced here. Prostitution, women working in public in occupations considered degrading, exhibiting their poverty in their lives (and deaths) on the streets of the city – all generated alarm, and were the objects of attention among reformers. At a more general level as well, crises such as the mid century cholera epidemic, the influx of Irish labourers to Newcastle, and the spread of urban squalor conjured visions of invasion, danger and encroaching pollution in the fearful imaginations of the bourgeoisie. A sense of moral panic and danger in society rose from time to time. Positioning these fears within a context which recognises the more constant and specific endemic site of infection and disorder from 'within' – the body of the poor working-class woman – provides some basis for exploring the metaphoric links between the two, the development of a vocabulary of (sexualised) disorder, and the subtle shifts in the 'discourse of danger' over a century. How was the identity of the poor Newcastle woman constructed, maintained, and, importantly, challenged over time, and how was her body implicated in the process?

The recent historical focus upon the body has been conditioned by the work of Michel Foucault,[56] as well as by developments within feminist theory which have brought the body to the fore, and which stress that, necessarily, the 'human body and its history presuppose each other'.[57] Foucault's conception of the body as the site deeply enmeshed in elaborations of power, despite considerable debate about the utility of his work in a gender-based analysis, has emphasised the historical specificity and materiality of the body. The anti-essentialism of Foucault's thesis, which envisioned bodies in modernity 'made' through discipline and also importantly through resistance, was a crucial early challenge to social constructionists who posited the body as a neutral, passive, biological 'given' to be later inscribed with meaning.[58] Feminist scholars in turn have considered the ways in which women's bodies are 'bound up in the order of desire, signification, and power', elaborating the concept of the social body as the crucial site 'of contestation, in a series of economic, political, sexual, and intellectual struggles' over gender meanings.[59] Indeed, in the complex theoretical debates on the concept of

---

[56] See Foucault, *Discipline and punish*, and *The history of sexuality*, Paris 1976, trans. R. Hurley, Harmondsworth 1978.
[57] M. Gatens, 'Power, bodies and difference', in M. Barrett and A. Phillips (eds), *Destabilizing theory: contemporary feminist debates*, Cambridge 1992, 120–37 at p. 132.
[58] On the conception of resistance as power in Foucault's work see *Power/knowledge: selected interviews and other writings, 1972–77*, ed. C. Gordon, Brighton 1980, 142, and *History of sexuality*, 101.
[59] Grosz, *Volatile bodies*, 17–19.

difference, the body has come to occupy a central place in critiques of dichotomies of sex/gender where the former is presented as the unmediated material of nature, the latter a product of social inscription.[60]

Of particular significance in the current context, historians of the nineteenth century too have begun to explore the ways in which the discourse of the body in Victorian England was positioned 'at the heart of so much Victorian social thought'.[61] While for earlier periods historians have traced the use of body metaphors in connection with social organisation,[62] Catherine Gallagher has argued that it was in the nineteenth century, through the influence of Malthus and others, that the body and its perceived needs were cast as intensely, and insolubly, problematic, and recourse to a language of 'biological economy' which intersected with views on the 'social organism', exerted a powerful influence on the shape of social criticism.[63] Inevitably, a focus upon the body, as Thomas Laqueur contends, confronts the historian with another version of a dominant theoretical tension, between the lived experience of the body as 'that extraordinarily fragile, feeling, transient mass of flesh with which we are all familiar . . . and the body that is so hopelessly bound to its cultural meanings as to elude unmediated access'.[64] Following John Fiske, here I proceed on the assumption that attention to metaphor is not to deny the material relationship between the individual body and the social body:

> the presence of bodies together in the same time and space, is where social relationships are grounded; and social relationships are the lived, material experience of those more abstract, structural social relations . . . [t]here is a continuum . . . stretching from consciousness through identities, bodies, relationships and relations that does not just extend into the social order but is constitutive of it.

The body is a useful (even pivotal) focal point, precisely because it is at once the primary site 'where social life is turned into lived experience',[65] and a powerful source of metaphor in the Victorian social imaginary.

In the middle of 1850, an unidentified investigator wrote a series of letters for the *Newcastle Chronicle* on the condition of the poor in that city. Referring at the outset to the 'extraordinary influence' of the press in pursuing a 'noble mission' to reveal the extent of wretchedness in the midst of Victorian

---

60 See Judith Butler, *Gender trouble: feminism and the subversion of identity*, London 1990, 128–41.
61 Catherine Gallagher, 'The body versus the social body in the works of Thomas Malthus and Henry Mayhew', in C. Gallagher and T. Laqueur (eds), *The making of the modern body: sexuality and society in the nineteenth century*, Berkeley 1987, 83–106 at p. 90.
62 Barbara Duden, *The woman beneath the skin: a doctor's patients in eighteenth-century Germany*, Cambridge, Mass. 1991, 26–49.
63 Gallagher, 'The body versus the social body', 97.
64 T. Laqueur, *Making sex: body and gender from the Greeks to Freud*, Cambridge, Mass.–London, 1990, 12.
65 Fiske, *Power plays, power works*, 57–8.

prosperity, the correspondent set about his task.[66] The result was predictable. The report combined a repeated insistence on the objectivity of the spectator's surveillance in the reports with the careful garnering of all relevant statistics to provide a 'scientifically rigorous' framework for his claims about the magnitude of the problem and the need for urgent action. Scientific rigour notwithstanding, the language in the letters was that curious (and now-standard) popular journalistic mix of shame, sensationalism, voyeurism and condescending sympathy.

The main object and location of the study was Sandgate. The area itself and its population had had a distinctive reputation well before the nineteenth century. Its proximity to the Tyne, the occupational groups which clustered there as a result – sailors, keelmen, fishwives – and a kind of 'rough and ready' pre-industrial culture that it supposedly spawned were all standard themes in local ballads and guides to the city.[67] Travellers to the area noted the tendency to riot and disorderly behaviour among its inhabitants. John Wesley in 1742 preached from the steps of the Guildhall near the quay, and was supposedly threatened by 'roughs' only to be saved by a sturdy fisherwoman who stood between Wesley and the crowd; he also commented specifically on the drunkenness and swearing he encountered.[68] To some extent, however, these incidents by the nineteenth century were cited as curiosities of a bygone age, when Sandgate was bounded by fields. In the middle of the nineteenth century, however, the dimensions of Sandgate went beyond its reality as a geographical area, or as a source of local characters and curiosities. For some, such as the *Newcastle Chronicle* correspondent, it came to represent the Novocastrian version of the vice-ridden underbelly of Victorian expansion:

> After exploring the town by day, I wished to survey it at night. . . . After the closing of the public-houses, the more sober move off in pairs at once. . . . It was pitiable beyond expression to see the desperation of those girls who had failed to attract even the most profligate to their abodes. I saw one going about, taking hold first of one and then of another. I saw another sitting in the gutter. . . . I asked one of the policemen . . . 'Is this the worst part of town?' 'Decidedly the worst. We call Sandgate the City of Sin, sir.' . . . Can nothing be done to roll back this surging tide of wretchedness and vice, or is it doomed that one generation after another shall remain the victims of systems and habits leading to such fearful results? I have merely described what I saw *exteriorly*. These outcomings of vice reveal the *inward disorder*.[69] (my emphasis)

Framed in the language of revelation, the letters were filled with descriptions

---

[66] *Inquiry into the condition of the poor*, 'Preliminary remarks', 1. The second series of letters was written by a Newcastle resident, Dr George Robinson, since the original correspondent had taken another 'engagement'.
[67] Anon., *The picture of Newcastle upon Tyne 1807*, facsimile edn, London 1969, 15–16.
[68] Tomlinson, *Comprehensive guide*, 21, 24.
[69] *Inquiry into the condition of the poor*, 1st ser., letter i, 12.

of crime, promiscuity and filth. Certainly, in some sections there were instances recounted of 'respectable' women who struggled to maintain their households. Stark contrasts were also drawn between the outward signs of bodily excess such as drunkenness in the streets and the 'swankey shops' of Sandgate, and those largely hidden results of bodily deprivation in nearby lodgings, such as an eighteen-month-old child who was 'a mere skeleton – the bones protruding – and the skin shrivelled and cold'.[70] But these exceptions to the general characterisation of the area, and the contradictions and extremes contained within it, merely strengthened the overall impression of Sandgate as a moral 'desert . . . overgrown with weeds and noxious plants'.[71]

The unfolding scene of vice, the environment of disorder which the reporter described, drew heavily upon portrayals of women who were 'out of place': a bar 'and behind it a girl, who seemed to be the mistress of ceremonies';[72] entries where groups of women stood 'retailing their gossip, and exchanging their powers of rhetoric in wholesale abuse'; female street sellers 'sitting till midnight on the damp ground . . . with a few articles of crockery ware gathered around them, and a single candle wasting away with the wind'; and the supposedly ubiquitous prostitute, in an area where it was claimed that prostitution was 'emphatically *the* traffic of the district'.[73] As Daphne Spain reminds us, 'femininity and masculinity are constructed in particular places'.[74] In Sandgate in 1850, female identity was constructed *by* particular places as well, and the places themselves were identified by the movements and activities which occurred within them. Women's passage through the space of Sandgate was often sufficient to identify them as disorderly, while such presence in turn further constituted the place as disordered. Certainly, there is evidence to suggest that women were *numerically* predominant in the population, and that the area contained a significant proportion of female-headed households. The *Newcastle Chronicle* writer reported that there were 760 adult males and 913 adult females in the area.[75] While the spectre of independent women may have been disquieting, it was neither simple weight of numbers nor household structure but the women's public activities which were the source of major concern. That women not only plied their trades or pursued their leisure in the open, but further did so noisily, and at night, involved a triple transgression of bourgeois norms in relation to gendered boundaries of space, time and speech. Women's bodies, and meanings constructed around their presence at particular places and times, formed a complicated circuit of identity in which each element derived definition from the other.

---

[70] Ibid. letter i, 14, 19, 10; letter iii, 28.
[71] Ibid.
[72] Ibid. letter i, 9.
[73] Ibid. letter i, 10–11; letter iv, 33.
[74] Daphne Spain, *Gendered spaces*, Chapel Hill, NC 1992, 7.
[75] *Inquiry into the condition of the poor*, 1st ser., letter iv, 29.

While the *Newcastle Chronicle* writer attempted to move systematically and critically through the area in his letters, describing the external environment as well as revealing a domestic geography of poverty and vice which usually remained hidden, neither his subject nor his emphasis upon women as a source of disorder was new. The existence of prostitution in Newcastle, for example, had long been acknowledged by observers of the city. Eneas Mackenzie recalled in 1827 that Plummer Chare

> was noted, a few years ago, as the receptacle of Cyprian nymphs, whose blandishments were of the most coarse and vulgar description. Indeed, most of these dark lanes were inhabited by 'very dangerous, though not very tempting females'. But the character of these lanes has been much altered in late years; most of the dwelling houses have been converted into granaries, warehouses, maltings [and] breweries.[76]

The language Mackenzie employs is in some ways suggestive of the approach taken to prostitution earlier in the century. As the focus of both the humour and condescension of the dominant patriarchal discourse, prostitutes were 'contained' and reduced to the space they occupied, viewed as some curious (and sometimes, as in Mackenzie's quote, exotic) human extension of the city's architectural impoverishment. The implication is that, rather like other problems of urban living, these living 'urban problems' would soon be swept away by the hand of Victorian progress. The emphasis upon simple containment is also seen in other records: in 1829, for example, Newcastle's constables were ordered by the mayor to keep the city's thoroughfares clear of girl street sellers and others creating a 'nuisance', and to present weekly reports listing brothels and prostitutes in their districts.[77] At times, the project to remove scavengers, paupers and prostitutes from the streets, and away from the public gaze, failed spectacularly. In 1838, for example, local newspapers reported at length on the case of Elizabeth Graham, an old woman who died from uterine cancer in a state of homelessness, emaciation and absolute destitution, and who was shunted between public authorities in the hours before her death. The *post mortem* report revealed her hitherto hidden disease, the concealed disorder within, and the whole case was a revelation to the coronial jury, which recorded their horror not merely at the individual's circumstances, but at the thought that in Newcastle, anyone 'might die as they are passing through the streets', or to be allowed 'to die as a dog'.[78] The visibility of the pauper, the possibility of public death, cut across optimistic visions of increasing prosperity and social improvement.

The theme of the separation and containment of the body of the poor

---

[76] Mackenzie, *Descriptive and historical account*, i. 164. Mackenzie does not indicate whom he is quoting within his text.

[77] H. A. Mitchell, *A report of the proceedings in the mayor's chamber, Newcastle upon Tyne, during the mayoralty of Geo. Shadforth esq., 1829–1830*, Newcastle n.d., 11.

[78] *Newcastle Courant*, 20 July 1838.

woman, and especially the prostitute, was evident in institutional and rhetorical terms throughout the century. Newcastle's Lock Hospital, opened in 1814 by two local surgeons, was designed both to treat venereal diseases and, importantly, to shield effectively the 'respectable' poor from the prostitute's presumed pernicious influence. Prostitutes were denied admittance to most of Newcastle's benevolent institutions for the poor, such as the Lying-In Hospital, and most privately administered charities designed to aid women specifically forbade the granting of relief to any who were not 'of good character'.[79]

The administration of poor relief too was increasingly based upon distinctions between 'deserving' and 'undeserving' applicants, and the gendered variants of these categories were clear. While for both women and men, allegations of drunkenness, lack of industry and criminality all operated to cast certain individuals as 'undeserving', each of these categories was formulated against ideal, 'respectable' forms of behaviour which drew heavily upon gender stereotypes. Moreover, the category of sexually 'inappropriate' behaviour applied to the female poor found no sustained parallel with their male counterparts, again reflecting predominant bourgeois ideals of passive, orderly and legitimate expressions of feminine sexuality. The taint of prostitution for women was sometimes the factor determining their treatment. In 1854, for example, Mary Moralee, a forty-year-old woman who was incurably diseased and a former prostitute, had been given medical attention and 'necessary whiskey [sic]' for her pain by the Medical Officer of the Poor Law Union, who recommended that she also be visited by a nurse. So incensed were neighbouring ratepayers at her treatment, and at the thought that 'their money should be appropriated for such a purpose', that they made representations to the Poor Law Guardians. In particular, they noted that she 'was constantly having with her 4 or 5 notorious prostitutes'. Relief thereafter ceased, a nurse was refused, and Mary Moralee was ordered to the workhouse.[80] Within the workhouse itself, the disciplining of women's bodies was effected both by architectural arrangements to separate the sexes and by daily regulation. While the Newcastle Workhouse was geographically separate from its main catchment area, and sometimes noted for its efficient operation, records of the institution suggest that its officials were keen to police behaviour and obliterate signs of bodily excess associated with slum living. Reports of opium use and alcohol consumption were dealt with swiftly, as were cases of sexual encounters between inmates, with punishments of extended confinement.[81]

---

[79] The Lying-In Hospital and Outdoor Charity for Poor Married Women, rules and regulations, 7, contained in the Lying-In Hospital minute book, 1859–78, TWAS 672/197.
[80] Charles Hammond to Poor Law Board, 19 Aug. 1854, Newcastle Union correspondence, 1853–4, PRO, MH 12/9099.
[81] Poor Law Guardians' minute book, 30 Aug. 1861, TWAS 359/1/20; Workhouse Visitors' Book, St Nicholas's parish, 12 Feb. 1828, 7 Oct. 1829, NRO, EP 86/124.

Both prior to the Poor Law Amendment Act of 1834, when grants of relief were subject more to the discretion of the local parish officers, and after, female applicants were keenly aware that their poverty made them liable to assumptions of immorality, and they often strenuously emphasised their 'respectable' characters. Casual surveillance of poor women and their occupation of 'dangerous' spaces provided ample opportunity for the construction of a general, immoral identity, a kind of presumed guilt by location as well as association, in the crowded environment and transient population of the slums. The economic or sheer physical necessity of public activity was usually lost on observers. Mention of women being in 'the entrances of their closes to breathe a little fresh air, escaping for a few moments from their stuffy . . . tenements' was rare enough:[82] acknowledgement that such space was possibly constructed differently in the minds of people for whom it was their home and neighbourhood was non-existent. Continuing emphasis on individual character assessment, of course, could obscure the links between women's economic status, poverty and prostitution. For the most part, discussions of prostitution positioned it primarily in the realm of deviant sexuality, rather than, for example, as an economic strategy.[83]

If earlier approaches to prostitution had been based upon the idea of containment, how did the terms of discussion alter in the face of urban expansion, and the increasing emphasis from about mid century onwards upon investigations such as that in the *Newcastle Chronicle*? In recent works, historians have considered the proliferation of discourses in response to the pressing problems of expansion and rapid urbanisation in Victorian cities, along with the implications of these constructions for gender and class identities. The work of Mary Poovey, for example, in relation to the development of the 'sanitary idea', is particularly useful.[84]

In relation to discourses of sanitation and disease in the Victorian period, it is as well to remember that fear of uncontrollable infection, of sudden and overwhelming invasion of the body from without, was certainly not without foundation. In the first half of the century in particular, Newcastle along with the other major urban centres of England was swept by a series of epidemics, which left not only death in their wake, but also a renewed urgency to investigate, explain and remedy their causes. While typhus was endemic in slum areas, and scarlatina and so-called 'Irish fever' epidemics occurred in the 1840s, epidemics of cholera provoked the greatest alarm. Its swift work, reportedly bringing diarrhoea-accompanied death in the span of just nine hours, its categorisation as a disease which 'spread inscrutably' to affect all

---

82 Sherard, *Cry of the poor*, 150.
83 Jane Long, 'Sex work and female poverty: the case of nineteenth century Newcastle upon Tyne', in P. Hetherington and P. Maddern (eds), *Sexuality and gender in history: selected essays*, Perth 1993, 144–66.
84 Mary Poovey, 'Domesticity and class formation: Chadwick's 1842 *Sanitary Report*', in David Simpson (ed.), *Subject to history: ideology, class, gender*, Ithaca 1991, 65–83.

classes,[85] was a terrible challenge to a society seeking to delimit more precisely the boundaries of the human body, and of the space within the city itself. Cholera was excess, uncleanliness and sheer corporeality, a shocking reversal of the Victorian mission to overcome perverse forms of nature, and to civilise and to progress through urban expansion and social planning.

Again, in seeking explanations for such disasters, slum areas and the bodily 'excesses' believed to occur there were the focal points. The 1832 epidemic, for example, was, according to one commentator, a 'terrible scourge from the hand of an offended God', brought about by lewdness and drunkenness. And though brought by the hand of God, it was carried first in the body of a woman, 'an aged female, who for many years has been remarkable only for her filthiness and intemperance. Her time was spent chiefly in begging and gathering up any kind of filthy offals which she could exchange for money.' [86] Lewdness, filth, offal, disease, drunkenness – and a disordering woman: the metaphoric links were plainly drawn. Analyses of the later epidemic of 1853 did not cite divine providence, but rather scientific and medical evidence about the disease's causes. Again, however, the focus was the slums of Sandgate, and again the rhetoric of infection was linked to images of other types of invasion thought to exacerbate if not explain the onset of the epidemic. Local doctors reported to the Poor Law Board in Westminster that the influx of Irish labourers to Sandgate for the harvest 'fearfully increased the evil'; at the very time that disease raged in the area, Irish workers could be seen walking up the hill 'in a Troop to the already crowded houses', disembarking from steamers which had docked on the quayside.[87] It was also 'the wandering Irish, who have continued to pour into the town during the greatest part of the year' who were blamed for the spread of typhus five years previously.[88]

In this hierarchy of danger and vice, the Irish commonly appeared as a primary example of foreign infection and invasion.[89] The Irish were the 'foreigners within', and consistently discussed in terms which cast them as such in sources from Newcastle throughout the century. As Gallagher has noted in relation to Henry Mayhew's treament of the Irish,[90] it was not any allegation of promiscuity that was the cause of consternation. Indeed, most observers in Newcastle were quick to remark that Irish women were distinguished from their English counterparts by their morality and religiosity.

---

85 Dr White, report on cholera, document received 13 Sept. 1853, PRO, MH 12/9099.
86 *An affectionate address to the inhabitants of Newcastle and Gateshead on the present alarming visitation of divine providence in the fatal ravages of the spasmodic cholera*, Newcastle 1832.
87 Second report from Mr R. D. Grainger, Medical Inspector of the Board on Cholera at Newcastle upon Tyne, 12 Sept. 1853, PRO, MH 12/9099.
88 Account of the Newcastle Dispensary for 1847, TWAS 1547/10, 6.
89 The Medical Officer of Health at Newcastle claimed that the city ranked fourth in England for the proportion of Irish in the area, after Liverpool, Manchester and Bradford: C. M. Fraser and K. Emsley, *Tyneside*, Newton Abbott 1973, 118.
90 Gallagher, 'The body versus the social body', 101.

Similarly, the Irish poor were described not as vicious and miserable, but on the contrary, as 'vivacious, happy, and contented in their circumstances'.[91] While not apparently linked, then, to disordering femininity, the concern expressed about the Irish none the less fell into that broader category of concern about the predominance of a regressive, brutish nature over civilisation and ordered culture. Such 'contentment' under these impoverished circumstances, alleged idleness in a society with a strong emphasis upon individual striving and self-help, could indeed be interpreted as a 'kind of perversity'[92] and a dangerous example. The Irish were portrayed as fundamentally corporeal, as a race whose supposed physicality and distinctive physiognomy placed them in a sub-human category of the racial hierarchy which extended from the most 'animalistic' and 'savage' states of nature – to be found, supposedly, among African tribes – to the 'pinnacle' of culture and civilisation, the white bourgeois English male, in whom all physicality was a mere adjunct to the dominant, rational mind which defined his being.

Indeed, the treatment of Sandgate and its inhabitants in the literature drew heavily upon such racial thought for its metaphoric punch. That the place was described as a 'desert' immediately suggested its dislocation from the *properly* cultivated and fertile soil (and bodies) of England. Entering its alleys required both a literal and figurative, almost proto-Wellsian, 'descent' into 'some cavern', marked by perpetual darkness, where people were compelled to eat 'their dinner at midday by candlelight'. The population had degenerated into a 'state of heathenism and social degradation as low as that of actual savage life',[93] and some dismay was expressed by those involved in reform work that it may have been as futile to expect the poor to ever actually change their character as it was 'to expect the Ethiopian to change his skin'.[94]

While the Irish represented the foreign, excessively natural 'other' whose presence was disordering, and the supremacist language of imperialism provided a ready supply of crude comparison, the local population of the slums repesented a fearful, endemic 'other'. Its corporeality was severely confronting, a corporeality which was often described with particular reference to the female body. Traditional ballads told of those particular occasions, such as the Newcastle Fair, when women from Sandgate, 'like bees from A hive/Like a bed full of fleas/They come jumping alive',[95] moved outside their usual location. As the city expanded, however, the presence of this disorder became an everyday occurrence, and more difficult to ignore. Writers to local newspapers, for example, complained at the time of the cholera epidemic of those 'squalid objects, ragged and barefooted children,

91 *Inquiry into the condition of the poor,* 2nd ser., letter iv, 34.
92 Gallagher, 'The body versus the social body', 101.
93 *Inquiry into the condition of the poor,* 1st ser., letter ii, 17; letter iii, 25; letter iv, 32.
94 J. Price, *NDG,* 1885, 279.
95 'The rigs of the Newcastle fair', BL, MS Bell 11621.i.2, vol. ii.

51

and wretched women' who sold wares and begged in the streets.[96] These embodiments of poverty were moving boldly towards the very households of the 'repectable' population. 'In many of our better streets it is almost one servant's work', complained a correspondent, 'to answer [the] knocks and rings of such people.' Even in the country's capital, there was no such infringement of space: in London, 'these persons have regular cries, and can be had when wanted'.[97] What was the solution to this encroaching disorder?

The bourgeois belief in domesticity as the core of 'civilising' influence was very strong. At the heart of this most gendered domain stood the body of the woman, exercising moral influence, bringing light, harmony, cleanliness and purpose to urban households: 'the best of all reforms begin at home, and cannot be accomplished without the voluntary aid of wives, mothers and daughters; it is important that we enlist them under the right banner', wrote one observer in 1885.[98] The ordering of the disordering female body, then, was an essential prerequisite to any further mission of widespread improvement. The task took on particular meaning in the rhetoric of generational progress, too, as women, once 'transformed', could not only exercise a critical influence upon existing conditions, but could help also to guarantee the continuation of improvement in the next generation.

According to the bourgeoisie, the animal state of nature in which the lower working classes were thought to exist could be overcome to the extent deemed desirable and functional,[99] fashioned into a cultural form which reflected their own priorities of progress, order and rationality. The rhetoric of a timeless, 'universal passion' amongst poor women for a 'natural but improper indulgence', of uncontrolled female sexuality and an innate inclination to vice, lingered throughout the century, suggesting perhaps that any scientific approach to transformative missions was destined to fail.[100] Such a position was fraught with difficulty, however. To argue an essentially biological model of female sexuality which propelled women to indulge their illicit passions logically implicated all women, regardless of class. Increasingly, a more complex interplay of forces was cited: notions of biological woman were retained, but were overlain with the idea that the degree to which 'natural' sinfulness was played out depended upon an array of specific cultural influences and constraints.

By mid century, then, a discourse of transformation came to predominate, which was strongly gendered and class based.[101] With careful handling, women could be educated away from their bodies' sinful excesses, which

---

96   *Newcastle Journal*, 5 Nov. 1853, 7.
97   Ibid. 27 Oct. 1853, 5.
98   Price, NDG, 1885, 280.
99   *Inquiry into the condition of the poor*, 2nd ser., letter vi, 102.
100 Mr Charles Lamport, in a discussion of the Contagious Diseases Acts, *Transactions of the National Association for the Promotion of Social Science, Newcastle upon Tyne meeting*, 1870, n.p., 231.
101 Poovey, *Uneven developments*, 11.

would then free this site for the development of socially approved forms of womanly behaviour and bodily functions, such as modest displays of wifely affection and (legitimate) maternity. The key to this process, George Robinson suggested, was for others of their sex, but not of their class, to visit the slums and to demonstrate by their deportment the virtues of bodies properly trained to cleanliness and natural delicacy. For men, the emphasis was more upon mental improvement. The exertion of control over the body, which had in the past been allowed to 'brutalise the mind', was the first step. Programmes of physical exercise could be used to liberate men's bodies and restore to them a state of 'childhood', from whence they could be led onto the paths of civilised 'manhood'. The rhetoric here, though, did not stop at the notion of transformation. For men, attention to the body could be the precursor of some degree of bodily transcendence: with the raw material of a re-educated body, the more important work of effecting an elevation in the position of the mind on the 'intellectual and moral scale' could commence.[102]

Transformation was thought possible for women if in the first instance their sexuality could be restrained or mediated. Young women were cited as the most likely beneficiaries of such a process, before they reached 'the brink of the moral hell of all that is vile and degrading'.[103] By the later nineteenth century in Newcastle, this growing belief in the capacity to transform poor women via the regulation of their bodies was clearly in evidence, and the systematic planning and zealous execution of schemes to 'rescue' poor women from prostitution took on appropriate missionary proportions. From about the 1860s, the involvement of notable local philanthropists such as Lady Armstrong in the establishment of refuge and training homes for poor working-class women began in earnest. By the 1880s, there were no less than twelve charitable homes and refuges for women in Newcastle, devoted to rigorous moral and occupational training and to 'preventive' work.[104]

Most of the homes were situated outside the recognised area of the slums, and usually emphasised a concern to separate the inmates physically from their usual environment for a minimum period. Many, too, imposed a regime of disciplined work and routine prayer, and attention to 'correct' appearance was cited as a means of elevation. In fact, as I detail later, many of the inmates of such homes were not recruited from the ranks of Newcastle's prostitutes, but were young women seen as being 'at risk' unless preventive measures were taken. Some of the inmates of establishments such as the Brandling Home for Penitent Women really had nothing to repent, except an 'inevitably' immoral identity preordained by accidents of class and gender. But both at

---

102 *Inquiry into the condition of the poor*, 1st ser., letter v, 44; 2nd ser., letter iv, 85; 2nd ser., letter vi, 105.
103 *NDG*, 1899, 35.
104 *Guide to the schools, homes and refuges in England for the benefit of girls and women*, London 1888.

Brandling and in other homes, the lines between actual and potential prostitution were blurred.

The themes of separation and transformation were exemplified in two major schemes in the reform establishments: emigration, which provided the ultimate means of separating women from their former lives, and laundry work within the homes themselves, which conveniently combined spiritual 'cleansing' rituals and the generation of income. Laundry work in homes was commonplace here and elsewhere.[105] Problems associated with the enterprises were common, and some homes, such as Brandling, were forced to close by the end of the century. At Brandling, staff turnover was high, and one laundress, whose occupation had clearly not done its 'cleansing' work, was dismissed for drunkenness, 'a common failing it wd. seem among these women'.[106] None the less, a range of other homes remained, and operated with similar imperatives – separation, cleansing and transformation.

Occasionally claims were made about the triumphs of transformation which had occurred. Hannah Clarke, a severely diseased young woman who had been turned to prostitution by a 'miserable woman' who accosted Hannah one day at the end of a Sandgate entry, lived in a state of 'gross darkness' and with an 'uncouth dialect' as well. She was completely 'cleansed', however, by her experience in Newcastle's Asylum for Female Penitents. At first Hannah threatened to get under the bed to avoid listening to a preacher; eventually not only were the 'scales from the eyes of her spiritual understanding' removed, she came from great tribulation and 'washed her robes, and made them white'. Unfortunately Hannah died shortly after her transformation, her body riddled with disease, but 'she was lovely in death'. Significantly, the Committee of the Asylum concluded, 'it may not be uninteresting to state, her body was carried to the grave by four ministers of God's word, as the underbearers, and the pall was borne by members of your Committee . . . to testify their respect for the deceased'.[107]

The interest in clothing the body in particular ways, as a part of the process of transforming it, again is a recurring theme in the literature. The Brandling Home, the Diocesan House of Mercy and the Salvation Army Rescue Home all had regulations about the attire of women, some grading their institutional uniforms to reflect the degree of penitence a woman had attained during her stay. The paid officers in some homes wore uniforms, or dresses 'of simple character . . . free from undue singularity'.[108] This emphasis upon dress could be seen as a simple correction of the prostitute's alleged fondness for gaudiness and finery. Nellie Guest, for example, was reported by

---

[105] Barbara Littlewood and Linda Mahood, 'Prostitutes, magdalenes and wayward girls: dangerous sexualities of working-class women in Victorian Scotland', *Gender and History* iii (1991), 160–75.
[106] Brandling Home register and diary, 1896, TWAS 583/4.
[107] Fifteenth annual report of the Asylum for Female Penitents, 1846, TWAS 586/1, 5–9.
[108] Diocesan Society for the Protection of Women and Children, minute book, statutes, 25 Oct 1897, NRO 3435.

the Salvation Army to have deliberately chosen 'the life, because of a love of dress and gaiety'.[109] Dressing in plain style, therefore, could be seen as one key element in the denial of former identity and the acts which accompanied it, actively involving a woman in the process of redefining the significance of her own body.

As well as the attempt to reorient perceptions of the body and its appearance, other themes arise in relation to dress and its meanings among poor women. The donning of silks, lace and feathers by 'low' working-class females was seen by some as a grotesque and disrespectful parodying of the upper classes. Clothing was also cited as the cloak for imposture, or of milder forms of dishonesty. A local ballad warned of the woman who wore 'fine frills and flounces' while 'underneath, all is not clean there'. The *Diocesan Gazette* recorded tales of landlords duped by apparently 'respectable' applicants for tenancy, who borrowed clothes for the occasion. A charity concerned with the 'rescue' of poor children related with horror the story of a teenage girl 'dressed like a woman' earning a living as a prostitute at the behest of her mother.[110] All these cases indicated a concern that clothing could not merely positively transform, but could also subvert or conceal bodily 'truths'. Masquerade through clothing, of course, was only part of a wider concern about the alleged proclivity of the poor to lie, adopt aliases, and manufacture circumstances to ensure undeserved access to resources. The Hebrew Friend-In-Need Society, for example, reassured its subscribers that the thorough investigation of applications for relief from the poor meant that 'imposture is well nigh an impossibility'.[111] Assumptions about the general dishonesty of the poor, of a culture in which deception was a commonplace strategy, appeared strongly as well in discussions of the work of women in the white-lead industry.[112]

There was no simple, single line of movement from attempted 'containment' of disorderly femininity to a belief in the possibility of transforming female bodies and the identities which clustered around them. Indeed, towards the end of the century, the inter-relationships between gender, class, sexuality and disorder continued to generate complex and sometimes contradictory views. There was the ongoing general challenge facing Victorians in attempting to make sense of their rapidly changing environment, a task complicated by the proliferation of specialist discourses which, paradoxically, claimed to simplify this sense-making process.

Moreover, a number of national and local events had brought gender-related issues in particular to the fore. The period is identified by a number of

---

[109] SAA Girls' statement books, vol. ii, case 413.
[110] 'C. T.': 'Famed filly fair', undated, BL, MS Bell 11621.i.2; J. Price, NDG, 1885, 279; Newcastle and Gateshead Poor Children's Holiday Association and Rescue Agency, annual report 1901, DU Archives 234/8, 26.
[111] Nineteenth annual meeting, Newcastle Hebrew Friend-In-Need Society, reported in *Newcastle Daily Journal*, 27 Dec. 1892, 6.
[112] See ch. 3.

historians as one in which notions of working-class family respectability and the need to forge 'respectable' female sexual and maternal identities as an integral part of this process were reaching new heights, spurred on by the growth of a distinctive working-class culture, trade unionism and feminism, and the campaigns around the Contagious Diseases Acts in the 1880s. There was also a trend away from paid work for the wives of skilled workers, as they attempted to consolidate their respectability. All these changes 'tended to rigidify gender divisions'.[113] Further, feminist historians have examined the ways in which 'gender relations are actively constructed in the workplace'[114] especially from mid century onwards, when issues of skill and protection of labour roles became more prominent and played themselves out in a gendered context.

How did these trends manifest themselves in Newcastle, and more particularly, what was their impact upon perceptions of the female body and female identity? One interesting example where the body of the working-class woman was again in the foreground of discussion and controversy, and where issues of sexuality, danger and women's work coalesced, is that of women's work in Newcastle's white-lead industry. In the chapter which follows, the specific example of white-lead employment is examined. Moving from the general environment of the slums and depictions of women within it across the century, to the more specific environment of the white-lead works of Newcastle close to the end of the nineteenth century, some closer basis is provided in which to consider the links between women's material conditions and the inter-relationship between these, and the cultural constructions of femininity which informed debate about their work.

113 Jeffrey Weeks, *Sex, politics and society: the regulation of sexuality since 1800*, London 1981, 74.
114 A. Game and R. Pringle, 'Beyond gender at work: secretaries', in N. Grieve and A. Burns (eds), *Australian women: new feminist perspectives*, Melbourne 1986, 273–91 at p. 275. For the nineteenth century see Rose, *Limited livelihoods*, 126–53; J. Scott, 'The woman worker', in G. Fraisse and M. Perrott (eds), *A history of women in the west: emerging feminism from revolution to world war*, iv, Cambridge, Mass. 1993, 399–426.

3

'You are Forced to do Something for a Living':
Women and White-Lead Work

The case of women's work in Newcastle's white-lead industry provides the opportunity to examine closely the discourses of exclusion which operated around one area of women's work, and to consider the inter-relationship between material conditions and cultural constructions of femininity. The particular debates around the work drew upon many of the broader characterisations of female disorder which were evident in the wider discussion of Sandgate and the slums of Newcastle. Such examination illustrates that the general, negative characterisations of women which clustered around activities such as prostitution were not confined, but spread outwards to inform judgements about a range of other activities. The women at the lead works bore the very real material costs of a system of labour which positioned them in 'unskilled' and dangerous occupations within the trade in the first instance. And the development of an exclusionary discourse which drew strength from, and in its turn contributed to, much wider constructions of working-class female identity and assessments of female capacity had material implications not merely for the women who were eventually banned from this particular form of wage-earning, but for the broader group of women from which they were drawn.

In 1855, a local directory listed five lead works in Newcastle.[1] While overall the trade was a relatively small employer of local labour, the concentration of women in the industry was high. Towards the end of the century, about 600 women were employed in the Newcastle lead factories,[2] many coming from neighbouring residential areas such as Sandgate or across the river from Gateshead. Lead processing was not new, nor was women's work within the industry. One writer in 1844 saw women's participation in the trade as a 'curious circumstance' which related to the propensity among Novocastrian women, as in the case of bricklaying, to 'have accustomed themselves to employments generally undertaken by men elsewhere'. Further, the writer implied that, just as bricklaying employment for women was dwindling as a result of the 'giant strides' Newcastle had made, so too would female employment in lead diminish with progress.[3] (The ideal of the

---

[1] Whellan, *History, topography and directory*, 351.
[2] *Daily Chronicle*, 15 Dec. 1892, unpaginated news cutting, TWAS 1512/14890, Lead Industry records, correspondence regarding female employment and lead poisoning.
[3] 'A day at the Tyne factories', *Penny Magazine* xiii, 797 (1844), 340–2 at p. 340.

non-working woman was so deeply embedded in the nineteenth-century bourgeois version of the great leap forward, that meaning here required no further elaboration.) On both counts, however, the writer was incorrect. Despite the 'progress' of urban industrial life, in Newcastle and elsewhere in the country, women continued to perform most of the work in the lead industry until government regulation in the late 1890s forced employers, despite their general reluctance, to cease hiring them.

With the exception of a few specialised positions within the lead industry, the bulk of the tasks performed were heavy, repetitive, dirty and designated as unskilled. In the Tyne works, lead 'pigs' were first melted, moulded into blue-lead cakes, and finally stacked in layers to a height of thirty feet. Each layer of lead in turn was spread with acid and oak-bark tan to begin the process of reducing the lead to carbonate, and then left for three months. The cakes with their white-lead coatings were at that time 'grubbed up from the bedding by hand', and carried to a rolling mill where the valuable product was separated from its blue-lead base. Residual white-lead was also retrieved by hand from the reservoirs. Once separated, the white lead was then scooped into dishes, and carried into stoves for drying. The white-lead carbonate thus produced was then marketed as a paste mixed with linseed oil, or as powder to add to yarn dyes, and especially to house paints, since its properties enhanced the 'hiding power' of the latter when brushed on walls.[4]

It was almost exclusively women who performed these heavy manual tasks: working in gangs of five, four women acted as carriers of the lead and the pots of acid in the first stages, while the fifth was engaged in stacking and arranging the cakes. It was women who later carried the cakes to the rolling mills, and then tended the lead in the stoves. The work of furnace-stoking and loading barrels of processed lead for transport, too, was their preserve. Men were usually employed in more skilled areas, supervising the smelting and desilvering processes or working as coopers within the factories.[5] 'Bed workers', as the women were called, toiled with bare hands and often bare feet stacking the lead cakes and treating the piles with acid. At many points in the processing of lead, white lead powder swirled in the air and was inhaled by the workers, became embedded in fingernails, and settled on the skin. The results of this labour could take a severe and obvious toll on the body. Some, but not all, women developed a distinctive blue line around their gums, a tell-tale sign of lead ingestion. Workers developed headaches and anaemia, and in more serious cases, excruciating colic, blindness and 'wrist drop', a partial but disabling paralysis which was frequently discussed in contemporary inquiries into the industry because of the disqualification from alternative employment it could impose upon its sufferers.[6] Disability from lead work

4 *Daily Chronicle*, 15 Dec. 1892.
5 See D. J. Rowe, *Lead manufacturing in Britain: a history*, London 1983, ch. vii.
6 See Dr Baumgarten, 1893 Report, 977.

could come quickly, and its results were often very visible. More extreme still were the severe encephalitic disorders and white-lead paralysis which preceded death from lead ingestion.

The introduction of new processing techniques and factory organisation in the nineteenth century underpinned expansion in white-lead production during the period. The drying of white-lead cakes, for example, had been made quicker and more economical with the introduction of special ovens in closed rooms, whereas cakes had previously been left to dry in open-sided sheds.[7] The increased speed and output of lead cakes with the use of machinery was reflected in the growth of the workforce: where works such as that at Elswick had commonly employed 100 people in the early period, by the end of the nineteenth century the labour force had trebled.[8] In the midst of such growth, however, women's occupation in white-lead processing became increasingly controversial. In the latter half of the century, a series of regulations regarding health requirements and the minimum age of workers was introduced. By 1898 women specifically were banned altogether from the industry. What were the sources of concern about lead work? A further question, sometimes overlapping but at other times quite distinct from the first, also arises: what were the sources of concern about *women's* work in the lead industry?

Given that lead work was not a new form of labour, understanding the growing controversy about women's employment requires an examination of the particular constellation of material conditions and discursive meanings in the nineteenth century which gave rise to new and widespread concern about its effects. There was considerable disagreement over the causes of workers' ill-health, as well as the measures which should be introduced as suitable remedies. An 1807 guide to Newcastle discussed lead processing: prior to the introduction of 'wet' processing, the circulation of dust and particles of white-lead generated in the factories had been 'extremely fatal to the health of the people employed'. Few lead workers lived beyond forty, it was claimed, until the 'most fatal' part of the process was remedied.[9] Despite such earlier claims, however, even at mid century the links between lead work and poisoning of labourers was far from clearly established. The writer of the 1844 *Penny Magazine* article on Newcastle's industry, for example, discounted claims that the women's work was injurious to their health. In this optimistic assessment, no account was taken of medical opinion: the very presence of female workers in the trade was taken as evidence in itself that the occupation 'was not so deleterious as it is often said to be'. Newcastle was a 'busy emporium' for the trade, and at its centre, bed workers 'certainly do not give countenance to the charge of unhealthiness brought against this manufacture; they look as healthy as the majority of females among the working

---

[7] Rowe, *Lead manufacturing*, 211.
[8] Ibid. 197.
[9] *The picture of Newcastle upon Tyne*, 104.

classes, and are said to feel but little inconvenience from their employment'.[10] The reference here to a class-based categorisation of female health, and to a dichotomy of health/unhealth based upon appearance, is revealing. This mid century writer's circular logic and reliance on the rhetoric of hearsay were not so much a failure of proper investigation but an expression of confidence in the general prospects of industry, and an affirmation of the superficial appearance of orderly progress. None the less, the focus upon the biology of class and gender, and upon the relationship between inner health and outward appearance, were to become recurring themes in discussion of lead work for women, as the sometimes hidden and relatively quick work of lead poisoning illustrated that, indeed, appearances could be deceptive.

The mood of the Victorians over issues of occupational health and safety was changing, and the translation of this concern into legislative regulation is well documented by historians of industry. In the case of lead, D. J. Rowe's major study provides a solid and interesting account of the trend towards intervention and regulation culminating in the exclusion of women in the 1890s, and later trends in the twentieth century when interventionist focus shifted to the regulation of anciliary industries.[11] While lead poisoning was first raised as an issue at the time of the Commission on Children's Employment in the early 1840s, it was not until the 1860s, with the extension of reforms to working conditions in dangerous industries, that any real consideration of the issue took place.[12] More regular comment on lead workers and their conditions appeared in the reports of factory inspectors from the mid 1870s onwards, leading eventually to the 1878 Factory Act which prohibited the employment of children, and women under the age of eighteen, in the most dangerous parts of lead processing. As Rowe points out, this act was a significant step in that it lent some formal recognition to the medical opinion that ingestion of lead dust into the bloodstream was the proximate cause of fatalities among workers. Once the initial restrictions of 1878 were introduced, there followed further regulations from 1884 under the Factory and Workshop Act (1883) which introduced minimum regimes of cleanliness and 'preventive' diets for workers within the factories, as well as compulsory medical inspection of ailing employees.

In the early 1890s, the publication of a medical treatise on lead poisoning by Dr Thomas Oliver of Newcastle, growing alarm on the part of poor relief authorities about disabilities among former lead workers, and newspaper exposés which took up the cause of workers in the 'white cemeteries',[13] contributed to growing pressure to further reform the industry. As well as introducing more stringent medical regulations, the Home Office appointed a departmental committee to investigate lead work in 1893. After taking

10 'A day at the Tyne factories', 340, 342.
11 Rowe, *Lead manufacturing*, ch. vii.
12 Ibid. 210.
13 *Daily Chronicle*, 15 Dec. 1892.

evidence throughout the country, that committee, which included Dr Oliver, recommended the exclusion of all women from white-lead processing. The measure was to be introduced in 1896. Consequent upon the protests of employers, however, it was not enforced until 1898. Rowe details the tensions between employers and the factory inspectors, and notes the contributions to the debate by individuals such as Chief Factory Inspector Alexander Redgrave. He also considers the varying interpretations of the economic position of lead workers by both radical and conservative contemporaries. In some respects, Rowe's view about the route of state intervention in the Victorian period based on the example of lead processing provides a useful general outline:

> Intervention was a slippery slope, on which one might stand still but could not move upwards and any movement was likely to send one downwards, deeper into legislative involvement. Often, therefore, within a decade of one piece of legislation which gave more or less general satisfaction, another would be passed enforcing restrictions rejected or not even considered by the former. Thus did society progress. As with poverty, there was, and is, no perfection, only relative progress as standards change over time.[14]

Yet Rowe's conclusions also alert the reader to the 'logical' progression often embedded in such chronologies of intervention, an inexorable movement from the regulation of child labour, to that of women, and from major industrial occupations to lower profile but none the less noxious trades on the periphery of the industrialising juggernaut of Victorian economic growth. This framework of progressive intervention can make the regulation of certain groups appear inevitable and natural: the orderly forces of social conscience, which at first tagged behind expansion, eventually moved in to police the 'obvious' disordering excesses of capitalism *en route*, to set to rights some of its graver consequences, but not to challenge the direction of its march. But what *were* the benchmarks for measuring the speed of progress, and *whose* standards change over time? Joan Scott has written about the hazards of representing the sexual division of labour, and protective legislation which flowed from it, as 'reflecting an objective process of historical development'. Instead, she maintains, it is the task of the historian not to naturalise or replicate the 'dominant discourse of the period, which conceptualised a standard woman and defined work as the violation of her nature', but to recognise it *as* a discourse which itself contributed to the construction of the 'problem' of women's work.[15] Rereading the sources on women and lead work with Scott's contentions in mind is fruitful, directing attention to the assumptions about gender, and working women as 'social pathology', which gave impetus to official regulation. In this way too, the connections

[14] Rowe, *Lead manufacturing*, 218.
[15] Scott, 'The woman worker', 401, 423.

between work, poverty, morality, and the perceived inherent disordering qualities of the female body are brought more clearly into view.

One of the specific triggers for renewed examination of the lead industry and women's role within it came with the inquests held into the deaths of women workers. The influence of the press in publicising such cases, as Rowe suggests, was instrumental in bringing the problem to the attention of the wider citizenry of Newcastle, and eventually to the country overall. But it was not merely the influence of the press; reportage of detailed coronial investigation of suspected work-related deaths was made possible in the first instance because the number of inquests themselves had increased, as a result of the more stringent medical regulations in the 1880s. The *Daily Chronicle* reported that in the two years to 1892, there had been 'ten inquests on the victims of lead . . . in Newcastle alone', quite apart from other lead-death inquests held on Tyneside.[16] In some respects, then, the growing interest in the lead industry and its fatal toll was a product of the increased regulation and surveillance of workers and work-related deaths which had previously been largely invisible, or appraised in a haphazard and inconclusive manner.

One particular case from this period, that of Charlotte Rafferty who died in November 1892, illustrates some of the interpretative tensions which arose around women's work in white-lead. The case of this unfortunate young woman in many respects appeared as typical: under-age at seventeen, she sought employment at Walkers, Parker and Co. in its Elswick works, situated close to her home in Mill Lane. Her father was unemployed during a period of strikes in Newcastle's industrial heartland, and so Charlotte 'had been the sole support of the house'. As a bed worker, she could earn 2s. a day, but Charlotte worked for a little more than five months; one Wednesday, she suffered a fit and lapsed into unconsciousness. Two days later, she died. On her death, Charlotte's family was given a sovereign by the firm. Walkers, Parker and Co. was subsequently prosecuted for employing under-age labour, and fined 5s. in Newcastle's Police Court.[17] It was then in death that Charlotte Rafferty's identity and motivations in life, and the state of her body, received intensive scrutiny. She provided, as did other individual women who suffered as she did before and after her death, the human marker around which broader arguments about the trade were constructed. The case prompted the writing of detailed articles in both the London and Newcastle papers, was subsequently raised in correspondence between officials in Newcastle and the Local Government Board in London, and was referred to in the minutes of the 1893 departmental committee which inquired into the state of workers in the trade.

Soon into the fray after Charlotte's death was Vaughan Nash, journalist for the *Daily Chronicle* in London. In two reports, Nash's focus was upon the poverty of women like Charlotte Rafferty:

16 *Daily Chronicle*, 21 Dec. 1892.
17 *Newcastle Daily Journal*, 30 Dec. 1892, 6.

THEY ASK FOR BREAD AND THEY RECEIVE WHITE-LEAD. The women who 'take to the lead' are mostly very poor and at the last gasp for the means of supporting life. Indeed, the white-lead works are for girls and women what the dock-gates are for men. . . . The elder daughter of a labourer's family, whose father may be out of work; the widow with the bairns looking to her for food; the wife whose husband is tempted to turn loafer by the knowledge that the woman can earn enough to find him in beer; the girl whose character does not stand scrutiny – these are the conscripts on whom the lot has fallen. . . . By a fatal process of selection these women go to the works ripe for death, their systems bared for the lead by poverty and impaired vitality.[18]

Nash's account, with its emphasis upon the implications of casuality in the labour market for women, was dismissed in the documents of contemporary officials. James Henderson, Factory Inspector at Glasgow, wrote to the Chief Inspector at the Home Office that it was 'an exaggerated and highly coloured statement of the case and contains just a sufficiency of truth in it to save it from condemnation as a piece of fiction'.[19] Rowe, too, criticises Nash's account in similar terms: 'much exaggerated and written in the language of righteous indignation, they contained enough truth (quoting, for instance, Dr Oliver) to compel belief and further investigation'.[20]

Such contemporary and historical appraisals of Nash miss the point. A number of interpretations circulated around the event of Charlotte Rafferty's death, the truthfulness of each depending upon the underlying discursive assumptions from which it was offered. Clearly Nash, writing within a framework of journalistic exposé, would produce a different truth to that constructed by the more formal and 'objective' language of officialese. For an historian to favour the official interpretation is perhaps to replicate those officials' privileged positions in the task of observation and explanation, and to neglect the critical interplay *between* contested truths. But it is that contest, which was informed by generalisations about the broader culture from which white-lead workers were drawn, and that interplay, which is most revealing here.

For Nash, women were the innocent victims of an exploitative trade which relied upon women's economic marginality for its continuation. Work practices were structured around an assumption that there would always be a ready, renewable supply of 'low class' workers. Documenting inadequate or poorly observed safety provisions in the works, where women wore mouth-guards which were makeshift and so open in texture they 'would serve as a kettle-holder', Nash concluded that culpability lay with 'the capitalist for his murderous process', abetted by the inertia of the Home Office. While he maintained that the issue had been 'hushed up for the credit of the persons

---

[18] *Daily Chronicle*, 15 Dec. 1892.
[19] James Henderson to HM Chief Inspector of Factories, 29 Dec. 1892, TWAS 1512/14884 [PRO, HO 45 9848 B12393A X/M 5983].
[20] Rowe, *Lead manufacturing*, 219–20.

. . . concerned',[21] evidence from other sources, too, also focused upon the economic position of the women workers. A local Board of Guardians five years earlier, for example, had reported the case of Mary Jane Todd, a worker at Walkers for four years, who had experienced sporadic illness. Deserted by her husband, a pitman, Mary had eventually been sent to the workhouse when she became too ill from lead-poisoning to continue her work. Citing such cases, the local Board pointed out that the manufacture of white lead cast 'great burdens . . . upon this Union . . . the victims of such work having to be maintained for a life long period in . . . premature decrepitude, palsy, and blindness'.[22] Witnesses to the 1893 departmental committee further testified to the lack of choice women faced in going to the lead works, if they were to ward off poverty. Dr Baumgarten, an examining physician for works in the area, stated that women turned to lead work sometimes as a stop-gap measure when 'there is poverty in the house'. Mary Ann Ingram, from the Hebburn works, explained that she was a lead worker because '[my husband] is a miner. I have the misfortune not to be with him. He is one of the bad husbands. I would not have been working now if he had been what he ought to have been.'[23]

While the link between lead work and poverty was quite commonly made, the interpretation of that link, and the conclusions about the moral state of the women drawn from it, varied substantially. To investigative writer Robert Sherard, poor women's preparedness to eke out a living this way was laudable: 'I cannot but hold in high esteem and honour a girl ready to sacrifice her beauty, her health, her chances of what is sweetest to womanhood, maternity, for a wage, albeit pitiful.' Dead but pure, women like nineteen-year-old lead-poisoning victim Elizabeth Ryan of Sandgate had preserved 'unspotted the white garment of [their] innocence', and she and her sisters comprised a 'very noble army of martyrs'.[24] The moral character of the women in the trade was the central issue which informed the oppositional frameworks utilised by Sherard and others. For Sherard, women were 'saved' by their work (and by their death) from the base and immoral destiny ordained for other women by their gender and class status. For others involved in the debate, however, it was just that baseness and immorality which was not warded off by death, but, rather, was actually revealed by it.

Considerable medical evidence had been amassed by the mid 1890s which in some respects appeared as scientific, neutral statements of cause and effect: the ingestion of white lead dust caused illness in workers. Studies by Oliver and others had made further links between lead poisoning and higher miscar-riage rates among workers, as well as early infant death and illness among

21 *Daily Chronicle*, 15, 30 Dec. 1892.
22 S. Robson, Clerk of Gateshead Board of Guardians, to Local Government Board, London, 14 Dec. 1887, PRO, MH 12/3096.
23 Mary Ann Ingram, 1893 Report, 77.
24 Sherard, 'White slaves', 526.

their children due to poisoned breast milk.[25] Yet beyond these observations lay considerable ground for further debate. Was the industry equally poisonous to all workers, or just to some? If only to some, what variables accounted for predisposition to lead poisoning? Was predisposition biological or social in origin? The questions multiplied, and as they did, so did the scope for confusion as the experts tripped over one another in the labyrinth of 'rational' explanation. In part, the generation of competing explanations was fuelled by the availability of information about both the public and private lives of the women. Indeed, as the sources amply illustrate, the division between these spheres became more and more blurred (and for some it was an alarming blur), as the trend to more detailed investigation of cases by the press and by officials grew.

While Vaughan Nash astutely suggested that the evidence taken to show that women were at greater risk than men of suffering from lead poisoning may have been linked 'to the circumstance of men doing the least dangerous work', the belief that women were more susceptible was stated more frequently in bald, unqualified biological terms. The report of the 1893 departmental committee, for example, stated that eight of the thirteen doctors who had appeared had agreed that women were 'more susceptible to lead poisoning'.[26] While views on women lead workers' biological weakness conformed to the tenets of general, gendered Victorian medical discourse, there were immediate and intense contradictions within these views which were logically insupportable in the class-based society of Victorian England. Sherard remarked that if women had been employed despite their weakness, then the reason for their employment was a 'mere economic one . . . they can be had at a much cheaper wage'.[27] Doctors who acted as employers' consultants were quick to deny the implication of grubby economic motives however, by arguing that women could easily perform the heavy manual work within the factories. Working-class women, said Baumgarten, were 'accustomed to hard work'. As for the trays of lead which women carried up ladders in the lead stacks and which weighed from 36lbs. to 56lbs. per tray, a manager explained that Newcastle women were particularly well suited to the task: 'I think it is all the training they are used to in this part of the country, in hawking about the streets here carrying baskets on their heads.'[28]

More difficult was the argument that lead-poisoning was attributable to hazardous conditions in the factories. Surely the white-lead deaths made it clear that the industry was poisonous to its workers? Not necessarily. Vividly illustrating the potent force of social prejudice fused with 'scientific' interpretation, the finger of suspicion was pointed at the victims: it was the

[25] Oliver's work and opinions are cited commonly during the period. See, for example, *Daily Chronicle*, 30 Dec. 1892; Sherard, *Cry of the poor*, 146.
[26] *Daily Chronicle*, 15 Dec. 1892; 1893 Report, 11.
[27] Sherard, 'White slaves', 525.
[28] Baumgarten, 1893 Report, 37; Mr G. Foster, Manager, James & Co., Ouseburn, ibid. 49.

pre-existing immorality and vice-weakened bodies of some women which probably predisposed them to illness. In this view, the body of the poor working-class woman was responsible, as much as the work which the women performed. In 1887, the north-east Inspector of Factories, William Chaytor, wrote that 'lead workers as a rule are of the lowest order[,] drink all they make & do not get proper meals of solid food besides living otherwise debauched lives'.[29] It was, said Inspector Henderson, not the honest married and single women in the works who suffered, but chiefly the 'weak, the careless, the ill cared for and the dissipated'.[30] Baumgarten claimed that some of those who suffered were 'women who have led a loose life'.[31] Dr Oliver himself was quoted as stating that, as well as some victims being poor, ill-fed, even starving, 'many of them lead a questionable life', while others included 'women who are labouring to support idle or drunken husbands or paramours . . . [and] betake themselves to the lead factories tempted by higher wages'.[32]

The language of desire linked to wages here suggests the strength of constructions of disorderliness which revolved around working women. While in other circumstances, the pursuit of wages in return for hard work was presented as the epitome of Victorian self-help and a mark of 'deserving' character among the lower working class, here the very activity of wage-earning was coupled with examples of sexual and corporeal excess, and had itself been transformed to become an activity which was enticing only because its continuation made possible the continuation of immoral life styles. It was a rhetoric in which economic and sexual identity became linked, and elided the distinctions between 'moral' and 'immoral' earnings: if the prostitute was the quintessential 'symbolic other', as Walkowitz suggests, she was not positioned in isolation from other women, but was one point in a continuum. That lead workers partook sufficiently of the same culture and so bore traces of that 'otherness', is strongly suggested in contemporary language.

In other respects, the very precautions introduced by employers, although given official imprimatur via government-enforced regulations, when administered to a disordered workforce could again contribute to the perception of disorder. The provision of a daily half-pint or pint of beer to stove-workers for medicinal and dietary purposes, for example, was mandated by the regulations. While the need for beer was duly recognised within the factory for labour which was hot, heavy and extremely taxing, drinking outside by the workers was condemned as a sign of moral looseness. In turn the fear arose that, among those women who were allegedly 'drunkards', the practical

29 Sir William Chaytor to W. E. Knollys, Local Government Board, London, 11 Nov. 1892, PRO MH 12/3096.
30 James Henderson to HM Chief Inspector of Factories, 29 Dec. 1892, TWAS 1512/14884.
31 Dr Baumgarten, 1893 Report, 37.
32 Quote from Dr Oliver in James Henderson to HM Chief Inspector of Factories, 29 Dec. 1892, TWAS 1512/14884.

intention and medical importance of the beer ration would not properly be recognised. Rather, the meaning of the ration would be distorted, perceived by the women as an opportunity merely to satisfy another addiction.[33]

The disorderly characteristics of women's lives outside the industry, then, could too readily be carried into the factory to subvert the meaning of the work they performed there. Such disorder permeating the space of the factory from beyond was further elaborated in allegations that women refused to observe particular regulations and safety requirements. A combination of deception, ignorance and neglect supposedly accompanied women into the factories, to ensure that any strategies devised for the safety of workers were mischievously evaded. The Local Government Board in London, in a draft reply to an enquiry from the Gateshead Board of Guardians, had stated that '[we] fear that in the cases of lead-poisoning which occur the persons employed are often themselves chiefly to blame for the evil results which follow from their neglect of the precautionary measures taken for their protection',[34] although on instruction from an assistant secretary, this conclusion was omitted from the letter which was finally sent. This instance of conscious editing, and others in which marginal comments are made only for consumption within the Local Government Board, illustrated the different layers of meaning which were generated within official circles, where controversial and unqualified views were expressed, but where a public position of administrative detachment was none the less preserved.

From the works themselves, some women interviewed by the departmental committee which visited Newcastle in the course of its proceedings spoke of the culpability of the poisoning victims. Isabella Hodgson, who at sixty-eight had worked in the same factory for fifty years, claimed that 'it is a great deal owing to their own carelessness, taking no care of themselves, and how they live has a great deal to do with it'. Similarly, Bridget Anderson, a blue-bed worker for thirty-five years in the same firm, stated that while it was hard work

> you are forced to do something for a living . . . [and] there is a lot of them who fall into sickness through their own dirty habits, and if you attempt to point this out to them they will fly at you and tell you to go to the Lord. So we let them alone, but they don't know the danger.

Mary Ann Ingram was less categorical: 'There are some very nice clean girls in, and there are others who are not. Of course, you cannot get them all alike.'[35] Indeed, few women actually interviewed complained of the work, or their treatment in it, a result in part perhaps of the profile of workers who appeared. Longer-term regular employees were more likely to appear and give

33 Sherard, 'White slaves', 530.
34 Draft of letter from Local Government Board, London, to S. Robson, Clerk to Gateshead Board of Guardians, 9 Dec. 1887, PRO, MH 12/3096.
35 Isabella Hodgson, 1893 Report, 43; Bridget Anderson, ibid.; Mary Ann Ingram, ibid. 77.

evidence than were those casual workers who predominated overwhelmingly in the industry. It was regular workers in turn, some believed, who were most likely to have benefited from the routines of washing and medical checks imposed by the regulations, rather than their more numerous casual co-workers.

As well as the suggestion of 'dirty habits', the neglect of 'indispensable precautions' which had already been introduced to ward off poisoning, such as daily baths, was attributed as well to biological characteristics. Bathing regulations were 'necessarily' not observed by women when they were menstruating, another characteristic which accounted for women's liability to become sick from work.[36] The fact that employers sanctioned the avoidance of baths at such times[37] merely heightened the sense of an insoluble dilemma presented by women's biology, a biology inherently at odds with precepts of industrial safety formulated in theory around a worker's body of unspecified sex. Just where the poison and disorder lay, and what was the active cause of the sickness – the environment of the works, or the body of the woman worker – were moot points.

Considerable attention was devoted by the departmental committee and by other investigating bodies, to evidence about those 'deceptive' practices among the women in the works which enabled them to circumvent regulations which, if enforced, would have curtailed their employment. Charlotte Rafferty's mother maintained at her daughter's inquest that she did not know of the age barrier to Charlotte's work. Charlotte's supervisor Mary Fountain, on the other hand, claimed that when Charlotte first began at the works, she had asked her if she could read, and drew her attention to 'the different rules that were printed and displayed in the works', some of which presumably dealt with age requirements.[38] As well as overstating age, casual hire provided an opportunity for women listed as sick by one works to seek work in another instead. When employers began to swap sick lists, one government official claimed that lead workers then would 'go from works to works with a different alias so they are difficult to trace' to secure continuous employment. Doctors checking the workers resorted to visiting the factories frequently, but in an unpredictable pattern, in order to 'catch any that have the least appearance of lead poisoning'.[39] Other means of avoiding detection and suspension from work were cited: Baumgarten claimed that if women ailed when at home at night or before work, rather than sending to the factory in which they were employed for a medical order and thus alerting the doctors to possible lead-related illness, the women went instead to the dispensary or workhouse for attention, to ensure that their return to work was

36 Dr Oliver, quoted in Sherard, 'White slaves', 525.
37 Employers referred to the difficulty in enforcing personal cleanliness regulations: Secretary, Walkers, Parker and Co. to under-secretary of state, 31 Oct. 1898, TWAS 1512/14889.
38 *Newcastle Daily Journal*, 30 Dec. 1892, 6.
39 Sir William Chaytor to W. E. Knollys, Local Government Board, 12 Nov. 1887, PRO, MH 12/3096.

free of problems. Such strategies on the part of the workers may have been taken as primarily another sign of their economic vulnerability; to Baumgarten, they were also a sign of these women's 'cunning'.[40]

Employer representatives, although mostly vehemently opposed to the exclusion of women from the works, had none the less resorted to some generalised condemnation of the women's ignorance or active subversion of regulations to safeguard their industry's reputation. There were three chief propositions running through the debates and inquiries, which employer representatives negotiated: the first was the proposition that the industry was inadequately regulated; the second was that women were biologically weaker and unsuited to the work; the third was that in the translation of regulations from the body of a written code, to practical application upon the body of the worker, their efficacy was being diminished by the workers themselves. Adherence to the third proposition was most common among representatives of industry, but, they concluded, was a problem which did not logically dictate the complete removal of women from the industry. Indeed, at times they would cite women's marginal economic status as an important reason for not excluding women or imposing further restrictions which might jeopardise their employment. At the Rafferty inquest, for example, the legal representative for Walkers, Parker and Co. argued that any further policing of age restrictions, such as compelling women to produce birth certificates at the morning hiring, would be onerous – for the women. Some, he said, did not even know when they were born, and if women were turned away from the works on this basis, 'in many cases that would inflict a very great hardship'.[41] Whatever qualifications were added, however, their adherence to arguments about the ignorance and disorderliness of (some) women could not help but add grist to the mill of the exclusionist cause.

The war of words to secure the dominant interpretative position about lead workers was fierce. On one side, inquests and investigations revealed the minutiae of personal family tragedies, economic need and physical pain of individual women: Charlotte Rafferty's mother had warned her daughter that lead 'was the worst employment she could have gone to', but she went anyway. Her father recounted pitiful tales of Charlotte returning home from the works to shake lead dust off her clothes which were like a 'poke of flour'. Other graphic accounts of deaths like that of Elizabeth Ryan, who tore out her hair in her agony, were accompanied by the comments of neighbours – 'such nice hair she had too . . . poor lamb' – and arrayed for sympathetic public consumption. Emphasis upon the screams and the visible bodily distortions of the sufferers threatened the boundaries which separated a public, healthy workforce and the ex-worker who usually ailed in a private world of invisible silence.[42] Many such reports also incorporated medical

---

[40] Baumgarten, 1893 Report, 37.
[41] *Newcastle Daily Journal*, 30 Dec. 1892, 6.
[42] Ibid; *Daily Chronicle*, 15 Dec. 1892; Sherard, 'White slaves', 524.

evidence from which a more general case was then argued about the urgent, scientifically-proven need for reform. On the other hand, employers and supervisors were at pains to prove that all their legal obligations had been scrupulously observed. Tragedy was the result of individual personal misman-agement, a mismanagement which carried with it strong implications of moral laxity.

For other groups of both sympathetic and less sympathetic observers the conclusion may have been reached via different assumptions, but was the same. Whether for their own safety, for that of future generations who were currently 'doomed before they are born',[43] or for the sake of the industry's continuation, women had to be banned, whether the cause of poisoning was biological predisposition, imperfectly exercised regulation, or individual irre-sponsibility and immorality. Indeed, that some commentators and officials who supported exclusion put forward generalised views of workers as immoral, and at the same time indicated that these characteristics were not evident in the cases of individuals reported in the papers and elsewhere, was not deemed a contradiction. James Henderson, for example, who had described the workers generally as 'dissipated', reported the case of a fatality at the works of Foster, Blackett and Wilson. A married woman had been seized with colic, and died soon after, neglecting to seek medical attention:

> Had she done so the probability is that she would have been cured but her hus-band was out of work[,] she was the only bread winner in the family and she knew that the reporting of her illness would involve the suspension of her work and the loss of all that gave food to her children[,so] she worked on and went to her grave in silence. This was a most painful case and illustrates the difficulty of dealing with exceptional cases.[44]

In characterising such cases as exceptional, the far less sympathetic general stereotype informing the impetus to regulation remained intact, and was probably strengthened.

The conflation of biological, social and economic identities of women workers underpinned the contemporary logic of their exclusion. The voices raised to contradict the composite identity of the 'standard' woman worker, forged as it was from shifting and slippery categories, were few. And even where opposition arose, such opposition itself was inevitably constrained by the terms of classification within the dominant discourse. Factory Inspector May Abraham, for example, was steadfast in her appraisal of the lead workers and aware of the prejudice against them since 'they have got the name of being a lower class', but to break away from the terminology of immorality in discussion of the women was virtually impossible in the question-and-answer format of the enquiry:

[43] *Daily Chronicle*, 21 Dec. 1892.
[44] James Henderson to HM Chief Inspector of Factories, 29 Dec. 1892, TWAS 1512/14884.

Chairman: [Are the workers] not more degraded than other women workers?
Abraham: I do not think so . . .
Chairman: We have been given to understand that in a great many places they like a free and easy life, that their wages compare fairly well with ordinary dressmakers' common hands, 10s. to 12s. a week; and we have been told that they rather like that, in order to have short days and fair wages, and those that like to drink a little, drink a little, and so on?
Abraham: I did find a few cases in which women were drunkards, but I found absolutely as respectable and nice women in those places as I found in others: taking them as a class, I should not have applied the term degraded to them.[45]

What term would the women have applied to themselves? In the interpretations around the work of lead processing and deaths from poison, as previously noted, the voices of the women are relatively quiet.[46] The evidence which exists from the women themselves almost universally stresses the factor of economic compulsion in their decision to seek employment, or to remain, in the lead works; they do not speak of free and easy lives facilitated by their employment. Overwhelmingly in other sources, however, women are discussed as the objects of investigation and surveillance, cast as passive victims of circumstance in the narratives. Where women are constructed alternatively as agents, they appear as partial agents only, whose behaviour and decisions are characterised in negative terms, defying the logic of regulation and thereby illustrating diminished responsibility.

As well as the predominance of atypical workers in the committee evidence of 1893, further reasons may be suggested to explain the silence of women. Two witnesses before the committee alleged that the women most likely to present damning evidence had experienced some coercion not to testify. Joseph Kelly, a representative from the Tyneside and National Labour Union, claimed that 'full liberty is not enjoyed by anyone coming here to offer evidence' for fear of employer boycott. At a previous enquiry, he went on, 'the women were afraid to come up for fear that they might lose their employment through it'. Later, May Abraham verified the claim that some women were fearful and may have changed their stories; such silence was typical of a wider problem for women at work. Even in routine factory inspections, she thought it was 'certainly' likely that women were not as candid in their complaints where 'the workwomen had to complain to men'.[47] In a similar vein, one of the women workers alleged that Dr Baumgarten's manner as the factory doctor was 'very strict', that he attacked women with a barrage of questions about their health and activities. Kelly described the threats women received in their daily work, supervisors 'horsing' them on to work

45 May Abraham, 1893 Report, 213.
46 On women's silence in the face of exclusionist legislation see C. Hall, 'The sweet delights of home', in M. Perrot (ed.), A history of private life, iv, trans. A. Goldhammer, Cambridge, Mass. 1990, 47–93.
47 Joseph Kelly, 1893 Report, 92; May Abraham, ibid. 213, 209.

harder: women remained at such work, he said, because of 'sheer force of circumstance over which they have got no control'.[48]

In the factories themselves, the controversy, especially the possibility that women might be altogether banned, produced tensions along gender lines. Male workers' skilled livelihoods depended, in the short term at least, upon the continuation of the rough work performed by women, and one foreman complained to Sherard 'that there has been too much writing about us'. It was perhaps concern over the sight of Sherard in the factory and an attempt to enforce women's silence in such company, as much as consideration of safety requirements, which often prompted foremen to shout to female workers, 'You there, go and get your muzzle on.'[49] (The 'muzzle' was the colloquial term for the rudimentary respirators which the women were supposed to wear on the job.) Although the committee members in 1893 asked Joseph Kelly to come forward with written evidence of the coercion of the women, he later reported that the women had been consulted, but had declined to provide him with letters. There are sufficient hints within the evidence, however, to suggest that women's general silence, both at work and in the committee, cannot be read simply as their having nothing to say, but was more likely the unrecorded testimony of their vulnerable economic position.

In the hotch-potch of identity construction of the lead workers, their economic circumstances were discussed, and they were characterised at times as poor women: but it was a poverty whose meaning was not embedded primarily in economic definition. Rather, it was the consequences of poverty which were seen as problematic and disordering, and which were deemed to generate a culture, a social life, a biology of poverty written on the bodies of the women which could not (or should not) be accommodated within the work environment. The removal of the source of disorder from the context of work was the primary focus, and at times this all but eclipsed considerations of the women's economic situation. Where the lack of alternative employment for women upon exclusion was raised, it appeared in passing, as an unfortunate consequence of a necessary restructuring. Nash was confident that 'prohibition would not . . . mean such a great sacrifice to the community. A very little sympathetic help would go far towards obtaining work for the women displaced, as those charitable people know who have helped again and again to equip some crippled victim of the lead turn to another occupation.'[50]

The taint of lead work not only jeopardised the health of the body, but also the future prospects of the worker. There was opinion expressed prior to the exclusion of women that the perception of lead workers as immoral would preclude them from occupations such as domestic service, where emphasis upon character was paramount. Abraham argued that for women seeking

---

[48] Bridget Anderson, ibid. 43; Joseph Kelly, ibid. 93, 92.
[49] Sherard, 'White slaves', 526, 527.
[50] *Daily Chronicle*, 21 Dec. 1892.

work outside the industry, 'the fact that they had been employed in a lead works at all told against them . . . they have got the name of being a lower class'.[51] Such concern appeared to be well-founded. A year after women were banned, Sherard's report on the fate of the women so displaced described their economic marginality: there 'has been a good deal of distress amongst those who have not as yet found fresh work. Some take their baskets and go hawking in the mining districts; some have gone to the paper mills, and others to the rabbit-downing works.' A slum worker reported to him that some women had gone to the rope works, but here wages were lower than they had been in lead processing. Wood-chopping and wood-hawking brought other women a penny for every six to nine bundles sold, and charring generated an income of 'perhaps 1s. 6d. a day'.[52] Others may have taken a path pursued by ex-lead workers like Elizabeth English, described by her Salvation Army 'rescuers' as being always 'engaged in the lowliest occupations, or in the lowliest forms of vice' in her working life, and who previous to the ban had turned to prostitution to earn a living.[53] Perhaps in this way, the disorder of women could not be expunged completely, but merely relocated away from the factory – that most important material and symbolic centre of orderly progress within capitalism – to the streets, where it would be greeted by a different but related alarm about women in the public domain.

There were telling signs that in the 1890s the exclusion of the woman worker – the 'standard' woman worker – had become an end in itself. At the time of exclusion, other 'remedies' to lead poisoning were simultaneously introduced. The installation of extractors to diminish dust in the works, for example, and the use of mechanical stoves to obviate the need for workers to enter them were part of the new regulations. One employer in Newcastle, Cookson and Co., had informed the Home Office as early as 1887 that the firm had abolished white-lead stoves to generally good effect; it was one of two firms commended for following best work practices. However, since Cooksons had also substituted male for female labour around the stoves at about the same time, the possible conclusion that the problem elsewhere was the work and not the women appears to have been overlooked.[54] Nash had certainly commented that one of the by-products of women's exclusion would be the complete cessation of the most dangerous work activities in the trade,

[51] May Abraham, 1893 Report, 213. See also Helen Ogle Moore and Edith Hare, 'Report to the Society for the Employment of Women on the work of women in the white-lead trade at Newcastle', in J. Boucherett and H. Blackburn (eds), The condition of working women and the factory acts, London 1896, 78–83 at p. 80.
[52] Sherard, Cry of the poor, 148, 156.
[53] SAA Girls' statement books, vol. iii, case 348.
[54] Rowe, Lead manufacturing, 221–2; Cookson and Co. to under-secretary of state, H. O. London, 27 Oct. 1898, TWAS 1512/14887.

and the substitution of machinery for human labour, since 'men could not be got to do the work'.[55]

Further, outside Newcastle the trend to voluntary exclusion on the part of employers had already begun before the new regulations were introduced, notably in areas where other occupational choices such as textile work were available to women. Where local economic arrangements permitted, employers acted upon assumptions about the undesirability of women as workers, assumptions which were entirely consistent with the broader views espoused by those of their own class and gender outside the industry. Dr Oliver was quoted by Sherard after exclusion, claiming that even though Newcastle employers had resisted his efforts, they were now 'most pleased with the new state of things. They have far less sickness to disturb them in their industry, and there is a general feeling of relief from the public odium which attached to this trade.' After the general exclusion, lead poisoning did not cease, as indeed it had not in those firms from which women had been earlier excluded. Oliver was again quoted by Sherard admitting that men continued to suffer, since they were now employed instead of women, but in less severe measure: 'they have more resistance'.[56] They also had the new and safer machines, but this did not form part of Oliver's observations. T. M. Legge reported on the industry run by an all-male workforce at the turn of the century, but here, a discourse constructed around gendered disorder was no longer available. Instead, the emphasis shifted to the structure of the industry: casual systems of employment which militated against the efficiency of precautionary measures, he concluded, were major obstacles to industrial safety.[57]

It is not the point here retrospectively and uselessly to castigate officials and professionals for reaching a 'wrong' decision, for not allowing one group of workers a disproportionate share of work which could bring disability and agonising death. As Rowe illustrates, the course of thinking about state intervention in industry was itself evolving, from an unqualified model of laissez-faire towards one which recognised that there were groups (such as female lead workers) which 'are not competent to take care of themselves'[58] – political economy with a conscience. Rather, the concern here has been to situate the subject, not within the internal logic of intervention in the industry, but within a broader field of reference which suggests the interconnectedness, the fluidity of discourse on gender and on poverty, and the ways in which meaning was created and contested in the context of work. The course of exclusion, the material conditions of the woman worker, and the

55 *Daily Chronicle*, 21 Dec. 1892. For the fortunes of the trade after 1898 see Rowe, *Lead manufacturing*, 206 n. 59.
56 Sherard, *Cry of the poor*, 146.
57 Rowe, *Lead manufacturing*, 225.
58 *Engineering*, 22 Dec. 1893, cited ibid. 223.

meanings constructed around her working life, at once both informed, and were informed by, views about the identity of poor working-class women.

In the white lead industry in the 1890s, the scrutiny of women's bodies, arguments that they were variously sites to be medically and morally protected, labour fodder for unscrupulous employers, or sources of weakness and disorder, was intense. As government workplace surveillance and poor relief bureaucracy grew, the scope for clashes between individual capitalists and the new caste of state bureaucrats increased. At the same time, the proliferation of specialist medical and scientific discourse, the expansion of investigative journalism, and the continuing concern of many groups pressing for social reform in the city contributed to the clamour. Whatever the confusion and contradictions within the debate, again the echoes of femininity as a disordered state or disordering force can be detected; again this was related to female sexuality and corporeality, and importantly, to class status, and was reshaped and particularised in ways rendered meaningful by the specific local and industrial context.

The interpretations of women's work in the lead industry drew upon many of the broader anxieties which were being expressed about working-class culture and women's position within it, the relationship between poverty and immorality, and generational progress. While only a century earlier, the processes leading to the disappearance of women from the area's coalfields had occurred leaving little trace in the historical sources, the perceived impact of women's lead work – past, present *and* future – drew considerable comment. The standard woman worker disrupted the orderly boundaries of public and private, when the poisoning of her body was made suddenly and alarmingly visible. Her plight was characterised by some observers as the human cost of Newcastle's mighty industrial status. Moreover, Sherard and others expressed the fear that the cost would be borne not only by the women 'flung out of the factories as it were on to the social midden', but also by their children, and by the city itself: 'it will be a generation or two before Newcastle recovers from these effects'.[59] Indeed, lead poisoning and its prevalence among women workers could be read as a potent metaphor of wider disorder in the city itself. Elizabeth Wilson, in tracing the impact of domestic ideology upon the creation of suburbs in the nineteenth century, argues that suburbanisation served in part as a means to separate women from the heart of the city, to mark the centre as an unequivocally 'masculine' space with strong associations of orderly growth. Conventional interpretations of industrial intervention notwithstanding, the dominant discourse of exclusion constructed around the lead industry could be read in a similar fashion: by positioning women 'as the objects of both regulation *and* banishment',[60] progress might be better secured.

---

[59] Sherard, *Cry of the poor*, 147.
[60] Wilson, *The sphinx in the city*, 46.

How did the women themselves respond to these imposed identities, not only in the 1890s, but throughout the century? There is ample evidence that women resisted simple categorisations, resented the imposition of priorites which they did not necessarily share, and at times refused to participate in regimes designed to discipline and transform their bodies. Women evaded the increasingly meticulous regulations which operated in the lead industry. Outside the specific context of the lead works and in the more general area of the slums, they absconded from refuges and homes, continued to exercise choice in the pursuit of leisure in the streets and in the pubs of Sandgate, and opted for sex work as a preferable and more profitable alternative to the drudgery of domestic service; in short, some women actively rejected or simply ignored the labelling obsessions of middle-class reformers. Certainly, while women's own views and priorities are vastly under-represented in the literature, the material which survives provides glimpses of a rich and complex working-class culture which operated in Sandgate, Quayside and other slum areas in which women were closely involved. In relation to the broad exercise of political, economic and social power in nineteenth-century Newcastle, however, these resistant practices of individuals had little impact upon dominant discourses. Women were keenly aware of the assumptions made about their identity, but their economic and cultural marginality left little alternative to participation in the dominant discourse.

That the Victorians in attempting to make sense of their rapidly changing world resorted to body metaphors should not surprise us. The challenges thrown up by a rapidly expanding and urbanising society, where the often grim accompaniments to such expansion at times severely threatened belief in progress and improvement, made the task of ordering social forces and human spaces a basic imperative. It was not primarily a material imperative, for material progress paradoxically created the conditions which threatened its own trajectory. Rather, the imperative acted upon and through the social imaginary of the bourgeoisie. The bourgeoisie's understandings of their world, and their belief in the moral value and scientific necessity of progress, were generated by a 'metaphorics of controllability'. Thus, the planned, 'public' city was a key signifier of control, of the triumph of culture and reason over the untamed disorder of both the hidden, 'labyrinthine' city and the excesses of nature, and it was indeed commonplace in literary and historical work to associate nature with 'woman'.

Such metaphorics relied upon the presence of both controlled and uncontrolled spaces and forces. It was as an uncontrolled vector of disorder that poor working-class women mostly appeared in the Victorian narrative of progress. Thus Elizabeth Grosz's insights into femininity as uncontrollability are particularly appropriate. I have attempted here to particularise these insights, to examine more closely the ways in which metaphoric links were made across a broad range of areas touching poor women's lives, to consider the forms which the 'formlessness' of femininity took at certain periods, and to elucidate the sense of urgency and moral panic which emerged and clustered around the female body. The example of Newcastle illustrates clearly that women's bodies, and their poverty, were indeed linked to specific and general disorder, and fear of invasion. The discourse of feminine danger shifted and fragmented across the century, moving, roughly, from an emphasis upon simple containment, to transformation, to specialised regulation. Consideration of the intersection of bodies and spaces is critical for the historian concerned with the formation of gendered identities in the past. It is by locating women in spaces such as Sandgate or the white-lead works that we can best understand the 'dangerous' femininity, the endemic 'otherness', which they were thought to embody, and begin to trace the ways those meanings were carried abroad into the everyday world of work, institutions and streets, and to the doors and factories of the middle classes themselves. Noting those links, we can detect some of the ways in which, whether real or imagined, actually or potentially disordering, the body of the poor woman occupied a similar space, metaphorically, to that of Sandgate itself: a precarious and frightening border territory somewhere between nature and culture, which threatened always to encroach upon the ordered space beyond, if left unpatrolled.

This kind of close application inevitably also raises questions about the constitution of feminine identity in different locations. How, for example, were female bodies and identities read in the context of rural Northumberland, where isolated geography and fresh air perhaps diminished any sense of looming danger or infection? The following chapter examines the work and life styles of women in rural Northumberland. Apart from the mobility which occurred between the two regions, the countryside provides a very different material context in which to consider the themes of gender constructions, and the perceived relationships between women, progress and disorder. As well as considering these links, in further exploring the dominant constructions of female identity in the north-east, a fuller context is provided in which to assess the relationship between patterns of work for women, and their experiences of poverty during the period.

4

'A Fine Race of Women':
Northumbrian Bondagers

In the centre of Newcastle at the junction of Grey Street and Grainger Street stands a towering monument to Earl Grey of Howick. Erected in the year of Victoria's coronation, it was perceived by city planners as a fitting centre-piece for the building improvements in that area of the city, and a celebration of Newcastle's connection with the prime minister who had steered the Reform Bill through the crisis of 1831–2, and who had presided over the statutory abolition of slavery in the British colonies in 1833. Later in the century, another smaller monument dedicated to George Stephenson was unveiled, close to the Central Station. Stephenson's pedestal is flanked by four figures of male industrial workers – a navvy, a miner, an engineer and a metal-smith. The reforming politician and the entrepreneurial inventor: these twin figures stood as larger-than-life parentheses flanking the improved heart of the city, attesting to the foundations of Newcastle's economic and social development and its industrial pre-eminence in the north. They served as focal points for the area's progress in the nineteenth century, and that focus appeared essentially urban in its character. Clear connections to the North-umbrian countryside, the vast stretches of sparsely populated agricultural land to the north and west of Newcastle, found little reflection in the history of the city as celebrated in its monuments.

The simplistic heroic distortions of statuary notwithstanding, the relation-ship between urban Newcastle and rural Northumberland – the economic, social and political interconnections between the two – were complex and constantly evolving. The example of Grey himself illustrates these continu-ing connections; while an astute and urbane politician, he was an aristocrat whose family's identity and political power base remained deeply entrenched in the agricultural landscape of Northumberland. Indeed, a year before the statue to Grey was raised, criticism of the proposed monument came which drew upon just this dual role as politician and local estate-holder, and at the same time questioned the urban basis of nineteenth-century Novocastrian progress, since it was the 'forgotten' countryside which allegedly bore the cost of those achievements. In a handbill, an 'old steward' from rural Northum-berland maintained that in the city, the 'proud pillar that perpetuates [Grey's] fame . . . will revive also the painful reflection, that perhaps its foundation has been laid, and its tablet . . . has been sculptured [sic] by some of the bitter fruits of Northumbrian bondage'. Slavery in the colonies may have been abolished, he claimed, but at home

[t]he unseemly and degrading employments in which Women are engaged under the bondage system operate as an effectual barrier to moral and social improvement, and are a humiliating disgrace to a civilised country. How revolting to all ideas of decency or propriety must it be to strangers to see Females of all ages engaged in the rudest agricultural Employments.[1]

The old steward here moved easily to connect provincial, national and even international spheres in advancing his argument, asserting strands of conti- nuity between the countryside, the heart of Newcastle, the nation and the colonies beyond. The figure of the working woman, here positioned nega- tively within a broad discourse of ideal femininity, provided the point of continuity which transcended geographical distance and mere local consciousness. In this context of protest, the working woman's continued labour was perceived as detrimental to the progress of civilisation in nineteenth-century rural England and was also taken to indicate something about the identity of the nation as a whole. Some local housekeeping was required, both to secure a more coherent form of national progress and to ensure that the country's reputation as a 'civilising' and 'reforming' power abroad could be sustained.

That the old steward chose slavery as the negative measure against which to characterise women's agricultural labour in the region is also telling. While abolitionist campaigns had drawn heavily upon arguments that personal independence and individual liberty underpinned civilisation, morality and progress, the old steward categorised women's *paid* labour – which arguably enhanced their status as independent economic agents – as a feature which positively *contributed* to some slave-like culture in England. In this respect the work of Catherine Hall is illuminating. Hall's exploration of anti-slavery discourse in Birmingham provides powerful illustrations of the ways in which that discourse, while relating to economic questions, was simultaneously and deeply embedded in 'a historically specific set of ideas and practices about gender, race, class, and ethnicity'.[2] What at first may appear as a paradox – the argument that women's exclusion from a form of paid labour would contribute to the country's reputation as a home of freedom and of personal independence which was in part based upon labour – appears less so when we consider the dominant construction of women as natural dependants and the gender-specificity of constructions of individual freedom.

Later in the century John Stuart Mill and Harriet Taylor would advance a very different argument, one which claimed that the independence of men in society rested upon the foundation of women's continued dependence and 'slavery' in marriage;[3] yet in Northumberland in the 1830s, the old steward expressed quite different links between women's work, slavery and the state

---

[1] 'Northumberland Bondage', handbill dated 6 Mar. 1837, enclosed in R. Robson to 3rd Earl Grey, papers of Earl Grey, DU Archives 121/9.
[2] Hall, *White, male and middle class*, 33.
[3] J. S. Mill, *The subjection of women*, London 1869, repr. Oxford 1974, 443–5.

of national progress which would have been readily understood both in the countryside and city alike. Even half a century later Richard Heath surveyed the countryside of Northumberland and remarked: 'It is curious to note . . . a party of women and boys turnip-hoeing, and all working in a line, with one man as overseer directing them . . . it unpleasantly recalls old scenes in the sugar plantations of Jamaica or of South Carolina.'[4]

Some modern observers and contemporary commentators have drawn clear lines between town and country in the north, suggesting that the rural hinterland could be identified more meaningfully with the border lands of Scotland[5] than with the more cosmopolitan setting of urban Newcastle: 'Geordies and Northumbrians are entirely different people, in their speech, character and humour',[6] contends Nancy Ridley. Contemporaries such as William Marshall too, describing the conditions of the Northumbrian 'peasantry', drew a divide: he claimed that his account 'will afford matter of amusement . . . to *English* farmers' and that the area had more in common with northern Europe.[7] Historian Keith Robbins has focused upon the growth of rhetoric concerning regional 'character' and national identity during the period. He presents a dense body of evidence to suggest that the notion of some cohesive, essential 'Britishness' increasingly underlay a relatively integrated political system in the nineteenth century. Yet he also argues, as an important corrective to any simple, strict divisions based on geography or linguistic differences, that in other spheres of life such national 'consciousness both did and did not exist . . . everything depended upon context'.[8] Hall, more alert to the interplay between 'the hierarchies of power formed through the axes of gender, race and class' which were drawn upon in the construction of English identity during the period, also portrays the identity-making processes of the nineteenth century as fluid and complex. 'Englishness', she states,

> is not a fixed identity but a series of contesting identities, a terrain of struggle as to what it means to be English. Different groups competed for the domination of this space and the political and cultural power which followed from such domination. Englishness is defined through the creation of an imagined community . . . built on a series of assumptions about 'others' which define the nature of Englishness itself.[9]

While Hall is specifically interested to explore elaborations of identity with

---

4 Richard Heath, *The English peasant: studies historical, local and biographic*, London 1893, 209; and see Plate 8, 30.
5 Keith Robbins, *Nineteenth-century Britain: England, Scotland and Wales: the making of a nation*, Oxford 1989, 42.
6 N. Ridley, *Northumberland then and now*, London 1978, 136.
7 William Marshall, *The review and abstract of the county reports to the board of agriculture*, i, n.p. 1818, repr. Newton Abbott 1969, 51.
8 Robbins, *Nineteenth-century Britain*, 97.
9 Hall, *White, male and middle class*, 26.

reference to the imperial context of mid nineteenth-century Jamaica, her observations may be applied usefully too, however, to the landscapes of identity – personal, regional, national – within England itself, and the gendered nature of the 'imagined communities' constituted in relation to them.

I have already considered discursive constructions of women's employment and female sexuality in relation to 'progress' in the urban context. What of constructions of femininity in the rural context? Did the countryside provide a different discursive terrain from that of Newcastle or did common themes appear which diminished the effect of spatial separation? To what extent were the conditions of working women in rural Northumberland and perceptions of them rooted in specific local conditions, or part of a wider discourse through which working women and poor women were marginalised as 'others' both in the region and, perhaps, throughout the country?

This chapter examines the culture and material conditions of working women in the rural environment, against a backdrop of such broader questions relating to female identity. The first section draws together evidence relating to the conditions of life and work for women in the Northumbrian countryside, to provide some basis for comparison between urban and rural employment structures and patterns of poverty for women. Further, the relationship between local rural conditions and broader discussion of women's position in rural society will be considered: the Northumbrian agricultural labour system, and women's role within it, exhibited distinctive local peculiarities which produced particular tensions and contradictions around the subject of women's work.

'Sufficient women workers': the bondaging system.

If the 'improving' heart of urban Newcastle was symbolised in its statues of Stephenson and Grey, and street names memorialised its nineteenth-century architects, the rural north too developed a pantheon of astute entrepreneurial heroes whose names were widely cited in contemporary accounts of scientific farming methods and capitalist organisation associated with the late eighteenth-century 'revolution' in agriculture. The Culley brothers of north Northumberland and John Grey of Dilston were just three such improvers whose systems of farming were nationally publicised and who contributed to a perception that the north, in its production levels and living standards, provided 'exceptions to all the rules'.[10] One such exception was the prevalence of the Northumbrian hiring system referred to as the 'bondage'.

While holidaying in Northumberland, the hero of Cuthbert Bede's novel, Mr Verdant Green, encounters a pair of 'lady labourers peculiar to that part of the country . . . – great strapping damsels of three or four woman-power'.

---

[10] T. E. Kebbel, *The agricultural labourer: a short summary of his position*, London 1893, 175.

Engaged to perform 'some of the rougher duties attendant upon agricultural pursuits', wrote the novelist, their distinctive dress of headscarf and hat (known as an 'ugly'), blue blouse, 'kerchief, winter leg sackings and striped woollen skirts 'not long enough to conceal their . . . clod-hopping boots', formed 'no unpicturesque subject for the sketcher's pencil'.[11] The workers so described were bondagers, a category of female labourer peculiar to Northumbrian agriculture, as well as to small areas of the Scottish border counties and northernmost Durham. While the bondaging system which persisted throughout the nineteenth century drew quite sustained contemporary consideration, with very few exceptions the opinions, attitudes and concerns of women so engaged are lost to the interested historian. Combined with contemporary conventions of speaking about, but not to, working women, the persistent use by some historians of definitions which render invisible their very existence, has indeed ensured that the bondager has remained 'a somewhat mysterious figure'.[12]

The peculiarities of bondaging were not confined to the women's attire alone. In Northumberland, annual agreements between farmers and male farm labourers (usually referred to as 'hinds') were made at local hiring fairs, which usually took place in May. Guaranteed or 'upstanding' payments to those male labourers were chiefly in kind, and a cottage on the farm was provided for the worker for the period of his year's employment. Agreements throughout much of the nineteenth century further stipulated that a hind's employment was conditional upon his employing a bondager for the coming year, or for six months.[13] The hind directly engaged the bondager, and provided her with food and lodging in his own cottage, while the farmer remained responsible for her cash wages.[14] Unlike the hind, whose wages or payment in kind were guaranteed regardless of sickness or weather conditions, the bondager was paid only for those days when she worked at the behest of the hind, and these wages varied from season to season depending upon the type of work which she performed.

Apart from working the bondage, there were two other categories of employment for women in the Northumbrian countryside. In the south of the county around Newcastle and other larger towns such as Morpeth, women were hired casually on a daily basis during peak periods of activity such as the annual harvest. The possibility of employing day labourers, however, depended to a large extent upon the farm's proximity to a town. In the south of the county, the casual employment of women during harvest was more common. Further north, the absence of a ready market of casual labour was

[11] Cuthbert Bede [Edward Bradley], *The further adventures of Mr Verdant Green, an Oxford undergraduate*, London 1854, repr. Liverpool 1908, 355–6.
[12] Hostettler, 'Women farm workers', 42.
[13] Andrew Hately's conditions for 1838, Middleton Hall [Simpson] MSS, NRO, ZS1/72/4. The shearing referred to in the agreement was corn harvesting.
[14] Agreements of William Kirkups and Alexander Lowrey, 1841–2, ibid. ZS1/72/7, ZS1/72/9.

reflected in the prevalence of longer-term hiring contracts. The other category of female labour in the region was that of cottar, where women (invariably single women or widows) were engaged directly by a farmer. Where a mother and daughter were so hired, they were called 'double cottars'. In return for a cottage, rent-free, and sometimes the provision of coals and potatoes during the year, cottars undertook to work on farms when required for a daily wage. Although these female-headed households provided both security of employment and basic living conditions for the cottars themselves, whose circumstances may otherwise have barred them from paid agricultural employment, as a category of labourer the cottar was relatively rare. While the employment of cottars had the advantage for the farmer of securing the ready service of women over an extended period, it relied upon both the availability of a vacant cottage and a scarcity of alternative forms of labour. As well as the increasing concern expressed about women living outside the orbit of a patriarchal family structure,[15] generally it was deemed more economical to house a hind and his family and/or a bondager, rather than an individual cottar, where cottage accommodation was in short supply.

This three-tier system of employment, of farmer, hind and women workers, and the contractual configurations it produced, varied slightly then from region to region within the county. As early as 1808 it was recorded that the duke of Northumberland expressed a 'benevolent determination to emancipate' tenants on his estates from any arrangements which required the hiring of bondagers. It was a policy pursued closely by successive dukes, who established more conventional farm tenancy arrangements.[16] But overall this arrangement appeared, at least in the early part of the century, as a specific Percy family quirk. The other major aristocratic landowners in the county – the Greys and Tankervilles, for example – exhibited no such compunction. Indeed, throughout the region the routine participation of women in agriculture within the bondage system was cast as an integral feature of the rural economy. Even by the 1890s, when rural populations were declining and women throughout the country were withdrawing from field labour, female farm workers in Northumberland accounted for one-quarter of its farm labourers and constituted one-eighth of England's female agricultural workforce.[17] Such heavy participation, in fact, led the Hexham Board of Guardians in 1867 to express the belief that 'to prohibit female labour in this district would simply be to prohibit farming'.[18]

The exact origins of the bondaging system are obscure. Ivy Pinchbeck

---

[15] *Royal Commission on Labour*, The Agricultural Labourer, PP 1893–4 [6894–iii] xxxv: report by Mr Arthur Wilson Fox upon the Poor Law Union of Glendale (cited hereinafter as *Royal Commission on Labour*, Glendale Report, 1893), 102.

[16] Bailiff of the duke of Northumberland to Thomas Robson, 17 Dec. 1808, NRO 2114/5.

[17] Hostettler, 'Women farm workers', 40. These figures do not include seasonal farm workers.

[18] *Report of commissioners on children's, young person's and women's employment in agriculture,*

suggests that it 'seems hardly possible that it existed in 1768, since Arthur Young, who was then in the district, does not mention it, but merely says that the labourer's conditions included a money payment of 5s. for his wife's work 'in hay and harvest'.[19] Other writers however, have traced the beginnings of the system to a feudal past, and have claimed that women became prominent in Northumbrian agriculture because of male labour shortages caused by raids and other 'warlike activities' along the Scottish border.[20] Confusion as to the origins of bondaging has arisen because while the term 'bondager' was in common usage in previous periods, the specific tasks of the bondager actually evolved in response to demographic, agricultural and economic changes in the late eighteenth century.

In the mid eighteenth century and earlier, labour agreements referring to the bondage in fact referred to the specific labour of the hind's wife. Importantly too, in this pre-industrial context, the bondage also included tasks such as spinning an agreed poundage of wool.[21] Gradually, as the factory system elsewhere grew and as cottage industry declined, the role of women in spinning yarn for sale diminished. At the same time, however, especially in the large-scale northern farming lands in the county, numerous improvements in agriculture led to expanded farm production and a more relentless timetable of regular farm work.[22] The agricultural economy in the county was based upon corn and sheep farming, as well as minor production of other crops such as potatoes. In many respects, parts of Northumberland appeared as text-book cases for scholars of the agricultural revolution.[23]

While the task of securing and retaining a reliable force of field labour had for long preoccupied Northumbrian farmers, in their region such improvements, greater yields and growing commercial incentives in some areas intensified the demand for field labour, and specifically for the labour of women. Turnip production expressly for sheep-fattening, for example, required an intensive year-round cultivation programme that previous grazing systems had not. Many of the innovations in agriculture resulted in the creation of tasks which were deemed particularly suitable for women,[24] and descriptions of women's work in the north attested to their intensive, year-round schedule. A bondager's employment required twelve hours' work in summer (longer at harvest) and from sunrise to sunset in winter. Her tasks varied from month to month:

first report PP 1867–8 [4068–1] xvii (cited hereinafter as *Women's employment in agriculture, 1867 Report*), appendix e, 60.
19 Pinchbeck, *Women workers*, 65.
20 Cuthbert Headlam, *The three northern counties of England*, Gateshead 1939, 130.
21 Hostettler, 'Women farm workers', 41.
22 J. D. Chambers and G. E. Mingay, *The agricultural revolution, 1750–1880*, London 1966, 35.
23 Ibid. 25.
24 Hudson, *The industrial revolution*, 128.

In January and February, pulling turnips and working in the barn . . . March, stoning . . . April, stoning, turnip hoeing and backing . . . June, quickening and hay-harvesting, constant; July, the same, constant; August, hoeing turnips and corn-harvest; September and October, corn-harvest, gathering potatoes; November, gathering potatoes in the beginning; December, pulling turnips.[25]

As well as this field work, the task of cleaning and maintaining animal byres was reserved for women.

Agricultural improvement and larger-scale commercialisation to some extent ruptured older patterns of family-based labour. For many hinds their daughters, wives and unmarried sisters (and sometimes, late in the century, their sons) continued to provide required bondage services. However, while the wives of hinds had been able hitherto to combine some cottage industry and domestic labour under the same roof, they were less able to contribute to the family economy in these traditional ways as domestic industry declined. None the less, if they worked the bondage as a field labourer, their economic contribution was still substantial. The demands for all-day field labour through the year in new agricultural systems though, may have been met only with difficulty during certain stages of a woman's life. Childbearing and rearing of younger infants precluded the hind's wife from working the bondage. For example, Alice Livingstone had been employed to work the bondage by a labourer whose wife had a year-old son.[26] Similarly, since the work of a bondager demanded a very high level of physical strength and endurance, older wives may have been precluded. An apprentice at Lilburn Grange in 1842 recorded in his diary that a hind with 'an Old Wife . . . is much worse off' than one with a wife 'able to work in the fields',[27] since in the former case, or where hinds were unmarried, the bondage role was filled by women hired specifically for the purpose. Bondagers outside a hind's family were almost always unmarried, and aged between about fifteen and thirty: indeed, the term bondager was, alarmingly for some contemporaries, virtually synonymous with single woman. The mobility demanded of these women, their live-in, shared accommodation often in very isolated areas of the region, were taken as clear prohibitions to the employment of married women, and those with children or other kin responsibilities, for bondage work.

While the nomenclature of 'bondager' remained unchanged,[28] then, the

---

[25] *Report of commissioners on the employment of women and children in agriculture*, PP 1843 [510] xii: report by Sir Francis Hastings Doyle on Northumberland and Yorkshire (cited hereinafter as *Employment of women and children in agriculture*, 1843 Report), evidence of Morpeth parish clerk, 372.

[26] 1851 Census returns, Carham Parish, Glendale, NRO, MF 23 (Glendale Ward, 562), 1, entry 3.

[27] Diary and notebook of an apprentice, Lilburn Grange farm, 1842, NRO 851, 20.

[28] Although certainly towards the end of the century, the term appeared less frequently. See, for example, the agreements at Thornborough farm, 1891–2, RU Archives, NORTHUM 2, 2/2/1.

bondaging system evolved to take on a different shape and new meanings in the late eighteenth and early nineteenth centuries. There were a variety of factors which served to sustain the system in some form into the early twentieth century. The most frequently cited reason for its persistence and the high participation rate of women in agriculture generally, was the chronic scarcity of farm labourers in the region. Contemporaries travelling in Northumberland, once out of Newcastle, were struck by the sparseness of the population. 'The country', wrote William Cobbett in 1830, 'seems to be almost wholly destitute of people.' Farms and cottages were isolated, and villages few, even compared with other agricultural areas.[29] Further, the availability of alternative employment in the countryside for women was low. Textile manufacture remained small-scale and geographically scattered and in villages there were only very limited opportunities for seamstresses, where 'perhaps one female . . . may carry on dressmaking',[30] although in areas close to Newcastle and towns such as Morpeth and Alnwick there was some work in small retail and service industries. Relatively high wage levels compared with other forms of work for women,[31] and consistent labour shortages may have served as inducements for women to remain in, or in some cases migrate to, the countryside at certain periods during the century.[32]

In a predominantly rural district such as Glendale, for example, the proportion of women to men far exceeded the county average.[33] While it would be wrong to designate such districts as areas of attraction for women, since the total population of areas like Glendale was in absolute decline between, say, 1851 and 1871, it is indicative of the different opportunities represented by town and country for the two groups, that women were slower to join the nineteenth-century rural exodus which was occurring. Women were abandoning agricultural labour and its attendant rural life styles, but men left slightly more quickly and in greater numbers.[34]

Looking more closely at the demographic conditions which prevailed in a rural area such as Glendale, a more accurate profile of the bondager, and the work and household configurations for female labourers, can be gained. The Glendale district in the north-west of Northumberland was bordered by the Tweed and Berwick District to the north, and Scotland to the west. Its villages were small and scattered, with the exception of Wooler, its principal market town. Its agriculture was dominated by sheep farming on the slopes of the Cheviots, and it was an area where the concentration of bondagers was high. Roughly speaking, while in 1851 about 8.5 per cent of all women in

[29] William Cobbett, *Rural rides*, London 1830, repr. London 1886, ii. 375.
[30] *Employment of women and children in agriculture*, 1843 Report, Morpeth parish clerk, 373.
[31] *Royal commission on labour*, Glendale Report, 1893, 121.
[32] Hostettler, 'Women farm workers', 41.
[33] *Census of England and Wales, 1871*, 1873 [c. 872] lxxii, pt ii, 'Ages of males and females . . .', 501.
[34] *1851 Census*, pt ii, 'Ages of the people . . .', 743, 746; *1871 Census*, pt ii, 'Ages of males and females . . .', 501.

Northumberland were connected with farm work, and about 3 per cent were designated specifically as full-time agricultural labourers, in Glendale, the comparable figures were 24 per cent, and 15 per cent. By 1871, the number of Glendale women over twenty years of age connected with farm work had declined to about 16 per cent, although at that time the category 'farmer's wife' had been excluded from the total.[35] In the district, many of the demographic features which were thought to characterise the Northumbrian countryside as a whole were here particularly evident. As well as high female participation, a far greater than average proportion of women over twenty were recorded as unmarried. In 1851, while 28.9 per cent of women over twenty in England and Wales, and 29.7 per cent in Northumberland, were unmarried, in Glendale the figure was 38.7 per cent.[36] In 1871, for the age cohort 20 to 45, a staggering 52.6 per cent of Glendale women were unmarried, compared with an average of 34 per cent for England and Wales.[37] Marriage rates for men too were significantly lower in Glendale than national averages.[38]

Specific information about household configurations in Glendale can also be gleaned from census material, and these conditions are interesting in the light of contemporary perceptions of rural life in the area, and the increasingly problematic status which certain aspects of it assumed. Analysis of 400 households in the Glendale parishes of Carham, Kirk Newton and Ford in 1851, reveal that in about one-fifth of households a bondager from outside the family had been employed. Women so hired most usually lived in households of between four and six people, including a hind, his wife and their children. Bondagers were only employed singly and it was extremely rare for both a bondager and an indoor servant to be employed in the same household. The majority of bondagers so employed were aged between fifteen and twenty-four years. A couple of women were forty years or older, but they were exceptions. In comparison, any indoor servants employed in the parishes were spread more evenly across age groups, a reflection of the different requirements of the two jobs, bondagers being hired on the basis of their assumed physical strength. About one-third of the women had been born outside the county, mainly in Scotland and a few in Ireland.[39] Whether from Scotland,

---

[35] *Census of Great Britain 1851*, 1852–3 [1691–1] lxxxviii, pt i, 'Civil condition of persons . . . division x northern counties', 753; *1871 Census*, pt ii, 'Civil condition of persons . . . division x, northern counties', 508–9.

[36] *1851 Census*, pt i, 'Civil condition of the people . . . division x, northern counties', 753.

[37] *1871 Census*, pt ii, 'Civil condition of persons . . . division x, northern counties', 507, 509.

[38] B. R. Mitchell and P. Deane, *Abstract of British historical statistics*, Cambridge 1962, 12, 15.

[39] Sample of 400 households from the Carham, Kirk Newton and Ford parishes, 1851 Census, NRO, MF 23 (Glendale Ward, 562).

Ireland or Northumberland, many lived well away from their birthplaces, and probably away from their own kin as well.

However, the analysis of economic or demographic data alone reveals little about the nature of women's work or the operation of gender relations in daily life. Reliance on such analyses can create a dangerous illusion that statements of 'objective' conditions carry obvious explanatory weight. Yet such could not yield any explanation for women's gradual withdrawal from agriculture in a system which provided some clear economic incentives for their continuation. Nor could the material provide an explanation for the degree of attention which a sparsely populated, remote and reputedly prosperous farming area such as Glendale attracted. Yet clearly, it did.

In certain respects, Glendale and its surrounding areas provided for the countryside what certain areas within the city provided for analysts and 'supertourists' of urban Newcastle: if one wished to learn about the inner life of the urban poor, one visited Sandgate; if one sought an exemplar of rural labouring conditions and sought to absorb country life at a glance, Glendale was becoming an obvious focus. Its reputation, strategically enhanced by the work of its farming heroes, was sustained and further entrenched during the nineteenth century through its starring role in three successive parliamentary reports,[40] as well as in the investigations and commentaries of other interested contemporaries. Theorists such as McDonogh have asserted that open space or emptiness rarely exists as an 'empty category' of spatial consciousness.[41] While openness, emptiness, remoteness, may describe physical character, the conceptualisation of such space is none the less deeply embedded in cultural definitions. As on farms generally, there were clear purposes and 'expectations govern[ing] activity'[42] on the holdings in nineteenth-century Glendale. Following McDonogh, however, the 'empty' spaces around and between these areas of specific land-use and economic value perhaps evoked notions of freedom, but also intense unease.[43] Despite any geographic isolation, the various meanings constructed around Glendale and its inhabitants, and assessments of women who worked there, made the discursive 'distance' between Glendale and Newcastle at times appear very small indeed. The interpretative tensions which arose in relation to the area again warrant some close scrutiny, as does the symbolic and material role of the bondager. For it was around this category of worker, *despite* the comparatively small proportion of women expressly hired for the purpose as evidenced by the Glendale census sample, that the most insistent concern was evinced. Again, arguments about the bondager drew heavily upon notions of ideal femininity, and so carried wider implications for women in the rural north.

---

40 *Employment of women and children in agriculture*, 1843 Report; *Women's employment in agriculture*, 1867 Report; *Royal Commission on Labour*, Glendale Report, 1893.
41 G. McDonogh, 'The geography of emptiness', in R. Rotenberg and G. McDonogh (eds), *The cultural meaning of urban space*, Westport, Conn. 1993, 3–15.
42 K. Lynch and G. Hack, *Site planning*, Cambridge, Mass. 1984, 326, cited ibid.
43 Ibid.

'Not worse than other women':
contemporary constructions of rural life and women's work

In August 1863, the inveterate traveller and voyeuristic seeker of 'authentic' working women, Arthur J. Munby, made a trip to Northumberland in search of female labourers. In language suggestive of a hunter tracking some exotic species, Munby described how his enquiries in preparation for the trip had revealed to him that bondagers were 'fewest about Newcastle; they increase and become universal as you go north and west from thence; they are most numerous in the country about Wooler'.[44] Further, the increasing geographic concentration of bondagers moving northwards was supposedly paralleled by a geography of measurable femininity, although in inverse proportion: 'the bondagers of the Wooler country are held to be coarsest and roughest of all. Those about Alnwick and southward are "more refined": they don't spread muck about nor drive carts, or at least, not often.'[45]

It was perhaps testament to the status of its employment system that Munby was attracted to the area. Armed with knowledge about the location and habits of the women, their rate of pay, their dialect, their supposedly distinctive physiognomy, and their work patterns, Munby set off to speak to bondagers in particular, but concluded that, ultimately, his visit 'has certainly been a failure'.[46] On four separate occasions, he recorded that bondagers had been in his sight – tantalisingly close for a 'collector' such as Munby – but yet too far off to engage in conversation. In a rare moment in Munby history, the geographic vastness of the Northumbrian countryside had imposed conversational silence on the man. More exasperating still, where Munby did encounter a bondager, she was not in her authentic working environment, which for Munby was so crucial in his examination of working-class female identity. She was found instead in a farmhouse kitchen: 'A bony strong girl of seventeen, who was standing barearmed at the washtub.' Even here, any plans for conversation were not realised, since with his arrival, '[she] shrunk out of sight thereupon: but only from sullenness'.[47] Four years before Munby's trip, Walter White had written that during their dinner hours, bondagers lay down near the roadside or path to look at passers-by.[48] There is no evidence to support the delightful thought that Munby, the observer himself, may have been unknowingly observed during his trip. None the less, White's casual note buried deep in his work alerts us yet again to the limits imposed by historical 'supertourism'; we may wish to read the significance of this reversal of the gaze, but are constrained from doing so through lack of 'hard' evidence of the kind supplied (in bulk) by Munby.

[44] A. J. Munby, MS diary, Cambridge, Trinity College, Wren Library, vol. xxi, 1863, 233.
[45] Ibid. 242.
[46] Ibid. 232.
[47] Ibid. 165.
[48] Walter White, *Northumberland and the border*, London 1859, 203.

Although Northumberland had not fulfilled its promise of close access to bondagers or 'country wenches', whose wearing of big boots and performance of dirty work were traits which loomed large in Munby's diarised universe of 'ideal' woman, the traveller was no less fulsome in his praise of the system in which they worked:

> it trains up the wenches to be hardy and lusty and familiar with out door ways: and it keeps up a wholesome protest against the molly coddlers, to see a whole countyful of stout lasses devoted to field labour only, not taking it as a parergon in the intervals of housework.[49]

Although in diary form, Munby's observations were written clearly with an audience in mind.[50] At his request, his work was not made public until after 1950. However, that Munby had not managed to consult bondagers themselves, yet saw fit to pronounce authoritatively on their work and their characteristics, certainly set him squarely within the dominant conventions of investigation and surveillance which were developing during the nineteenth century.

Assessment of contemporary reports relating to the bondager immediately suggests the ambivalent status she occupied. On the one hand, the bondager was part of a wider population of Northumbrian rural workers who were elevated to a pre-eminent position in the hierarchy of English rural labour. A considerable literature throughout the century celebrated the numerous advantages which northern farm workers enjoyed in comparison to their southern counterparts, and the 'superior' strength, skill, education and organisation of workers in the region. They were, reported a vicar in Alnwick in 1867, 'a very intelligent, thoughtful, and calculating race . . . [and] possess brains of a very superior order'.[51] In 1843, Sir Francis Doyle concluded that the northern peasantry were 'intelligent, sober, and courteous in their manners',[52] while Richard Heath fifty years later concluded that the labourer here was undoubtedly 'a *superior* animal'.[53] In some accounts, bondagers were positioned securely within this celebratory discourse: they were 'physically a splendid race; their strength is such that they can vie with men in carrying sacks of corn, and there seems to be no work in the fields which affects them injuriously, however hard it may appear'.[54]

For others, however, such examples were alarming: to them, muscular femininity appeared as a contradiction in terms, and discussions about the bondager are suffused with contrasts. Moreover, there was a sense among

---

49 Munby diary, vol. xxi, 1863, 241.
50 Ibid. 31.
51 *Women's employment in agriculture*, 1867 Report, letter of George Hans Hamilton, appendix a, 222.
52 *Employment of women and children in agriculture*, 1843 Report, 299.
53 Heath, *The English peasant*, 87.
54 *Women's employment in agriculture*, 1867 Report, 53.

critics of the existing structure that the identity of the bondager was in many ways that of a disordering woman, one whose presence and conditions of employment militated against the recognition and maintenance of 'appropriate' boundaries of gender and class. Unravelling the strands of contemporary discourse around the bondager cannot proceed with a simple division between urban and rural conditions in mind: the discursive interconnections are more complex, implicating the body of the bondager, the spaces she occupied and moved between. These themes suggest that while the bondager's conditions and behaviour were interpreted in ways which positioned her as marginal, 'peculiar', even threatening to order, such definitions relied constantly upon the strength of normative definitions of femininity. Again then, hired bondagers could be viewed as numerically 'peripheral'; but the place they occupied in a wider discourse on women's work and economic position rendered them more central in cultural representations of gender.

In the Northumbrian countryside, writes Nancy Ridley, a woman was invariably referred to as 'a body'.[55] For bondagers, this association of identity with the body was particularly evident. The premium upon physical strength was clear from accounts of bondagers at the hiring in the region, which usually took place in March. Women were judged on the basis of their assumed strength alone. Again drawing upon analogies with a slave or a cattle market, observers described a general process of employers critically scanning labourers, 'as the slave merchant would have scanned a negro, and naturally [they] regard them in no other light than that of animals'.[56] Their arms would be examined, and enquiries made about their health.[57] There is only scant evidence about women's own responses to the process. One woman recalled that late in the century, as a person of small stature, the hirings were an immense ordeal: she stood in 'the town square feeling like an animal, and being so ashamed' because no-one wanted to hire her.[58] For women like Mary Rutherford however, who had been a bondager over the border, the hirings were a source of personal pride, since she 'was always away [hired] by eight in the morning'.[59]

Wearing distinctive uniforms which were neither provided by nor insisted upon by employers, but made and maintained by the women themselves and for some women a source of pride,[60] ready identification through clothing further heightened the associations made between the bondagers' identity, and their outward bodily appearance. At the hirings, well-recognised emblems were pinned to the uniform to provide ready reference to observers

---

[55] Ridley, *Northumberland: then and now*, 109.
[56] Kebbel, *The agricultural labourer*, 174.
[57] 'Rambler' [Revd A. S. Wardroper], *Rambles in Northumberland*, Newcastle 1924, 13.
[58] L. Taylor, 'To be a farmer's girl: bondagers of border counties', *Country Life*, Oct. 1978, 1110–12 at p. 1110.
[59] Idem, 'The days of the bondager', *Scotsman*, 5 July 1978, 8.
[60] A. M. Scott, 'Women's working dress on the farms of the east borders', *Costume* x (1977), 41–8 at p. 41.

as to whether or not a woman had already been hired. Tickets before hiring were attached to the women. Once an agreement had been made, and a bargain sealed with a token shilling from her future employer, the ticket was replaced with red ribbons.[61] Increasingly, this reliance upon appearance as a major guide in the hiring process prompted criticism from observers who argued that in the process of any engagement, consideration not merely of body, but also of character, was indispensable. Equal payment of servants without respect to their character was 'a monstrous injustice', claimed a local newspaper writer in 1861.[62] The practice promoted dissipation by exposing 'good servants to be corrupted by the bad'.[63] The engagement made between the bondager and the hind was viewed as particularly suspect in moral terms, since the hind himself was 'but a servant on the lowest scale',[64] without references to vouch for his own good character.

The hirings themselves were associated with various forms of bodily excess, all of which attracted more consistent concern around women's participation than that of men. Once business was completed, in the afternoon dancing, 'a passion which . . . prevails to an enormous extent' among the women,[65] drinking and other 'boisterous merriment'[66] took place, adding to the list of features which made the hirings appear to some reformers, and especially the clergy, as an abominable nuisance. The Northumbrian Mirror in 1840 displayed a tolerant attitude to the labourers' leisure pursuits, asking whether they were to be 'too severely blamed? These meetings are few and far between, such indulgence but annual.'[67] For locals like the Revd Dr Guthrie, however, the spectre of large crowds and the drunkenness and illicit sexual behaviour deemed to be an inevitable consequence of unsupervised leisure demanded that alternative 'agreeable recreation' be created.[68]

If the hirings were designated as a dangerous space in the cultural geography of rural life, where corporeal excess was linked to the unfettered sexuality of working women, other places too loomed large as 'blots' in any ordered rural landscape. Once hired, unmarried bondagers were accommodated in hinds' cottages, which invariably contained only one room. The ideal rural home would provide a private, 'sacred asylum for the females of the family' and space in the garden for growing the vegetables which would

61 'Rambler', Rambles in Northumberland, 12.
62 Dr Guthrie, 'Farm hirings', Alnwick Mercury, 1 Mar. 1861, 7.
63 A. Lawson, The farmer's practical instructor, Newcastle 1827, 138.
64 Revd H. Stuart, Agricultural labourers as they were, are, and should be, 2nd edn, Edinburgh 1854, 25.
65 Kebbel, The agricultural labourer, 177.
66 Samuel Donkin, The agricultural labourers of Northumberland: their physical and social condition, Newcastle 1869, 11.
67 'Agricola', 'Domestic condition of the Northumbrian peasantry', Northumbrian Mirror xi/12 (1840), 253–362 at p. 317.
68 Guthrie, 'Farm hirings', 7.

'inspire a man with a nobler feeling'.[69] The hinds' cottages fell far short of the ideal. Here, the uncontrolled sexuality of the bondager could work its particular disordering mischief: undressing in close proximity, both single and married hinds were unsettled by these 'coarse, blowzy girls'.[70] A committee organised expressly for the purpose of improving cottages in the area maintained that under such conditions, 'the wonder is not that instances of . . . intercourse occasionally occur, but that these are so rare'.[71] The identification of separate rooms with guaranteed female chastity was as complete among the moral reformers of Northumberland as it was in discussions of the working classes elsewhere. Meticulous attention to cottage floor plans and furniture consumed local reformers. The use of box beds, for example, which afforded some degree of privacy and separation, were discussed at length, although even here there was ambivalence about the use of such furniture. The boundary between the virtuous preservation of modesty through privacy and the maintenance of privacy for the concealment of sexual improprieties was bound up in the bed; it was feared that in any event, a box bed alone could never 'conceal what should not be there'.[72]

Worse still than bondagers housed with hinds, in the eyes of contemporary critics, was the 'objectionable' practice of housing single women on their own in vacant cottages: 'this is a great cause of immorality'.[73] No such equivalent concern was evinced about single men occupying cottages. Although relatively rare given the employment structures which operated, occasionally a group of men on a large farm would share quarters. Late in the century Anderson Graham visited one such cottage, applauding its neatness, and describing how cooking and cleaning were happily rotated on a weekly basis, each man in turn playing 'Bessie of the household'. The walls of the cottage were 'a dream of fair women', adorned with pictures from calendars and cheap newspapers. The men, he knowingly reported, had women to the cottage for dancing and for other visits: 'youths placed as they were are almost certain to indulge in more or less wild "larks" '.[74]

It was not the bodies of the youths but women's bodies which were most obviously and significantly implicated in illicit sex through the production of illegitimate children. Illegitimacy rates in rural Northumberland were considerably higher than those in its urban areas.[75] The high rate, however, cannot be attributed easily to the bondaging system alone, although that system constituted a primary focus among contemporary critics. Reasons for the illegitimacy rate are obscure, and difficult to assess. Yet one piece of

---

[69] *Report of the Cottage Improvement Society of North Northumberland*, London 1842, 11.
[70] White, *Northumberland and the border*, 203.
[71] *Report of the Cottage Improvement Society*, 32.
[72] Revd W. S. Gilly, *The peasantry of the border: an appeal on their behalf*, Berwick upon Tweed 1841, 24.
[73] *Women's employment in agriculture*, 1867 Report, appendix a, G. McDouall, 223.
[74] P. Anderson Graham, *The rural exodus*, London 1892, 101.
[75] *Women's employment in agriculture*, 1867 Report, 59.

evidence relating to fifty-eight mothers of illegitimate children suggests that hired bondagers constituted only a small proportion of the group, compared with women who still lived at home, and domestic servants.[76] The rates were probably influenced by late age at marriage in rural areas, and contemporaries claimed that an illegitimate child acted as no impediment to future marriage. According to Archdeacon Hamilton, the proximity of north Northumberland to the border, where 'irregular' marriages prevailed in the past, contributed to 'lax' attitudes about sexuality. The matrimonial institution, he claimed, was not taken seriously in the region.[77]

To those moral reformers such as Hamilton, the apparent willingness of the farming community to 'overlook' the stigma of illegitimate motherhood was troubling. Certainly the evidence from the region suggests that there was a degree of tolerance exhibited. Women with illegitimate children were hired and housed as cottars, while others were employed as labourers.[78] Evidence from Glendale too suggests that mothers were not necessarily precluded from housing, employment or kin networks.[79] From a later period, a farmer's wife remembered an event which indicated the matter-of-fact attitude that some adopted towards the 'problem'. When a hind informed her husband one day that he had 'sent Jessie [a bondager] off the field', the farmer's wife enquired about the reason. ' "[I]s she ill?" He just looked at me strangely and said "She's just had a wean in the barn".' Some time after the birth, the woman resumed her work.[80] The reaction to illegitimacy rates from outside the farming community, however, was shocked and at times extremely punitive. Late in the century Kebbel suggested a means of economic punishment of women throughout the English countryside for such alleged moral 'lapses', through a co-operative boycott: 'masters [should] combine together, so that girls who had met with "misfortunes" found themselves experiencing every year greater difficulties in getting employed'.[81]

Some small consolation was found by reformers in the interpretation of illegitimacy rates, however. Contemporary commentators on the problem assumed that their size reflected the greater impossibility of either concealing birth in the countryside or of women committing infanticide, 'supposed to be very common in some towns . . . [and] quite unknown in Glendale'.[82] Women in the country perhaps had less access to the means of procuring an abortion, and the isolation of female farm workers may have hindered them in acquiring knowledge about contraception. No other evidence exists in relation to these matters, except in an oblique reference made by William Nicholson, a farmer, in 1867. Young women migrating from the town to the

---

76 Ibid.
77 Ibid.
78 Ibid. appendix c, Mr Hunt, 237.
79 For example, 1871 Census, NRO 958/22, parish of Carham, 6, entry 19; 10, entry 51.
80 Taylor, 'To be a farmer's girl', 1110.
81 Kebbel, The agricultural labourer, 180.
82 Women's employment in agriculture, 1867 Report, 58.

country, he maintained, had usually already lost 'their own character . . . [and] also contract habits and ideas which are sufficient on their return to the country, to hide the results of their fall, and to poison a whole community'.[83] Again, the association of female bodily excess with the spread of infecting disorder through the transgression of ordering boundaries of town and country saw women's mobility being interpreted as peculiarly dangerous.

If the bondager was her body, the disorder she represented was carried within it through her sexuality, and played out in the danger zones of hirings and cottages where 'normal' boundaries of respectability became so blurred as to be rendered meaningless. There were other specific sites, moreover, where the bondager appeared not merely as a potent agent of a *threatening* femininity, but as one whose femininity (however dubiously characterised by some contemporary observers) was itself under threat. Again, the environment in which the reciprocally disordering qualities of women's bodies and particular spaces could be seen was at work in the fields. While some question was raised in the rural, as in the urban, context regarding the capacity of women once exposed to vice to be then transformed – 'female modesty is not a possession which can be parted with and resumed'[84] – for many observers the introduction to fieldwork and employment in it over extended periods dangerously entrenched behaviour and sentiments inimical to bourgeois ideals of femininity. Although farmers like William Hindmarsh confidently asserted that conditions of labour were most satisfactory, and that bondagers 'are not worse than other women',[85] others condemned the 'bad conversation' which took place at work beween men and women, and claimed that field workers were 'more immoral than those in service'.[86]

As well as the inevitably immoral outcome of mixed-sex work portrayed in contemporary constructions, the very nature of some aspects of women's labour apparently bore visible testimony to their fading or even 'inverted' femininity. 'Constant labour and exposure by day in the field, and the absence of decent accommodation at night must tend materially to unsex them, both morally and physically, and unfit them . . . for their future spheres as wives and mothers', asserted John Wilson in 1864.[87] It was a 'species of toil which weakens the frame and blunts all finer feeling . . . already in the prime of life [bondagers are] hastening to decay'.[88] There could be no more telling material measure of their distance from true femininity and its concerns of cleanliness and domesticity than that bondagers spent their days 'up to their ankles in reeking filth'.[89] Even a strong supporter of the system such as Sir

---

83 Ibid. appendix e, Richard Huntley King, occupier, 250.
84 *Report of the Cottage Improvement Society*, 38.
85 *Employment of women and children in agriculture*, 1843 Report, William Hindmarsh, 375.
86 *Women's employment in agriculture*, 1867 Report, appendix b, Thomas Carr, 229.
87 John Wilson, 'Notes on northern farms and farming', *Newcastle Chronicle*, July 1864, 21.
88 'Agricola', 'Domestic condition of the Northumbrian peasantry', 254.
89 Wilson, 'Notes', 21.

Francis Doyle reported that bondagers' 'occupations render them somewhat masculine'.[90]

Little value was placed upon women's considerable farming skills by rural commentators like Wilson, Howitt and others, since these were assumed to exist in inverse proportion to their domestic capacities:

> They can hoe turnips and potatoes to a miracle, but they know very little of the approved method of cooking them. They rake hay better than comb children's hair; drive a cart or a harrow with a better grace than rock a cradle, and help more nimbly in the barn than in the ingle.[91]

The degree of knowledge of housewifery was as standard a source of controversy around working women in Northumberland as in other areas of England in the nineteenth century. None the less, the particular conditions of the bondage, which required no domestic work from the women for the period of their engagement, contributed to a widespread perception of their domestic ignorance. In the cottage, 'she may lounge about like a lad and whistle or snooze until she be ordered afield', reported Munby.[92] 'A woman in Northumberland's not worth house room', responded an old shepherd to one investigator, when asked why he had remained unmarried.[93]

In some ways, then, the bondager was interpreted by critics of rural life as another 'quintessential' female figure who represented the worst features of rural disorder. That she was young, female, mobile and corporeally identified was not merely incidental, but central to this symbolic significance. The want of 'proper' control she embodied, a lack whose results were supposedly manifest at hirings, in cottages and fields, provided a focal point for wider concerns about the maintenance of social cohesion, stability and order which were evinced consistently in the rural context. Again, the priorities and concerns of rural reformers seemed not far removed from those of bourgeois urban Novocastrians, when we consider the impetus to contain or even to eradicate the sources of social disorder believed to inhere in the bondage system. Rural paternalism was dwindling and any suggested means of promoting moral responsibility through supervision and education 'from above' were difficult to carry out among an isolated, very mobile population. For those contemporaries who were so alarmed at the system's alleged potential for creating disorder, the standard practice of 'flitting' in the region brought with it significant concerns, and was seen to hamper any attempts to regulate and transform the behaviour of workers.

Throughout Northumberland, annual removal to new farms after the hirings, called flitting, was widespread. On 12 May each year, horses and carts criss-crossed the county carrying bondagers, hinds, family members, furniture

---

90 *Employment of women and children in agriculture*, 1843 Report, 300.
91 W. Howitt, *The rural life of England*, London 1838, i. 181.
92 Munby diary, vol. xxi, 1863, 236.
93 Heath, *The English peasant*, 210.

and personal belongings to the site of new employment.[94] The flitting was seen as a 'crisis', a great social earthquake which 'begets a spirit of unsettledness in all . . . [and which] means the negation of the idea of home'.[95] Significantly, the clergy were vocal in their condemnation of a system which undermined the influence of 'employer, schoolmaster, or clergyman', and local philanthropists complained too, that the practice diminished their ability to perform 'good works'.[96] It was a system in which, it was feared, 'no public opinion can be brought to bear' upon the labouring population.[97] Workers moved when they had been given notice, but could also choose themselves to leave, without explanation to their employer. Late in the century, some evidence was given that the hind moved at the behest of his family, with one member or another becoming discontented.[98]

Attempts were made to discourage mobility. The Northumberland Agricultural Society, for example, awarded prizes to workers who had remained longest in the same employ. In 1843, Anne Armytage was awarded £3 for long years of service at Kirkwhelpington.[99] Cautionary tales and ballads warned against the hazards of frequent removal.[100] Advice was offered to employers about the means of securing their labour force. For example a local minister, Dr Guthrie, encouraged farmers to allow open courting, thereby dissuading young women from pursuing 'dangerous' alternatives.[101] However, although bondagers were represented as flighty, they could not always choose where they went, nor could they depend upon remaining at a farm they liked; the decision rested with the hind, to whose employment her own was tied. In fact, workers like Mary Rutherford in later life maintained that the thing she liked the best about her retirement was 'not having to flit every year. It was awful, thon flittin.'[102]

To some contemporaries, the annual mass movement of workers made for a 'kind of vagrant population'[103] in the countryside, an intensely disquieting image. Certainly, the sight of people selling goods or in search of work in the region was not uncommon. Hucksters moved through the countryside selling tea and coffee to 'women . . . [who] indulge four times a day in [these] enervating' beverages,[104] and later in the century 'cadgers' allegedly sold alcohol and

---

94 A lesser 'flit' sometimes occurred six months later.
95 Hastings M. Neville, *A corner in the north: yesterday and today with border folk*, Newcastle 1909, 10, 29.
96 *Women's employment in agriculture*, 1867 Report, Archdeacon Hamilton, 59.
97 *Royal Commission on Labour*, Glendale Report, 1893, Dr Walker, 127.
98 Ibid. William Hindmarsh.
99 *Newcastle Journal*, 2 Sept. 1843, 3.
100 'Lucy's flittin', in Revd J. Christie, *Northumberland: its history, its features, and its people*, London 1904, 21.
101 *Alnwick Mercury*, 1 Mar. 1861, 7.
102 Taylor, 'Days of the bondager', 8.
103 *Women's employment in agriculture*, 1867 Report, appendix a, unidentified correspondent, 224.
104 *Women's employment in agriculture*, 1867 Report, 57.

'in consequence some women have acquired drinking habits'.[105] Munby encountered three people on the tramp during his short trip. A pair of teen-agers in Hexham, 'the girl almost in rags', told Munby that they were *en route* from Glasgow to Newcastle in search of kin and work. He passed 'a lone tramping woman' at Stamfordham, but did not speak to her.[106] In other areas, the synonymity of poverty and agricultural labour may have been in evidence:[107] in Northumberland, the regular movement of workers, not as vagrants, but in a disturbingly 'vagrant-like' manner, was perhaps yet another 'proof' to observers of the perversities of a system which was deemed to be increasingly ill-suited to Victorian priorities of order and progress.

Fixing boundaries of space, movement and gender was imperative in the cause of progress. In examining the figure of the hired bondager in the light of these preoccupations, her symbolic significance becomes clearer. She attracted concern among contemporaries to an extent which otherwise appears disproportionate to her demographic weight in the population of Glendale or elsewhere. The role of bondager blurred important ordering dichotomies of respectable Victorian life. Her work conditions had clear implications for arrangements within the household, and ruptured the ideal separations of home and work, public and private, which were the foundation stones of domestic ideology. In the face of urban expansion, as some writers and artists turned to the countryside to 'recapture' a vision of an undifferenti-ated natural idyll,[108] the bondager's corporeality and sexuality contributed instead to the perception of a rural landscape dotted with dangerous spaces. In the same idealising tradition, where the labour of a ruddy peasantry could be propagandised as outgrowths of a naturally benevolent paternalistic order, the bondager intruded as a blemish upon the complexion of 'organic' master/servant relations. In the particular constellation of workforce distribu-tion and labour power in the county, the bondager's position served to dangerously blur the discourse of order of which a labour hierarchy was a visible sign. All such concerns about her were underpinned by alarm that she was a feminine force which operated within, but was not clearly controlled by, patriarchal power at home or work, in a period when gender relations were seen as naturally ordered.[109] As a single woman, she belonged to that wider group which supposedly suffered 'from the weight of too much liberty'.[110] Labour shortages and terms of employment allegedly enhanced her

---

[105] *Royal Commission on Labour*, Glendale Report, 1893, 110.

[106] Munby diary, vol. xxi, 1863, 142, 185.

[107] R. A. E. Wells, 'The development of the English rural proletariat and social protest, 1700–1850', *Journal of Peasant Studies* vi/2 (1979), 115–39 at p. 120.

[108] See, for example, Paul Street, 'Painting deepest England: the late landscapes of John Linnell and the uses of nostalgia', in C. Shaw and M. Chase (eds), *The imagined past: history and nostalgia*, Manchester 1989, 68–80.

[109] Hall, *White, male and middle class*, 92.

[110] 'Our single women', *North British Review* xxxvi (1862), 62–87 at p. 67.

disruptive power, while simultaneously ensuring that such disruptive potential remained unfettered.

Contemporary perceptions of the bondager, however, were not uniform,
nor were they formulated without producing considerable contradictions.
The bondager was, after all, only one category of worker in rural Northumberland. What of women who were married to hinds, and performed bondage
services? What of casual workers and cottars whose labour, alongside that of
hired and family bondagers, was portrayed as indispensable to the maintenance of productivity and prosperity for landholders? And what of the implications of controversies about bondaging for the general economic position
of women in the countryside, as workers, and in some cases, as poor women?
As has been illustrated in the case of the exclusion of women from the lead
factories of Newcastle, the cluster of arguments about working conditions for
women drew heavily upon broader assumptions about gender identity. In
turn, the cultural representation of femininity in that context did not remain
separate from the sphere of material conditions, but was in constant interaction with it, fashioning the web of constraints and opportunities within
which women operated. In the rural context, from the 1830s a growing
clamour to dismantle the bondaging system and to modify women's work was
heard. In the following section, the course of this debate is examined, again
affording some insight into the ways in which gender meanings were actively
constructed in the work environment, and also how the material implications of such constructions affected women.

The 'irresistable march of civilisation'?
The bondage debate and constructions of rural femininity.

As the experience of Munby perhaps indicates, the possibility of undertaking
any sustained surveillance of rural labourers in Northumberland was
hampered by distance. For this reason, the observation of outsiders was often
confined to occasions such as the hirings or the kirn feasts at harvest time. At
the hirings, wrote one local author, 'nature always turns out hundreds of our
best specimens of unsophisticated workmanship',[111] and such crowds of
labourers gathered together made observation an economical, if incomplete,
task. In comparison to the kirns and hirings, we 'do not know a great deal
about the nature of relationships within the rural household',[112] or of relationships in the fields, and how these were viewed by observers, or experienced by the labourers themselves. None the less, in the Northumbrian
context, the three major parliamentary reports compiled at intervals across
the century convey some sense of the ways in which these relationships were

---

111 *Alnwick Mercury*, 1 Aug. 1859, 2.
112 M. Reed, 'The peasantry of nineteenth-century England: a neglected class?', *History Workshop* xviii (1984), 53–76 at p. 59.

characterised and how such characterisations evolved; these are dealt with here, and in the following section.

The first two reports, in 1843 and 1867, were specifically concerned with the conditions of women and children in agricultural employment. The third report, presented in 1893, dealt more generally with the agricultural labourer, and was part of the extensive 1892-4 Royal Commission on Labour. The report in 1843 was almost uniformly celebratory. Sir Francis Doyle, in gathering evidence, relied almost solely upon the opinions of large landowners and significant farmers in the region. No evidence was gathered from hinds or bondagers, nor indeed from any category of farm worker. In fact, Doyle himself stated clearly that the workers in the area were 'represented to me' by the 'experts' from the region.[113] In this respect, the Northumbrian evidence diverged from that collected in other regions, where workers themselves were more extensively consulted. The report did not include reference to the criticisms of the system levelled two years earlier by the Revd Mr W. S. Gilly, whose book had called both for cottage reform, and the extension of education to improve the 'moral culture' of the people, and the education of young females 'in a manner worthy of their sex' to counteract the 'rude tendencies' of field work.[114] While Doyle mentioned the shortage of cottages and the state of disrepair of existing accommodation, with the exception of a lone dissenting voice about the effect of field work on the morals of young women raised by the Clerk of Morpeth Parish,[115] his conclusion that women farm workers were 'the best attired and most healthy of the population' indicated his more general approval.[116] With reference to William Cobbett and others who had characterised the system as akin to slavery, moreover, he maintained that this was merely the result of 'some confusion of thought'.[117]

By 1867, the enquiries carried out by J. J. Henley, a magistrate, Poor Law Guardian and landowner from Oxfordshire, yielded less uniform results. In a more extensive report, Henley had consulted a wider cross-section of the population, and had spoken with a few women farm workers themselves. One could argue that the diversity of opinion expressed was the result of this wider consultation alone, that such diversity had been masked through Doyle's report, and certainly, other sources would indicate no unanimity of opinion about women's work in the 1840s. Yet Henley's report exhibits two interesting features. First, in a list of 190 witnesses, nearly a third were drawn from the clergy, and from fields of medicine and education.[118] The prominent inclusion of these professional groups, and in particular the clergy, paralleled a growing trend for the publication of tracts by clerics about rural morality

113 Employment of women and children in agriculture, 1843 Report, 300.
114 Gilly, Peasantry of the border, 31.
115 Employment of women and children in agriculture, 1843 Report, 372.
116 Ibid. 378.
117 Ibid. 298.
118 Women's employment in agriculture, 1867 Report, calculated from appendices a–e, 219–68.

and women's work in the area. Indeed, increasingly throughout the country in the second half of the century the generation of comparative material on rural areas illustrated a gradual shift in the discourse, away from a focus upon general productivity and labour force arrangements, and instead towards social measurement and comparison. Such emphasis in the literature, which drew heavily and selectively upon the evidence about women furnished in successive parliamentary reports, saw Northumberland cast as a problematic area. Second, the range of issues covered by the 1867 report deals far more extensively with fluctuations in the sexual division of labour and the tensions it generated, as the introduction of machinery to the farms became more widespread.

As in industry, agricultural improvements and the adoption of machinery brought with them constant redefinition of what constituted 'women's work'. While observers such as Hastings Neville constructed the sexual division of labour as eternal, with men's and women's work being different 'to the world's end',[119] sources reveal the historical and cultural specificity of such divisions. Increasing adoption of the scythe, earmarked as 'an exclusively male instru-ment',[120] had, for example, gradually excluded women from the primary task of reaping corn. With sickles, contemporaries such as Henry Stephens main-tained, women were as efficient, or more efficient, than male reapers: 'what is called a *maiden-ridge*, of three young women, will beat a *bull-ridge*, of three men, at reaping any sort of corn'.[121] Scythes harvested more quickly than sickles which women had used previously, but left the corn in disarray. In scythe harvesting, women were relegated to a kind of outdoor housewifery, tidying the mess by gathering and tying up the crop.[122] With the introduction of the threshing machine, too, women usually assisted male workers rather than operating the machines themselves. Ploughing and cart driving were usually reserved as male occupations. Witnesses in 1867 told Henley that cart-driving was dangerous, and that females lacked the necessary talents to negotiate winding country roads.[123] Although the women themselves enjoyed driving, and in fact argued among themselves when an opportunity arose to perform the task, it was assumed by most to be a male preserve.[124]

Superior strength and ability were often given as reasons for these divi-sions. A local folk song warned women against attempting 'men's' work such as reaping, since 'it takes wit and method too, and strength to carry it through'.[125] Yet clearly, on the basis of contemporary evidence, such claims were spurious. Strength? Henley himself recorded the sack weights carried by

---

[119] Neville, *Corner in the north*, 17.

[120] Hostettler, 'Gourlay Steell', 97.

[121] Henry Stephens, *The book of the farm*, n.p. 1844, cited ibid. 96.

[122] Michael Roberts, 'Sickles and scythes: women's work and men's work at harvest time', *History Workshop* vii (1979), 3–28 at p. 13.

[123] *Women's employment in agriculture*, 1867 Report, appendix c, George Davidson, 238.

[124] Ibid. appendix b, 'M. M.' of Lanton, bondager, 234.

[125] 'Bonny Peggy', in Neville, *Corner in the north*, 52.

women upstairs into the granaries at eight stone (wheat and barley) and nine stone (oats).[126] Wit? One man who advised against women driving carts admitted that his own wife drove, and was 'a splendid coachman'.[127] (In a relatively rare explicit reference to the inconsistencies brought about by the dual vision of femininity refracted through the lens of both biology and class, Henley himself drily observed that, with regard to wealthy women who rode and drove horses, 'few would be bold enough ... to propose legislative inter-ference'. So farming women were 'undoubtedly as fit to be trusted'.)[128] As well as specific exclusions, the range of tasks delimited as women's work bore all the hallmarks of women's work elsewhere: their jobs were heavy, repetitive and considered particularly menial and dirty. Forking dung and loading manure were female tasks, one farmer observing that 'we cannot get males to work' in the kind of labour which bondagers undertook.[129] John Wilson observed that during manure loading, men invariably stood 'idle, merely looking on during the operation'.[130] Moreover, in any case where women performed 'men's' work, the status of that work was protected by assigning two women to the task which a lone man would customarily undertake.[131]

Adherence to, and development of, these divisions found ready support from two different quarters. Bourgeois observers of the system, as previously mentioned, were shocked by some of the work women performed, supported exclusive work practices, and indeed wished to extend them to curtail women's most 'offensive' jobs. For rather different reasons, hinds had an obvious interest in retaining 'skilled' work for themselves, and strongly upheld exclusionary practices. In 1893 Fox hit the nail on the head, stating that women's work 'is almost as effective as men's at nearly half the price ... if men were substituted for women workers the additional cost would impose a greater burden on the employers than they could bear'.[132] The stricter differentiation of male and female labour therefore, was perceived as 'protection' for the hinds in an economic situation which they perceived as unfavourable to them.

In a fascinating examination of the ways in which evolving sexual divisions of labour were reflected and perpetuated, Eve Hostettler traces the early inclusion but eventual erasure of women from the farming illustrations used in Stephens's *Book of the Farm*. The book gave an account of northern farming practices, was published in successive editions from 1844 to 1901, and illustrations by Gourlay Steell of women reaping with scythes were included in earlier volumes. By 1899, not only were new illustrations

---

126 *Women's employment in agriculture*, 1867 Report, 54.
127 Ibid. appendix c, Mr Dickson, 240.
128 Ibid. 54.
129 Ibid. appendix e, Charles Borthwick, occupier, 251.
130 Wilson, 'Notes on northern farms', 21.
131 *Women's employment in agriculture*, 1867 Report, 53.
132 *Royal Commission on Labour*, Glendale Report, 1893, 102.

included which reflected changing techniques and technology: an older illustration of sheep-feeding with turnips had been doctored, with the woman worker featured in the first version erased from the centre foreground of the picture.[133] Such visual representations of farm practice contributed towards creating an unproblematic division of labour which denied the history of women's participation, and reflected a picture of how the process should look ideally (without women) according to some reformers of farm work and conditions in the late Victorian period.

Hinds felt sorely aggrieved that their employment was bound to the engagement of a bondager. In the 1830s when the old steward wrote his handbill, a meeting of hinds declared that 'hiring a Servant Girl is ruinously burdensome, most harassing and tyrannical . . . [we] consider it a duty to ourselves, our families, and the oppressed class to which we belong, determinedly to resist' the bondage.[134] In the 1860s and 1870s as well, hinds attempted unsuccessfully to organise to defeat the bondage condition. In 1861, the Alnwick hiring saw some hinds combine to refuse to hire bondagers, but their attempt failed. At the same time in Belford, hinds who pursued such action were simply 'left without being engaged'.[135] By contrast, and attesting to the considerable demand for scarce female labour, women farm workers at Haydon Bridge in 1873 succeeded in their strike for higher harvest wages.[136] Other sources suggest that informally too, bondagers negotiated individual labour and living conditions with employing hinds at the time of hire.[137] In a sometimes fragile employment position – in 1863, a hiring agreement between a hind and a farmer was subsequently cancelled 'on account of J[ohn] Macanalty being unable to find a satisfactory bondager'[138] – gender-based constructions of skill could be used to preserve the status and wage levels of the hind.

It appears that the respective position of hinds and hired bondagers in the labour market produced tensions which were transferred to and played out in both the fields and the households of the region. Neville describes the practice of 'kemping' at harvest, for example, where men in the fields 'fond of a joke' would inform different bands of women shearers that each intended to outdo the other in the speed of their work, thus creating a battle between the bands. 'The strife is fast and furious, angry passions are aroused, especially among the women', while the speed resulted in badly-harvested corn[139] which in turn reflected poorly on the shearers. Within the cottage, bondagers, 'knowing that they must be had', were reputed to 'stir up mischief

---

133 Hostettler, 'Gourlay Steell', illustrations reproduced at p. 100.
134 Handbill, Feb. 1837, enclosed in R. Robson to 3rd Earl Grey, papers of Earl Grey, DU Archives 121/9.
135 *Alnwick Mercury*, 1 Apr. 1861, 4
136 J. P. D. Dunbabin, *Rural discontent in nineteenth-century Britain*, London 1974, 161–2.
137 Taylor, 'To be a farmer's girl', 1110.
138 Middleton Hall MSS, NRO, ZSI/72/37.
139 Neville, *Corner in the north*, 45.

among the families of the hinds'.[140] Domestically some alleged that bondagers were useless, and able only 'to mind the bairns a bit about the door'.[141] The wives of hinds reported the particular distress they experienced through lack of privacy in the household: Mrs Nesbit, for example, told Henley in 1867 that the 'girl must undress with her husband in the room', and this together with the hard conditions of labour, she deemed 'a disgrace to a Christian country'.[142]

However differently motivated, the hinds' objections dovetailed nicely with the broader rhetoric which cast the 'independent' woman worker as a social, economic and moral problem. There was some support provided in the report for the Revd Mr Stuart's view, expressed some years earlier, that for bondagers, away from their 'natural protectors', there were few checks upon them, or upon the general 'sinful indulgence of the animal propensities of our labourers'.[143] At this stage any prospect of legislative intervention to curtail the employment of women was deemed unnecessary by nearly all witnesses. It was believed that any intervention may have adversely affected the economic position of the hinds, may jeopardise the continuation of wives' work, and thereby would operate to the detriment of the rural family economies in the county. There was also a corresponding faith in the capacity of informal 'correction' to operate in relation to problematic areas. In the area of women's work, for example, the bank manager at Wooler maintained that '[p]ublic opinion will cure any objectionable work':[144] there was a sentiment too, that the moral excesses generated by the system could be checked through containment and better surveillance. An Ilderton farmer informed Henley, for example, that his superintendent 'has strict orders to prevent levity between the sexes' in the fields, and added: 'I believe when females are strictly superintended their morals may be kept correct.'[145]

Significantly, most attention was focused upon traditional labourers' festivities associated with hirings and harvest, as clergy and other bourgeois observers manifested the kind of cultural imperialism within England that is usually associated with the country's 'civilising' missions in its colonies,[146] which had been occasionally evidenced already in the plans of more zealous reformers. The Cottage Improvement Society, for example, had emphasised the need for the education of the population in the virtues of good, clean cottages with separate rooms. While they admitted that there might be some resistance to any changes since 'uneducated minds are not easily excited to innovations', the lessons of colonialism supposedly revealed the value of

---

[140] Stuart, *Agricultural labourers as they were*, 23.

[141] Howitt, *Rural life of England*, 181.

[142] *Women's employment in agriculture*, 1867 Report, appendix b, Mrs Nesbit, 234.

[143] Stuart, *Agricultural labourers*, 35.

[144] *Women's employment in agriculture*, 1867 Report, appendix b, William Wightman, 235.

[145] Ibid. appendix e, George Pringle Hughes, 250.

[146] Alun Howkins, 'Rider Haggard and rural England: an essay in literature and history', in Shaw and Chase, *Imagined past*, 81–94 at p. 86.

perseverance: 'The islanders of the Pacific Ocean had to be *taught* the advantages of decent clothing; but having once commenced the practice they were not in a hurry to lay it aside.'[147] The 1867 report attested to similar attempts at 'educative' reform. Witnesses related the attempts which had been made to 'improve the tone of the fairs' by bringing hirings indoors, establishing employment registers, and providing supervised entertainment for the labourers over the previous decade. All attempts had failed miserably; people preferred the open air, and women refused to enter halls reserved for them without being accompanied by their 'partners for the day'. One consolation by 1867 was that the railway system could transport some labourers on the actual morning of the hirings, rather than on the previous night, thus reducing the 'danger' period.[148]

The kirn feasts were deemed morally suspect as well. James Hardy in 1844 had described the harvest season as one of 'care-defying rites . . . poured into one impetuous, uncontrolled, headstrong tide' which culminated in the kirn. Here, the revelry exhibited many of the characteristics of carnival, an occasion for 'fantastic mummery . . . [and] rude masquerade':

> Some [men] dress themselves in female attire, others are encased, from head to heel, in straw ropes wound spirally around the body and limbs; others again have recourse to some animal's skin, to mask the face . . . [and are] secured beneath these 'guisings', from every embarrassment.[149]

By the early 1860s, in place of these festivities, reformers advocated the peaceful, 'rational enjoyment' of carefully organised and monitored suppers, where it was usual 'for the Clergyman and Squire, with the farmers, to join the dinner, and by their presence they contribute to the pleasure and good order of the day'.[150] The contrast between the disorder of nature and the animalistic body lived through and represented by the traditional kirn, and the externally-imposed discipline of the bourgeois-dominated supper, is marked.[151] If the geography of Northumberland and the nature of agricultural work impeded the ordering mission of the clergy and village-based bourgeoisie, they none the less attended strenuously to the task of ordering those individual spaces which were located within their orbits of influence.

Yet the strength of opinions in favour of the system expressed by farmers and landowners in the report was overwhelming. Arguments in terms of economic interest were expressed, not merely in relation to personal gain, but in relation to the wider prosperity brought through the gainful employ-

---

147 *Report of the Cottage Improvement Society*, 28.
148 *Women's employment in agriculture*, 1867 Report, 70
149 James Hardy, *Harvest customs in Northumberland*, Newcastle 1844, 4, 10.
150 Anon., *Harvest homes (by the authoress of Enshrined Hearts)*, printed for private distribution [Newcastle, c. 1862] (held at NCL).
151 Here, the echoes of Bakhtinian carnival and grotesque are compelling: M. Bakhtin, *Rabelais and his world*, Cambridge, Mass. 1968.

ment of workers. Further, while those who disputed the merits of the system on moral grounds deployed arguments about the damage which was done to the femininity of the women employed, farmers and doctors from the area developed a very different set of alternative propositions for consideration, arguments which were constructed around the notion of the essentially healthy rural female body. A local doctor claimed that field work fitted women to be 'good bearers of children'.[152] Another claimed that 'women are less subject to female complaints'.[153] One doctor expressed reservations about the strains of field work, especially for married women who in his experience had suffered uterine prolapse as a result.[154] But Henley himself overall favoured the interpretation of the farmers and doctors who supported women's work: 'there is no evidence that such employment is morally injurious. On the contrary, it tends to rear a fine race of women, who make the best wives for labourers, and are invaluable in a national point of view as producing and rearing a fine population'.[155]

Yet positive assessments of women in the area at times relied upon the shadow of a 'lesser' or even more disordered femininity elsewhere, particularly in the towns. Mr Brown, a Berwick surgeon, stated that farm women 'are by far the finest women physically', adding that the disordering blots came but from the town and were brought into the countryside by women travelling to rural areas at harvest time: 'these are very loose women and girls, who almost all smoke'.[156] Land occupier Richard Huntley King was quick to point out that in respect of morals, while there was 'a considerable amount of bastardy extant', yet again, 'at the same time it is to be remarked that prostitution does not exist'[157] as it did in urban areas. The farm worker was 'better and her life happier than that of a woman occupying the same social position and following any of the various employments open to her in manufacturing towns'.[158] The comparative element in moral discourse continued unabated well beyond 1867. At the turn of the century, a local clergyman concerned with the continuation of the 'evils' of the hirings stated that 'The Hiring Day is the day when town cuteness comingles with country innocence; and too often country innocence returns home with bedraggled skirts.'[159]

Whatever the economic gains to be made from the system by its advocates, the debate was cast primarily in terms of gender in the varying construction of the bondager's identity around the pivot of femininity, and domestic ideals of future marriage and motherhood. Here there was no woman of official or

---

152 *Women's employment in agriculture*, 1867 Report, appendix c, Dr F. Cahill, 237.
153 Ibid. Dr Paton.
154 Ibid. Dr Brummel.
155 Ibid. 70.
156 Ibid. Mr Brown, 236.
157 Ibid. appendix e, Richard Huntley King, 249
158 Ibid. appendix d, Mr Joseph Bainbridge Fife, 242.
159 'The hiring day . . . by a country vicar', *NDG*, May 1900, 72.

professional status of the like of May Abraham in the Newcastle lead works enquiry to challenge the validity of the discursive frameworks established in the report, or at least none was interviewed. One female land occupier from the south of the county made brief comments voicing her disapproval of women in the north 'doing the hard work' and her constant shock whenever she saw women filling manure carts.[160] But labouring women's own voices were largely silenced through a focus on 'expert' witnesses and substantial economic stakeholders. Even so, the material which does exist from the report and elsewhere suggests an alternative reading of the bondager's position which does not necessarily coincide with these dominant views.

Women themselves did not necessarily subscribe to the ideal of healthy womanhood: some women complained that their work was particularly onerous. As well as carrying sacks on their backs in the granary,[161] women disliked turnip work in wet weather and snow, and the extra demands of harvest time.[162] Mothers complained that their daughters were debilitated by their labour.[163] Far from the image of the independent, mischievous worker, the bondager once hired was faced with often gruelling tasks in all weathers, and 'can't shirk it'.[164] While daily payment rates for her work appeared generous by contemporary standards, and some of her wages were paid in kind, the bondager was only paid for her work when it was required. In periods of bad weather or sickness, her pay was not guaranteed, and so actual earnings could vary considerably.[165] While few enough women in the city could afford the contributions required for membership of female friendly societies which provided some rudimentary insurance against illness or other misfortune, in the country even this slight protection was unavailable. Since the wages of men were guaranteed during bad weather or illness, there was a total absence of benefit societies in the region.[166]

Moreover, the precondition of physical strength in her employment made the role of hired bondager a relatively short-term proposition. While for young men there was some future career path in agriculture as hinds and stewards,[167] for older women there were few alternatives. For them, identity and some economic security were offered not through independent labour, but through the prospect of marriage to a hind. Quite aside from individual sentiments regarding any such prospect, in simple demographic terms the low

---

160 *Women's employment in agriculture*, 1867 Report, appendix d, Mrs Colbeck, occupier, 244.
161 Taylor, 'Days of the bondager', 8.
162 *Women's employment in agriculture*, 1867 Report, appendix c, 'A. B.' of Bamburgh, 240; appendix b, 'M. M.' of Lanton, 234.
163 Ibid. appendix b, Mrs Gibson, 234.
164 Munby diary, vol. xxi, 1863, 239.
165 *Women's employment in agriculture*, 1867 Report, 53. The daily rates in 1867 were quoted as 1s. (winter), 1s. 6d. (summer), and 2s. 6d.–3s. (harvest).
166 *Royal Commission on Labour*, 1893, analytical index, 5.
167 *Women's employment in agriculture*, 1867 Report, p. xv.

number of men in the region made even this option a problematic one to pursue. Munby encountered a dairy worker on his travels, and remarked with surprise that 'she was nine and twenty . . . and not married yet!' She informed Munby that there were few men in the area, 'and none I could set my mind on'. Echoing the prevalent notion that for women identity was secured through marriage, Munby provided reassurance that she would yet 'be Mrs. Somebody' in future. She laughed.[168] As a hind's wife, the work was no less taxing. Mrs Anderson described the necessity which drove younger family members out to work to contribute to the family income, and recalled how she had herself 'slaved at harvest to earn the bondager's money'.[169] The women were 'sair wrought' at some times during the year,[170] but working the bondage provided money to send children to school, and was deemed preferable to the 'piece-work' of harvest.[171]

By 1867 then, despite the optimistic conclusions in Henley's report, a considerable degree of tension was elaborated about the bondage system by various witnesses. In comparison with earlier periods, there was a rise in the drive to control, supervise and redefine work and leisure in the countryside and this momentum was elaborated around the pivot of gender identity. The rhetoric of womanhood, marriage and uncontrolled sexuality figured significantly in the discussions. As well as overarching conceptions of femininity, there were also more particular, subtler deployments of gender representation as various relational frameworks were brought into play. Categories of femininity were constructed around divisions of town and country, north county and south county, and Northumberland and other regions, and these divisions in turn were suffused with meanings about the greater or lesser morality, greater or lesser disordering qualities, of individuals and groups of women within them. Even divisions between indoors and outdoors were pertinent here, as gender was elaborated and interpreted within these very specific local sites. The instability of definitions of femininity is evident both in the characterisations of the bondager as a problem, and in the arguments advanced by adherents of the system for its perpetuation – better a bondager than a 'loose' town woman – and hence the struggle to fix meaning, given these underpinnings, was defeated by the very terms of the discourse. The language of the report shows clearly that the landscape of gender in rural Northumberland was as muddied and complex and shifting as that of urban, industrialised areas.

The 'logic' of the arguments employed by opponents of bondaging was claimed by some of them to be so compelling that the decline of the system was cast as inevitable. In discursive terms, both in the report and elsewhere, that tendency to conflate 'what ought to be' with what actually was, was very

168 Munby diary, vol. xxi, p. 175.
169 *Women's employment in agriculture*, 1867 Report, appendix b, Mrs Anderson, 234.
170 Ibid. Mrs Gibson.
171 Ibid. Isabella Humbleton.

strong. In commenting on the report in 1869 in a speech to the Newcastle upon Tyne Farmers' Club, Samuel Donkin declared that 'the bondage system had to give way; it fell before the irresistable march of civilisation'.[172] The declaration was certainly premature, but indicative none the less of a frame of reference in which women's identity was cast in terms of morality and progress, and in which their economic identity was all but eclipsed.

'There are no poor people at all here': work, identity and the contours of rural poverty

By 1893, when Arthur Wilson Fox conducted further enquiries in Northumberland as part of the broader 1892-4 Royal Commission on Labour, the bondaging system of the nineteenth century was in decline. The same problems with cottages and unsupervised work were noted in the report, but overall Fox concluded that the labourer in Northumberland had reached 'the high water mark of prosperity'.[173] While there had been sustained criticism of the system for decades, there had been no legislative enactment or protest activity which had brought any decisive end to women's employment as bondagers. When the system began to decline, the process was gradual, patchy and, even by 1893, incomplete. In part, the decline was explained by Fox as an element in a more general rural exodus in late nineteenth-century England. In part too, the resistance of the hinds to hiring bondagers, perhaps in conjunction with the growing tide of opinion against this form of work for young single women, had seen the relaxation of the conditions of employment in some areas.

Yet it would be wrong to cast the young women affected by the decline as the unwilling 'victims' of a discourse, as though they existed separately from it. In the late nineteenth century, there is evidence that women actively constructed 'feminine' identity, and that this activity played a role in the decline of bondage work. Women's desire to constitute themselves as 'feminine' manifested itself as the rejection of the bondage. For example, by the last decade some women who might previously have 'naturally' worked the bondage were instead employed in country towns, meeting the increased demand for servants and shop assistants.[174] Some women sought to entrench their non-rural status by seeking marriage outside the rural community: socially, 'a hind's daughter would think she was bettering her position by marrying anyone not connected with agricultural employment', even if that person were a railway porter.[175] In 1893, bondagers like Mary and Alice Black

---

172 Donkin, *The agricultural labourers of Northumberland*, 12.
173 *Royal Commission on Labour*, Glendale Report, 1893, 109.
174 Ibid. 125.
175 Ibid. 103.

stated that they would 'rather go to service than work in the fields'.[176] Some women, perhaps, chose (to the extent that 'choice' is possible) to take on worse economic conditions, with less work freedom in return for the possibility of a self identity – a subjectivity – that in contemporary terms was unambiguously feminine.

Some bondagers at the same time were abandoning their traditional woollen uniforms, the 'ugly' and hobnail boots, in favour of less practical dresses and frilly blouses.[177] It was reported with alarm, too, that a fad had begun among women field workers of chewing raw rice in the expectation, some claimed, that this would whiten their suntanned complexions.[178] At the hirings, one witness told Fox that women now went wearing 'their best clothes, and their white veils and bonnets. They often look a lump better than the gentry, for they look fresher like.'[179] Rural women lived within and contributed to dominant cultures of 'feminine' display. The attractions of crowds and display added to the excitement of hirings, where women said they went 'for sport',[180] but most contemporaries claimed that women were more attracted by the permanent amusements of towns and cities. In an ironic twist of imagery, Anderson Graham stated that migration from the countryside was because towns were looked upon by women 'as a kind of Eden'.[181]

It is difficult to interpret such evidence and make unqualified claims about the degree of agency the women exhibited. The adoption of particular work clothing and the uniform of the bondager had, perhaps, traditionally been a mark of independence: but in the increasingly moralistic gendered discourse on 'progress' in the nineteenth century, this independence itself was subject to varied interpretation. The proud traditional uniform of the early century may well, by century's end, have become instead a sign of perverted femininity or, indeed, of masculinity. To some extent, the issue cannot be satisfactorily conceptualised within a framework which assigns simple agency or simple passivity in the face of overwhelming external gender constructions. In the Northumbrian countryside there were really two discourses at work – a traditional one which unproblematically assigned value to bondaging, and a 'progressive' one borne by the reverends and other reformers – which conflicted, especially from about mid century onwards.

Even within families, individuals sometimes gave voice to strikingly different ideas about women's work, rooted perhaps in different gendered experience, economic position and cultural concerns. While William Hindmarsh as an occupier claimed that women's labour made for 'a fine life for

---

176 Ibid. 127.
177 'Rambler', *Rambles in Northumberland*, 51.
178 *Royal Commission on Labour*, Glendale Report, 1893, 110.
179 Ibid. Mrs Black, 126
180 Ibid. Mary and Agnes Black.
181 Anderson Graham, *Rural exodus*, 99.

them', his wife argued that it was 'bad for the women to get wet. They age very soon with outdoor work and it makes them rough.'[182] Henley in 1867 recognised the increasingly contradictory impulses at work in the countryside which operated to define women's roles. If hinds' daughters remained at home, he said, they were compelled economically to contribute to the family economy by working the bondage where possible, accepting 'any description of work that is offered to them, including perhaps that which has been censured'.[183] But such contemporary insights were rare, and there was no simple victory of one discourse over the other: they existed side by side and thus rural women were forced to negotiate not just a subject position, but a subject position between and across two discourses.

In the histories of identity formation, the construction of the bondager and the implications of such constructions for other women in rural life occupies a complex position. There were fleeting glimpses of the economic circumstances of a woman who worked the bondage: women 'must work for a livelihood'; and more strongly, restrictions on employment 'would inflict a great hardship on many industrious females, especially widows and aged spinsters'.[184] Yet while a woman was often defined by her work role, the significance of her work was only rarely discussed primarily in economic terms. As in the Newcastle lead works debates, rural labour provided the vehicle for generalisations about wider cultural meanings attached to the morality and femininity of women's activities, and it was in this respect that the bondager attracted such sustained examination. These cultural generalisations provide some greater insight into the statements of the old steward which appear at the beginning of this chapter. If we consider the bondager's cultural position, and its relation to the wider terrain of gender definitions in the nineteenth century, any apparent contradictions observed in his arguments vanish. The slavery to which he referred was not something which was perceived as inhering in the work of women. While that work may have been cited as a hideous by-product, a material yardstick with which to measure the degradation of the system, the slavery to which he and others[185] referred was that of the hinds. It was the compulsion that the hinds were under to employ women which was perceived to undermine the independence and freedom of *their* labour, and render *them* slaves. That they were compelled to hire women to perform the role constituted a fundamental part of this degradation.

The precondition of her hire meant that the bondager occupied a disordering position in the world of master/servant relations. It is very illuminating too that where the wife worked the bondage, no such detrimental impact upon manly independence was perceived. Davidoff has persuasively argued that in the Victorian universe, the elision of categories 'servant and

[182] *Royal Commission on Labour*, Glendale Report, 1893, 127.
[183] *Women's employment in agriculture*, 1867 Report, 54.
[184] Ibid. appendix e, Christopher Atkinson, occupier, and John Angus, occupier, 251, 252.
[185] See Howitt, *Rural life of England*, i. 165.

wife'[186] was clear: in the Northumbrian context such elision was manifest, since the role of the family bondager was viewed not only as unproblematic, but as peculiarly fitting. In the 'imagined community' of rural Northumberland, women thus appeared at best as an adjunct to the principal processes of identity formation which were forged around notions of the 'free, educated and independent' male labourer. Achieving and maintaining that independence was vitally connected to an ability to create harmonious homes and working environments, where clear hierarchies of gender were to operate. The adjunctive nature of a woman's identity relied upon the performance of roles as wife and mother; where she fulfilled no such role, her position was at best ambiguous. At worst, she was a disordering 'other', a reminder of the ground yet to be traversed in the Victorian march towards civilisation.

The push to modify or contain female labour in rural Northumberland, then, operated within a matrix of cultural and economic conditions which in many respects cannot be separated. Cultural meanings attaching to town and country for women and for observers of their work, had clear material implications when we consider the limited employment opportunities for women in the city of Newcastle. A vision of rural Northumberland as a prosperous region of independent labourers was dominant. It was a vision which may have held true for some, but one whose 'truth' relied largely upon the exclusion of women from the formulation, and which served to mask the existence of poverty in that society, and the factors which contributed to it. 'There are no poor people at all' in rural Northumberland,[187] appeared as a proud but incorrect boast. Although the evidence about poverty in the region is scanty beyond the material generated by poor relief officials, glimpses of quite widespread need are at times given. In Wooler in 1843, in the heartland of supposed agricultural prosperity, for example, a soup kitchen was established to dispense food to 'upwards of 60 poor families' at the cost of a penny a pint.[188] Later in the century as well, emergency food relief and clothing, paid for through public subscription, was provided from an outlet in Wooler High Street.[189] In the country the general lack of organised charity on a scale such as that witnessed in Newcastle, should not necessarily be taken to indicate that extra sources of relief were simply not required: the isolation of the villages and, as Ridley had intimated, the mobility of the workers, militated against the expansion of organised charity. In particular, conditions in the countryside militated against the establishment of groups such as the Charity Organisation Society, which emphasised the importance of close and ongoing surveillance of any charity recipients' circumstances.

---

186 L. Davidoff, 'Mastered for life: servant and wife in Victorian and Edwardian England', *Journal of Social History* vii (1974), 406–28.
187 *Women's employment in agriculture*, 1867 Report, appendix d, Mr McCabe, 242
188 *Newcastle Chronicle*, 4 Mar. 1843, 2.
189 C. Collier and L. A. Stewart, *Wooler and Glendale: a brief history*, n.p. n.d. (NRO, shelf mark 942.82 WOO), 44.

None the less, both through poor relief records and more incidental sources, poverty, and in particular women's vulnerability to it, figured as a constant (if obscured) feature of rural life. Many factors contributed to rural women's poverty. In 1895 Jane Wilkinson, the daughter of a hind, wrote to Earl Grey seeking his charity and in the process provided some sense of the economically precarious position of women who through older age or lack of male relatives experienced difficulty in securing work. Wilkinson was one of six children, of whom only Jane and her older brother had survived. Upon her father's death Jane emigrated to Montreal to better her circumstances, but returned to Hexham when her own mother became ill. Nursing her mother, she was unable to work, and became sick herself. Once her mother died, Jane faced destitution. She applied to the earl for assistance, 'so that I may get my strength gathered to work for myself', and included in her letter her mother's death notice, 'so that your Lordship will see that it is no fraud'.[190] That combination of age, and responsibility for caring, appeared to have contributed to Jane's situation, although it is not known if Grey provided her with any help. Certainly in the city at this time, the Charity Organisation Society and other groups which advocated close investigation of charity applicants were strong in their insistence that begging letters should be ignored. None the less, that Wilkinson made application to the earl suggests that she, at least, still operated in some belief that more traditional ties of social obligation and aristocratic benevolence were relevant.

As well as underemployment and age limitations which curtailed the earning power of hired women, the threat of accidents and ill-health loomed to disrupt their earning capacity. Although not featured in parliamentary reports, evidence from newspapers and other sources during the century attested to the dangers of farm work. A gashed hand, probably a common accident at harvest, meant unemployment for one bondager for two months;[191] as well as general fatigue, one specific case was reported of a young woman dying in the fields as she was pulling turnips in winter, from 'softening of the heart'.[192] Serious accidents dramatically damaged ability to earn a livelihood. In 1841, a young woman from Dunfermline caught her arm in a threshing machine. Her arm was subsequently amputated. 'Without relations to assist her, and entirely dependent on her own labour for a livelihood', she was at least fortunate in living near Alnwick. Her case came to the attention of the duchess of Northumberland, who supervised her recovery and instruction so that she could earn a 'decent and honest' livelihood.[193] The records of the Bamburgh Dispensary for the 1880s also attest to more chronic levels of illness among working people which undermine the notion of the essential healthiness and invigorating nature of farm work. Of the 212 patients who

190 Jane Wilkinson to Earl Grey, 27 Apr. 1895, papers of Earl Grey.
191 Taylor, 'To be a farmer's girl', 1112.
192 *Alnwick Journal*, 15 Nov. 1859, 77.
193 M. A. Richardson, *The local historian's table book*, Newcastle 1846, 224–5.

sought charitable medical relief in April 1881, for example, 70 per cent were women, one-quarter of whom were young field workers. Most of these women were treated for anaemia and respiratory complaints.[194]

For many different reasons, as one mother of ten girls from the area explained, 'it's no easy . . . for the lasses to help themselves, and earn their own living, as 'tis for the lads'.[195] Yet just as the bondager occupied an ambiguous position in both the literal geography and imagined community of rural Northumberland, there seemed to be little recognition of poverty in the area, or of the connections between work and poverty for women. The experience of poverty, however, cannot be separated meaningfully from the experience of work for many women in nineteenth-century England. As the previous chapters have illustrated, in many respects the identity of the working woman was problematic in the Victorian north-east. Experiences of labour, the patterns of constraint and opportunity which working women negotiated, were squarely positioned within discourses of gender, and the inter-relationships between cultural meanings and material conditions were many and complex. Constructions of poverty in that society were similarly gendered, and it is the shape of that gendered discourse and women's experiences within it, which are addressed in the following chapters. The formalised structures of poor relief are considered, as well as the work of private charitable concerns operating both in Newcastle and in the Northumbrian countryside. Women's changing experiences within these institutional frameworks, and examination of the tactics which they adopted to 'make ends meet' also constitute an important theme in the treatment. The relationship between these activities, and the themes of progress, containment and disorder developed already in relation to both urban and rural environments, forms a further link.

[194] Cases, 29 Mar.–29 Apr. 1881, in Bamborough [sic] Castle Dispensary case book, 1881–5, NRO 452/D8/13.
[195] White, *Northumberland and the border*, 447.

114

5

Regulating Poverty, Regulating Gender: the Administration of Poor Relief

If the meanings of work for women in the Victorian north-east bring into focus a complex interplay between cultural and material conditions, the meanings of poverty and their relationship to gendered identities appear no less fluid. The patterns of opportunity, constraint and exclusion already examined in relation to female labour in the north-east assist in understanding poverty as experienced by women during the period. Despite the sustained and detailed attention of scholars to the contemporary concern with poverty, the gendered dimension of poverty – its perception, its treatment, and the actual experience of want in that society – has, with some notable exceptions, received scant attention.

While this chapter acknowledges and explores this omission, it seeks to go beyond a task of historical 'redress'. In the first two sections, the dimensions of female poverty in the area and the inter-relationships between work and poverty are elucidated, and considered against the dominant strands of poor relief historiography. That historiography has invited historians, variously, to consider the lines of continuity and rupture between older systems of relief and those which were administered under the New Poor Law of 1834,[1] the relationships between poor law policy and the increasingly centralised administration of relief,[2] and the relative influence of individuals, interest groups and schools of thought in the processes of writing and reworking legislative measures.[3] All these lines of enquiry are potentially significant in broadening understanding of poverty and gender. Yet such examination cannot simply proceed within the parameters established by a more traditional historiography. At best the inclusion of gender perspectives within these parameters can be achieved only partially, and only then at the

---

1   The classic statement of the new poor law as 'rupture' was provided by Sidney Webb and Beatrice Webb in 1929: *English poor law history*, II: *The last hundred years*, London 1929, 52. Interpretations which have emphasised the continuities between the old regimes of relief and those operating after 1834 include A. Brundage, *The making of the new poor law*, London 1978, and A. Digby, *The poor law in nineteenth-century England and Wales*, London 1982.
2   E. P. Hennock, 'The measurement of urban poverty: from the metropolis to the nation 1880–1920', *Economic History Review* 2nd ser. xl (1987), 208–27.
3   See, for example, Peter Mandler, 'The making of the new poor law *redivivus*', *Past and Present* cvii (1987), 131–57, and the subsequent debate between Anthony Brundage, David Eastwood and Peter Mandler, 'Debate: the making of the new poor law *redivivus*', ibid. cxxvii (1990), 183–201.

substantial cost of diminishing the analytic potential of gender perspectives overall. Some critical rereading and some different lines of enquiry are required.

The links between poverty, work and constructions of femininity which are suggested through a rereading of contemporary source material in the first sections of the chapter, are then explored further in relation to the discourses of poverty revealed in debates about poor relief and its administration in the region. The correspondence between northern officials and the bureaucracy in London from 1834, as well as the local documents generated by poor law authorities, provide further insights into the discursive construction of the female poor and that series of tensions and contradictions which arose around the category over time. As well, the practical workings of relief systems in Newcastle and rural areas – the regulation of bodies and spaces in the specific environment of the workhouses, and the gendered disciplines of relief – provide a further avenue for consideration of the links between material conditions and representations in culture, and suggest that the traditional line of division between 'policy' and 'experience' deny the constant interplay between the two in a way which further erases the significance of the Victorians' own gendered vision of their world.

Discourses of poverty and discourses of labour were linked, and both were fundamentally gendered. The overarching schemas of femininity which informed these discursive categories cannot be overlooked. Indeed, it is the argument here that in order to better comprehend the complexity of contemporary views on progress, civilisation, social reform, women's work and women's poverty, and the strength of ordering dichotomies – of morality and vice, 'fecklessness' and industry, 'deserving' and 'undeserving', regulation and disorder – the fluidity of ideas between these categories, and the processes through which identity was constructed within them, must be highlighted. The limitations of historical sources and their utilisation can reinforce a sense of the staticity, the fixity of definition of the poor woman *or* the working woman, 'captured' and experientially frozen in those snapshot moments of census-compiling, pauper head-counting, or event-recording. Some Victorians were only too aware of the difficulty in developing adequate definitions to encompass the varying circumstances of poor people in their society. Harriet Martineau wrote in 1839 that poverty 'has many shapes, aspects almost as various as the minds and circumstances of those whom it visits'.[4] None the less, in general some Victorians' drive to quantify can at times convey an illusion of certainty and confidence which administrators and reformers may have deemed necessary in order to build and streamline the machinery of state, but which militates against consideration of the overlap between experiences of work and experiences of poverty for women, and the ways in which their gender identity at once informed and was itself informed within the terrain of those experiences.

---

[4] Harriet Martineau, *Deerbrook*, London 1839, repr. London 1983, 427.

116

Attention to the perception and operation of femininity in relation to poverty is made richer through previous reference to women's work, women's bodies, and the spaces they occupied: at the same time, recognition of the dynamic between work and poverty contributes to a wider understanding of gender boundaries and their operation. To this point, it has been clear that the 'conversations in cold rooms' of the poor in the slums of Sandgate, of women in the lead works of Newcastle, or the cottages of rural Northumberland usually passed unrecorded, vanishing into the air of the Victorian north-east. None the less, both through the existing sources in which the voices of women may be heard, and in the more voluminous writings of observers, reformers and critics of working-class life, some better sense of the meanings and implications of that unequivocally gendered world in which women worked and lived, and also died, may be suggested.

The 'shadowy world of the very poor': rereading the case of Elizabeth Graham

Elizabeth Graham's life ended in Newcastle in the midsummer of 1838. An inquest was held following her death, in the course of which sketchy details of her social and economic circumstances emerged.[5] Her precise age was not known, but it was thought that she was between seventy and eighty years old. She had migrated from Scotland a few years earlier, and since her arrival in Newcastle she had lodged principally in and around Sandgate. It was from Sandgate that Elizabeth plied her trade, 'hawk[ing] tapes and threads about this town'.[6] Through her work and her poverty, she became known to local authorities such as police officer Robert Leslie, who recalled that he had 'seen her frequently pass through the streets' carrying her basket of goods.[7] Although no estimate of her income from this source was provided, and while she was not on the 'pauper list' at the time of her death, it was probably a meagre and inconsistent living which had led her to seek aid from charities and poor relief officials in the past. She was apparently well known to the keeper of the Mendicity Office for example, a private charity which provided relief specifically to vagrants.[8]

Little more is known about the daily life of Elizabeth Graham. It has been suggested that she was the same Elizabeth Graham who had been arrested for disorderliness in the company of two men some years earlier, but the evidence

---

[5] 'Inquest on the body of Elizabeth Graham', *Newcastle Courant*, 20 July 1838, news cutting included in correspondence, Newcastle Board of Guardians, 21 July 1838, Newcastle Union correspondence, 1834–40, PRO, MH 12/9096.

[6] Ibid.

[7] Ibid.

[8] Sir John Walsham to Newcastle Board of Guardians, 21 July 1838, Newcastle Union correspondence, ibid.

for this is not conclusive;[9] nor is there direct evidence relating to her marital status, family circumstances, or other aspects of her personal history. But for Graham's movements immediately preceding her death, which could be charted because they brought her into contact with a variety of public authorities, and but for the later outcry about the treatment she had received, Elizabeth would probably have remained one of the anonymous poor, rendered individually invisible by virtue of her class, her geographic situation and her poverty. Nevertheless, in some important respects her situation serves to illustrate some of the dimensions of poverty as it was experienced by women in nineteenth-century Newcastle. Before considering the case in this broader context however, some further discussion of the case and its treatment by contemporaries, as well as later interpretative responses to it, is required.

Elizabeth Graham had been turned out of her lodgings by an allegedly drunken landlady on 9 July 1838; she sought shelter at St Nicholas's workhouse, but was refused admission by the relieving officer there because he deemed her to be a tramp, and therefore ineligible for indoor relief. She wandered about the streets until a local woman, Eleanor Pattison of Castle Garth, took Elizabeth into her coal yard to rest. A *post-mortem* examination would reveal that she had been suffering from uterine cancer. Weakened by her illness, but apparently not aware of its nature, Elizabeth told Eleanor that she 'thought she would die that night'.[10] Other neighbours again sought aid for Elizabeth at the poor house, but as the keeper was not present, they then sent for a local police officer.

Soon after Officer Robert Leslie arrived in the afternoon, there began another journey to secure relief and overnight shelter for Elizabeth which began at the Mendicity Office. The official there refused to provide assistance, but on opposite grounds to those given by the workhouse officer: since Elizabeth lived in Newcastle, she could not be defined as a tramp or vagrant. He remarked that 'we have often been bothered with her', and suggested that she be taken instead to St Nicholas's workhouse. Returning to the workhouse, Robert Leslie was informed that Elizabeth had been there earlier in the day – indeed, too sick to eat, the bread that she had been given there on her earlier visit remained in her pocket. Questioned by the police officer, the relieving officer, George Rutherford, maintained that he could do nothing more, could provide no shelter, and that any discretionary power he had had in such cases had been stripped from him by the 1834 poor law legislation. Having exhausted these options, Leslie took Elizabeth to the police night-house, offered her food, and provided her with a cell. Later in the evening,

9 An 1830 case mentions an Elizabeth Graham: Mitchell, *Proceedings in the mayor's chamber*, 147, 40. This may be the source referred to in McCord, *North east England*, 92. However, the report on the inquest suggested that by 1838 Elizabeth Graham had lived in Newcastle for only four or five years.

10 Ibid. The street where Eleanor Pattison lived is shown in the frontispiece.

she was moved to another cell where some female prisoners had agreed to attend her, but she deteriorated rapidly and died on the morning of 10 July.[11]

Newspaper coverage of the inquest held the following day was not confined to the Newcastle press. *The Times* also carried the story, and the Newcastle Board of Guardians determined that its own investigation be held in the presence of the regional assistant commissioner, Sir John Walsham.[12] Medical evidence from the inquest itself suggested that Elizabeth died from cancer, rather than from want. However, it was noted that her stomach was empty and her body emaciated.[13] The coroner's jury determined that she had died 'by the visitation of God', but further recorded in the verdict their unanimous regret that

> no better provision is made for people who are found under such circum-
> stances. And we beg to suggest, in the first place, whether those who have the
> care of the poor-houses might not be induced to act with more kindness to
> people who are so absolutely destitute that they might die as they are passing
> through the streets. And, secondly, whether it was proper, in this place, to put
> a woman, in a dying state, into a cell, to die as a dog. . . .

The jury awarded their individual appearance fees to Robert Leslie, as 'a mark of his humanity'.[14]

The coroner was informed by a poor law official that Rutherford had erred in insisting that he had no discretionary power to provide urgent relief: he in fact had 'full power to do what was required'. Rutherford was suspended from duty on 16 July. Walsham reported to the commission after further investiga-tion that Rutherford appeared simply to have discounted Elizabeth Graham's 'plea of being houseless and ill', and 'persisted in adhering to his own very erroneous view of the case in despite of the "poorly" appearance of the woman'.[15] Rutherford refused to resign, and so was dismissed from his job by the Poor Law Commissioners later in the month.

Norman McCord, in his discussion of the case, places it in the context of the haphazard and sometimes difficult development of regional poor law ad-ministration. Rutherford had been 'tragically wrong' he states, but the case illustrates the daily problems which faced officials who worked in the 'sha-dowy world of the very poor'. At a time when there was little training, it was 'not surprising that some officials failed'.[16] McCord's assessment here relates to his more general conclusions, which invite consideration. Elizabeth Graham's case, and one other with which he deals, were 'more significant in

---

11 Ibid.
12 *Times*, 17 July 1838. The investigation was conducted on 16 July.
13 Surgeon H. P. Brummel to Sir John Walsham, 23 July 1838, Newcastle Union correspon-dence, 1834–40, PRO, MH 12/9096.
14 'Inquest' news cutting.
15 Sir John Walsham to Newcastle Board of Guardians, 23 July 1838, Newcastle Union correspondence, 1834–40, PRO, MH 12/9096.
16 McCord, *North east England*, 92.

illuminating a variety of aspects of contemporary society than in their ability to represent the mass of poor law cases'. In short, Elizabeth Graham's case was 'distinctly unusual'.[17] Yet just how unusual was it?

Within McCord's context of local poor law history, the case provides one illustration of administrative failure in the immediate post-1834 period. Such a focus on the poor law too is apparent in the contemporary reports and investigations which examined Rutherford's culpability as a representative of the system, and which cited the case as one means to gauge its current weaknesses. Certainly, Elizabeth's age, gender and physical condition added a particularly tragic dimension to the reports which was compatible with the imagery employed by anti-poor law polemicists of the period.[18] The timing of the case was potentially further damaging to the reputation of both the New Poor Law and the local administration of it. Just a fortnight prior to Elizabeth's death on the occasion of the queen's coronation holiday, an anti-poor law demonstration on the Newcastle Town Moor had heard addresses which alleged that reform of the relief system had not brought benefits; instead, 'murder was its result'.[19] However, apart from the sympathetic response of the coroner's jury, the subject of Elizabeth's poverty itself was nowhere raised for examination in the contemporary records.

That the case appears in the historical record, as McCord states, makes it unusual. That the aged and infirm in nineteenth-century Newcastle in fact constituted one of the main groups to which relief was directed and for which workhouse facilities were provided renders Elizabeth Graham's treatment unrepresentative in the statistical sense.[20] However, when the focus is shifted away from the poor law structures and the debate generated by Elizabeth's death, and instead towards the case's backdrop of poverty, fresh lines of enquiry may be suggested. First, how widespread was Elizabeth's experience of destitution, which drove her to the streets and to relief authorities? Second, to what extent did the dilemmas of definition which arose in the Elizabeth Graham case influence other women's experiences of poverty? And to what extent can the contemporary scrutiny of Elizabeth's case and its press

---

[17] Ibid. 93.

[18] Robert Blakely, *Cottage politics; or, letters on the new poor law bill*, London n.d. [*c.* 1838], 41–7.

[19] *Northern Liberator*, 30 June 1838, cited in Knott, *Popular opposition*, 5.

[20] Throughout the period, the numbers of old and infirm men and women who received relief in the workhouse were roughly equal. For outdoor relief, the Poor Law Inspectors' returns are very difficult to analyse along gender lines because of the phenomenon of 'constructive pauperism', whereby women's poverty was obscured in the construction of the records. None the less, of the groups of women for whom outdoor relief was recorded, the old and infirm were by far the largest group, at least twice as likely to be in receipt of this form of relief as able-bodied women. Within the workhouse, a significant group as well was that of able-bodied women, whose numbers equalled, and at times exceeded, the numbers of older women in the house. By comparison, the number of able-bodied men in receipt of indoor relief remained negligible. Statistics of indoor and outdoor relief are contained in Poor Law Inspectors' returns, 1848–69, TWAS 359/300–1.

coverage be viewed as characterising a growing trend of surveillance and public comment on the problem of poverty, and its relationship to progress? If the evidence about Elizabeth Graham is reread in this light, it appears more as representing certain dimensions of female poverty in nineteenth-century Newcastle, and rather less as a 'distinctly unusual' case.

In her life Elizabeth Graham was economically and socially marginal. Claiming attention only in those moments spent in public spaces and institutions, and scrutinised in the terms of local authorities, she appears in newspaper and poor law records as a fragmented identity, both metaphorically and literally. Recognised, seen, 'known of' but not actually known, accounts of Graham's last day do evoke a kind of shadowy world of movement, punctuated by the sharper light of her episodic encounters with officialdom, while her ribbons and tapes, a basket, a piece of bread, a tumour, appear as the material fragments of her poverty and ill-health. No stable identity was to be forged for Elizabeth: a lone Scotswoman, any family ties remained unknown, and as an aged female wandering the streets in the hours before her death, the relevant authorities would not or could not even accord her certain status in her poverty, but focused instead on what her status was not. Certainly, after the Graham case, poor people still died from want in appalling circumstances in the streets and houses of Newcastle. Starvation, absolute destitution and tragic deaths were reported throughout the century, a fearful reality to those whose own circumstances presented a constant challenge to make ends meet.[21] For many more poor people, however, extreme destitution and death was not the immediate outcome of their poverty as they sought to negotiate relief for themselves and their families.

The dimensions of female poverty in nineteenth-century Newcastle

Brief glimpses into the construction of economic and social marginality among other poor women are provided in relief records for Newcastle parishes such as All Saints'. Here, Eneas Mackenzie's easy assumptions expressed early in the century about solid, male-dominated families in Newcastle providing for women[22] are quickly dissipated by accounts of desertion, death or imprisonment of male spouses; the experiences of the female household head – widow and single mother alike – are brought more clearly into focus.

Surviving applications for parochial relief in the parish of All Saints in Newcastle cover the years 1820 to 1837, a period incorporating both the passage of the 1834 poor law legislation and its implementation in Newcastle

---

[21] For example, see Henry Ingledew to Poor Law Commission, 1 Jan. 1840, PRO, MH 12/9096; *Newcastle Journal*, 19 Dec. 1892, 8; 20 Dec. 1892, 5.
[22] See above ch. 2.

in 1836.[23] All Saints' parish, which encompassed much of the Sandgate and Quayside areas, was one of four parishes whose select vestries determined the provision of relief and oversaw the running of poor houses within the inner city of Newcastle. St Nicholas's church (which in 1882 became a cathedral) dominated in its sheer architectural scale, but St John's and All Saints' churches and their attached parishes were only a few hundred feet away, to the west and east respectively. Even St Andrew's parish was separated from the others by only a short distance, but lay to the north-west near the old city walls, and was furthest away from the crowded heartland of urban poverty. All four parishes, however, were deeply involved in the administration of poor relief in the city.

The All Saints' applications are particularly interesting in two respects. First, the printed form which individuals (or in the case of illiterate applicants, a relief clerk or friend) were expected to complete, provides important insights into the formal priorities and considerations which had been set prior to 1834 to assess claims for relief and, as will be suggested below, convey some sense as well of the ways in which bureaucracy functioned to channel or construct the applicants from the outset as passive, dependent individuals. The text of the relief applications did not alter immediately after the introduction of the Poor Law Amendment Act in 1834, and these printed documents contained thirty-three questions which applicants were required to answer in order to be assessed. Second, the applications provide rare direct evidence from women themselves: even for those cases where there was transcription by a poor relief clerk or friend, the nature of the material and its purpose in assessment meant that the recording of women's own circumstances and views were immediately relevant and still very directly expressed. The majority of the applicants were women, and the majority of these in turn were widows. The applications serve to remind us that in negotiations for relief, authorities found themselves dealing mostly with women who fell outside the boundaries of 'conventional' family and household structures. As well as providing information relating to the economic and social histories of the women seeking relief, the All Saints' applications also provide interesting evidence of the relationship between the relief bureaucracy, and women's concerns as they sought relief within the system.

Some of the material conditions outlined in the applications for relief echo the economic and social position of Elizabeth Graham. A woman such as Bridget Hair, for example, had supported her family for years after the death of her *de facto* husband on earnings from selling ribbons in the streets.

---

[23] Applications for parochial relief, parish of All Saints, TWAS, T241/1, 2, 4 (cited hereinafter as 'application' with call number). These applications are not uniformly dated, although information provided within some of the applications themselves provides a means for approximate dating, and suggests that they were ordered according to date of receipt, so that the T241/1 series was for applications in the 1820s and the T241/4 series related to the period of the 1830s.

She had borne eight children, four of whom had survived to depend upon her, and she struggled to pay her rent of 6*d*. a week. 'Afflicted upwards of 3 years with inside disease', she no longer had sufficient work, although she stated that she would 'do anything to make a livelihood . . . [but] i have been employed by no body'. Her case became more urgent: '[T]he Bed tick is in pawn for 3s and rug for 3s6d and as for Bed clothes or body clothes we have none. . . . I have nothing But what comes from the parish of All Saints and the mercies of God.'[24] The circumstances of women such as Bridget Hair make strict division between those who were employed and those who were not, artificial. While casuality, seasonality, occupational hazards and the risks brought by heavy manual labour operated across gender in the Victorian labour market, other gender-specific factors overlaying these general patterns exacerbated women's economic vulnerability. Designations of low skill, low status and low pay relative to men in a trade all acted to further diminish women's economic security, and their ability to effectively survive short-term economic crises.

Sickness, old age, unemployment and chronic underemployment figured strongly in the All Saints' applications. In a number of cases women had worked for long periods, but slipped into poverty through a variety of circumstances. Elizabeth Garrett at fifty-eight, for example, had been a servant 'but from infirmities she is unable to make Place'.[25] After the desertion of her husband Grace Wilson had provided for herself and her two children by teaching, but increasing disability made her living precarious: 'Having two children to look after and being of weak constitution I cannot go out to do heavy work, and the small earnings I do get will not keep us without assistance.'[26]

The scope of underemployment and unemployment in that society is clearly emphasised in the relief applications. As the more detailed case histories of Bridget Hair and others indicate, Elizabeth Graham was not alone in selling ribbons in the streets to make a living, and this mode of earning a living itself was sometimes difficult, or even dangerous. There were regular prosecutions of street sellers, and the sellers so prosecuted were almost exclusively women, who were fined 10*s*. each, but were usually sent to gaol for a month instead because they were unable to pay.[27] Violence could also erupt as women attempted to guard their 'pitch': two women selling oysters on the quayside fought when one encroached on the space of her 'rival'.[28]

As well as the street selling described in the 1850 *Inquiry into the condition of the poor*,[29] and the work women performed as carriers in the streets of the city, most female applicants pursued incomes by providing domestic services.

[24] Bridget Hair, application, T241/1.
[25] Elizabeth Garrett, application, T241/4.
[26] Grace Wilson, application, T241/2.
[27] Mitchell, *Proceedings in the mayor's chamber*, 26, 77.
[28] Ibid. 50.
[29] *Inquiry into the condition of the poor*, 1st ser., letter i, 11; letter ii, 14.

Such work could, in theory, provide greater choice in working hours, while the home-as-worksite could further enhance women's ability to mesh the separate strands of social and economic responsibility. Discussions of the practice of 'dovetailing' employment, where women contributed financially to the family economy at those particular times of the year when work was seasonally unavailable for any male providers in the family, have provided insights into the ways in which family economies were structured around fluctuating gender-specific work activities.[30]

Yet while such considerations enrich perspectives on women's work, any generalisations must, as ever, be refined in the light of enormous chronological and regional variation, as well as fluctuations in family circumstances – where, for example, the 'dove' had died or flown away. Similarly, while working at home appeared to be a 'logical' solution for those faced with childcare responsibilities in the absence of a cheap and reliable alternative system, any financial advantage could be lost when work was scarce. Perhaps contributing to the scarcity of home-based work and domestic services as well, particularly in the second half of the century, Newcastle's proliferating charitable and reformatory institutions employed inmates in domestic work, particularly sewing and laundering. At times of economic downturn, moreover, older women like Elizabeth Graham or those with young children were less likely to be able to travel further afield each day to secure employment, while the reliability of the strategies of 'penny capitalism'[31] adopted by women in poor areas like Sandgate would inevitably have fluctuated as customers themselves became unemployed, or tightened their family budgets.

The capacity to earn through work at home was also necessarily diminished by the time and energy required to oversee children. Sarah Cadwallidar was young and fit, but with two infants 'which cannot be left. . . . I am obliged to abide by them'.[32] In 1850 other cases were recorded of poor women as sole breadwinners who, pursuing a living outside the home but unable to afford childminding, left their young children unattended on workdays.[33] The unreliability of work taken into the home was also clearly in evidence in the relief applications. Ann Harper could make no more than 2s. a week sewing at home.[34] Work outside the home was similarly inadequate. Isabella Black, a widow with a nine-year-old son, went out to perform domestic work, but even going out each day, 'I don't make more than 1s. 6d. and 2s. per week. . . . My income is so small it will not support the boy and myself.'[35] Indeed, time

---

30 See, for example, Stedman Jones, *Outcast London*, 85–7.

31 Roberts uses this term, drawing upon John Benson's work: E. Roberts, 'Women's strategies, 1890–1940', in J. Lewis (ed.), *Labour and love: women's experience of home and family 1850–1940*, Oxford 1986, 223–47 at p. 231.

32 Sarah Cadwallidar, application, T241/1.

33 *Inquiry into the condition of the poor*, [letter numbers, series] 27, 41.

34 Elizabeth Harper, application, T241/4.

35 Isabella Black, application, T241/1.

divided between fulfilling family responsibilities, chasing haphazard employment, and completing poor relief applications, meant that in this as in other periods 'being poor was itself a busy occupation'.[36] Perhaps a sufficient, although patchy contribution to a family income where there was another working adult in the household, self-supporting women and those responsible for children constantly emphasised the uncertainty of their work and complete inadequacy of their sole earnings. Many of the women had experienced considerably better times, sometimes as a result of their independent exertions: Mary Wrightson recalled that from being a servant at twenty-one she had then become a public house keeper in mid life and had actually paid poor rates to the parish, to which, at age seventy-one, she was now applying for relief.[37] Much more frequently, however, the more secure economic circumstances enjoyed in the past had been in large part the result of marriage to fully employed men. It was primarily the death or sickness of a spouse, sometimes coinciding with old age for women, which proved disastrous.

Economic dependence upon a male breadwinner was also apparent in the numerous cases of desertion and other absences. Jane Hutchinson had 'no knowledge' of the husband who had deserted the family, and she had since worked for a year at 'anything I can get to do' to support her two children. She hoped that relief for a month or two would be sufficient to tide her over until more work was found.[38] Mary Ormiston's husband, a soldier, had been transported for fourteen years. With three children, Mary was granted 3s. by the parish.[39] Clementina Carr's husband had been lost at sea coming home from Quebec eight years prior to her making application.[40] Declining economic situations in many instances did not lead to immediate destitution. Particular misfortune was followed by an intermediate period, often of some years' duration, during which women made adjustments to new circumstances, eking out a meagre living, and trying to provide for themselves and their children. Poor relief was sought reluctantly when strategies failed or circumstances worsened. Jane Brown at seventy-four explained that she made application because while she 'began in trouble Several years [ago]' and now lodged with her niece, the rest of her family was dead and she was 'not Able to do any thing to gain a livelyhood[sic]'.[41]

Other questions in the parish relief application forms sought to establish the kind of relief which applicants had received from private sources of any kind. In establishing existing family arrangements, the parish was clearly concerned to ensure that family members contributed to the applicant's

36 P. Rushton, 'The poor law, the parish, and the community in north-east England, 1600–1800', *Northern History* xxv (1989), 135–52 at p. 139.
37 Mary Wrightson, application, T241/2.
38 Jane Hutchinson, application, T241/1.
39 Mary Ormiston, application, ibid.
40 Clementina Carr, application, ibid.
41 Jane Brown, application, ibid.

support wherever possible. Some applicants cited the care and provision of shelter by kin, but this source of relief was limited by the very poverty of those who provided it. Sarah Cadwallidar's parents were 'very poor, I have a little food and cloths [sic] just what they can afford'.[42] For other women, particularly women who had been deserted or who were young widows, even these forms of piecemeal relief were sometimes unavailable. Mary Unwin's children were not old enough to contribute to her relief, and she had 'no sopart [sic] from any body whatavar [sic]'.[43] Elizabeth Harper's relief was cut by half from 4s. to 2s. when it was calculated that her three children still living at home earned between them 12s. a week.[44]

Kin support was not always forthcoming, and when it was, it was not entirely without problems. Local court records from the late 1820s attest to some level of violence and dispute within extended family households of the poor, and certainly too between poor women and men. William Row was brought up before the Mayor's Chamber in 1829 for allowing his wife to become chargeable to All Saints' parish, 'not having been bound more than nine weeks in the sacred chain of Hymen'. His (unnamed) wife had apparently left the household they were compelled to share with William's parents due to their poverty because, it was reported, his mother 'was apt to raise her voice at her a little higher than was quite agreeable'. The magistrate provided informal counselling to the couple and the case was dismissed.[45] Richard Carrick was charged with not supporting his son and daughter when they left the house after severe ill-treatment by their stepmother, and their plight was brought to the attention of the authorities by 'three or four decent women, whose humanity did them great credit'. Carrick was sentenced to one month's hard labour.[46]

Domestic violence between partners also figured in the proceedings. Occasionally, women were charged with violence towards husbands. Ann Haupt, the wife of a musician, was charged with assaulting her husband and threatening his life. Unable to pay a fine, she was committed to the house of correction.[47] Much more commonly, men were charged with assault on their wives. Thomas Sandridge, for example, was brought before the court on three occasions between October 1829 and May 1830 for ill-treating and threatening his wife. Unable to pay his fine on the first occasion, he was committed to the house of correction for a short period. On the second occasion, a fortnight later, his wife Margaret intervened; Thomas avoided imprisonment because 'she did not wish to have him punished'. He was committed to gaol again, however, a few months later for assaulting his wife.[48]

---

42 Sarah Cadwallidar, application, ibid.
43 Mary Unwin, application, ibid.
44 Mary Hall, application, T241/4; Elizabeth Harper, application, ibid.
45 Mitchell, *Proceedings in the mayor's chamber*, 12–13.
46 Ibid. 9.
47 Ibid. 26.
48 Ibid. 3, 13, 111.

The reluctance of women to prosecute was probably due to that range of reasons suggested in Hammerton's recent study of conflict in Victorian marriages: 'wives' fear of further violence after prosecution and conviction, from anxieties about jeopardizing an already marginal family income, or . . . a genuine wish not to punish the husband, only to stop his violence'.[49] The economic risks of prosecution were considerable. William Dougal, a journeyman tanner, was brought up on a charge of refusing to support his family. Although earning 17s. per week, he had given his wife on average only 5s. per week to maintain the family. He was adjudged 'to be an idle and disorderly person', and sentenced to one month's hard labour.[50] While the evidence regarding the allocation of resources within families with male breadwinners is scant, such a case reminds us that 'survival strategies were not necessarily arrived at by an unchanging, uniform, and uncontested consensus between husbands and wives', and that practices inside the family economy could 'make living more difficult for women than for men'.[51]

The degree of support provided for All Saints' applicants through previous subscriptions to friendly societies, funds or local 'boxes' was also examined, and questions posed regarding any amount which would be paid in funeral expenses or as a bequest upon their death from such sources. Clementina Carr was in receipt of 9d. per week from a sailors' fund after her husband's death, and Hannah Davison was likewise situated.[52] One or two women had in fact paid funds to funeral boxes, and indeed the various articles governing the establishment and administration of some of these small, local, private schemes of aid and sickness or death insurance referred to the specific 'vicissitudes to which womankind are liable'. Women who lived in a 'comfortable competency' when in health: but when sick, or when 'death has put a period to the head and hope of the family, involved in penury and woe, what language can convey the horrors of their situation?'[53] But the vast majority of All Saints' applicants were not covered by any of these rudimentary forms of insurance, which required a joining fee of around 2s. 6d., and usually monthly contributions of around 6d. Such regular contributions, wrote Mary Unwin, reflecting the lot of most women, were simply 'not in my power to uphold'.[54]

Indeed, undertaking financial management to avoid poverty appeared impossible. Sarah Ayres, for example, a widowed staymaker with four young children, was unable to find work. Ten years earlier, she had rented a shop in which to ply her trade. By the first anniversary of her husband's death, she

---

[49] A. James Hammerton, *Cruelty and companionship: conflict in nineteenth-century married life*, London 1992, 40.
[50] Ibid.
[51] Rose, *Limited livelihoods*, 89.
[52] Clementina Carr, application, T241/1; Hannah Davison, application, ibid.
[53] Articles of the Byker Hill Female Union Society, 1826, NCL, Women's Friendly Societies, L334.7, p. vi.
[54] Mary Unwin, application, T241/1.

was in debt, without property, and without means to secure the more consistent employment a shop-front had provided.[55] Sarah Ayres's experience exemplified one of the problems faced by poor women. Even the most common or basic means of earning an income could require some financial outlay which the very poor could not afford. Rent on small premises, the cost of renewing equipment and purchasing new materials could become unsustainable expenses. Similarly, a mangle or even a spare bed in which to accommodate a lodger had no value except as pawnable items when work fell off or when visitors were scarce. Decisions by women about converting such 'tools of trade' to cash varied. Some applicants pawned all but their clothes before seeking relief. In other applications, the pathetically short lists of property sometimes included one or two campbeds for which lodgers, where available, would pay from 2d. per night, to 2s. per week.

To meet the needs of the present, but in the process to undermine the possibility of future earnings, placed these poor women in an unenviable position. Certainly, the intricacies involved in 'making ends meet' through pawning have been well-documented by Melanie Tebbutt,[56] as has the contemporary middle-class disdain for the poor's supposed inability to conceive of and plan for the future.[57] Ironically, conditions laid down in relief applications did little to promote such an outlook. Applicants were questioned specifically on their preparedness to have their goods surrendered to the select vestry, to cover costs. These questions prompted the most telling responses from some women, who resisted a structure which provided little scope for expression of their own views, priorities, and circumstances. The questions were as follows:

> Question 31: State here any other peculiar circumstances in your case, that induce you to solicit any Relief from this Parish.
>
> Question 32: Supposing that the Select Vestry should agree to sustain your Application, are you willing to subscribe to the annexed Declaration, bequeathing all you have at your death to the Parish, in repayment of what they may now advance to you?
>
> Question 33: If the Select Vestry find that they cannot grant you any Outdoor Relief, are you willing to give up all you have to the Parish, and to become an Inmate of the Workhouse; and when admitted, do you promise diligently to labour at such work or Service as you may be able to do, as may be prescribed to you by the Master or Mistress in the Workhouse?

In response to Question 31, mothers like Mary Unwin, Isabella Black and Jane Kay were emphatic in their insistence that the relief they sought was not

---

[55] Sarah Ayres, application, ibid.
[56] M. Tebbutt, *Making ends meet: pawnbroking and working-class credit*, Leicester 1983.
[57] Paul Johnson, *Saving and spending: the working-class economy in Britain, 1870–1939*, Oxford 1985.

for themselves, but for their children.[58] Having earlier detailed individual possessions which frequently amounted to little more than 'what covers my nakedness with, Gentleman'[59] (as the 98-year-old applicant Barbara Bennett responded), some bedding, and perhaps odd furniture such as chairs or camp beds, Question 32 met with some wry responses. Clementina Carr wrote that the parish 'wont thank me for any thing that I have'.[60] In other responses, a sense of women's frustration with a procedure whose meticulous questions seemed far removed from the urgent realities of their everyday lives is clearly conveyed. When Sarah Clark applied for relief for her three children when her husband was injured at work, she wrote next to the question

> I have Nothing to [offer?] up But a Distressed Family that can Neither work nor want we have Ben Many Day sitting down to a pece of Bread and a D[r]ink of Watir and the young child [ ]you may judge what state we are in if you will take the trouble to come . . .[61]

The last two questions in particular were significant in that they moved from the realm of apparently straightforward description, and required instead that applicants make clear their degree of preparedness to submit to the possible demands of the select vestry and to the disciplinary regimes it administered. Framed as hypotheses, the questions at one level invited judgement and the exercise of individual agency; yet simultaneously, the terms used in the questions – bequeathing all, giving up all, labouring diligently under orders as an inmate – conjured a future of relinquished agency, and conveyed the state of passive dependence which could be the possible outcome of an application. Women proceeded to answer the questions in a variety of ways, but frequently, whether or not they assented to these terms, their responses revealed that they were prepared to argue against them or to cite constructive alternative measures. Isabella Dixon was a rare example of a woman who assented to the terms regarding the workhouse. Single, ill, with no possessions and with no kin support, she said she was 'quite agreeable to come if the Doctor can say that I am fit to be moved and to work if any doctor can say I am able'.[62] The workhouse in such circumstances could appear, perhaps, as a reasonable destination.

More guarded and qualified were the agreements of other women, who expressed a view that they had no alternative to providing their assent: 'What can I do else?', asked Jane Marr.[63] Martha Bell, bedridden at thirty-two

---

58 Mary Unwin, application, T241/1; Isabella Black, application, ibid; Jane Kay, application, ibid.
59 Barbara Bennett, application, ibid.
60 Clementina Carr, application, ibid.
61 Sarah Clark, application, ibid.
62 Isabella Dixon, application, ibid.
63 Jane Marr, application, T241/2.

with asthma for four years and unable to work, reluctantly conceded: 'if you cannot grant out Door Relief I Must Go In'.[64] Despite Eneas Mackenzie's characterisation of the All Saints' poor house as one which 'possesses every requisite convenience', and which he believed compared so favourably with the neighbouring house in St Nicholas's parish – whose conditions motivated even 'those who are steeped in poverty and acquainted with misfortune' to survive outside the house[65] – there was very little evidence in All Saints of women willingly submitting to indoor relief.

Perhaps reflecting more complex family circumstances and concerns, however, others refused to assent, and offered explanations for such refusal. Widowed mothers struggling to support their children viewed any suggestion of entering the workhouse and the disposal of all their property as too abso-lute, or as an unjust blindness to their own keenly-felt obligations to provide for their children, even in the most modest ways. Margaret Cunningham responded to Question 33, stating 'No! I would rather work hard night and day with the little assistance the Parish is kind enough to assist me, and as soon as it is in my power to do without it, I will most willingly [do] without it.'[66] Her refusal was noted boldly on the front of their applications by the clerk, as though non-compliance was the critical key in assessing such cases: yet she was granted a small sum in out-relief none the less.

Old women, too, seemed more inclined to refuse the terms outlined. Elizabeth Wheallans, a widow who lodged with her daughter and who had worked carrying water around the city for nearly three decades, launched a persuasive argument against any idea of committing her to the workhouse as a condition of relief. Her earnings from her trade had declined, she said, since a new water company in Newcastle had been established, in some ways making her a 'victim' of the city's material progress. Meeting the select vestry on the discursive terrain of economic imperative which, she possibly anticipated, would inform their deliberations, she requested that her relief of 1s. per week out-relief continue:

> I am convinced that it would be as much against the interests of the parish as it would be against my inclination to leave my own daughter and come into the House. . . . [In] my foremost occupation of carrying water. . . . I can work to an advantage to the parish at my time of life; and the parish could not keep me in the house for the sum of 1/– per week.[67]

Her economic analysis convinced the parish, which granted her the sum on the terms she sought.

While widowed mothers and the aged appeared at times to be given some latitude, in other cases outright refusal led in turn to a denial of any relief.

[64] Martha Bell, application, T241/1.
[65] Mackenzie, *Descriptive and historical account*, ii. 541–3.
[66] Margaret Cunningham, application, T241/1.
[67] Elizabeth Wheallans, application, ibid.

Mary Marton, a 76-year-old widow with no kin, no money and no belongings, refused to comply and was told what the outcome of her decision would be. She left the relief office saying 'it was a great hardship'.[68] More commonly, women showed an awareness that they were addressing a bureaucracy which was masculine, a bureaucracy composed of officials who were presumed to be of a different class to their own. Jane Boyer's entire application was peppered throughout with deferential references to 'Sir',[69] and the tone of other applications was similarly deferential. Applicants constructed themselves and their children as 'helpless', relying upon the kind benevolence and 'mercy' of the parish, and some expressed gratitude to the select vestry when their need for relief in some cases terminated – perhaps against the day when they would reapply.

The insistence upon applicants complying with the terms of the final questions appears at first sight as a bureaucratic superfluity given the amount of out-relief which continued to be provided. Yet that those who refused outright to respond to such questions were automatically denied relief in any form suggests that some concern existed on the part of the select vestry to establish clearly the relations of dependence between applicant and parish. That the vestry's power was enforced with discretion rendered its power no less.[70] The relief forms required applicants to detail the materiality of their poverty, a painful and confronting process. Simultaneously, applicants elaborated their experience of poverty within the discursive bounds prescribed by the questions, questions which were predicated upon a notion of limited and self-defeating agency. This agency had to be exercised to complete the form satisfactorily but in the end meant that successful applicants channelled themselves towards formal submission and passive dependence which marked them as 'proper objects' of relief. Yet this reference to object should not be misread. From the point of view of the select vestry, the women were objects of poor law procedures. Yet from the point of view of the applicants, the process was one of *subject*-formation since they themselves had to co-operate with the process, actively constructing themselves as persons suitable for relief. In this way the vestry mobilised the power of the poor law: women had to give up their claim to a freedom in the process of forming their own *identities* to secure for their *bodies* (and often those of their relatives) a different freedom – freedom from the threat of material suffering, or even extinction.

The material conditions of poverty expressed in the applications suggest the many points of continuity between working women and poor women who sought relief. Applicants' occupations were typical for women in the

---

[68] Mary Marton, application, ibid.
[69] Jane Boyer, application, ibid.
[70] In relation to the 'examination' aspect of the vestry's work in assessing applications, again the work of Foucault is useful. He suggests that various mechanisms of examination hold individuals 'in a mechanism of objectification', made visible for classification and judgement, and that it is this process through which power 'manifests its potency': Foucault, *Discipline and punish*, 187.

area.[71] For both groups, responsibility for childrearing and their consequent lower mobility at such periods in their lives, their relegation to secondary roles in paid labour, and their reliance upon work which was haphazard and economically peripheral, increased the potential for women to experience hardship. The difference in circumstances between many working women and those women who were actually compelled to seek relief often appears merely as a hair's breadth difference between the potential of hardship (often precariously) averted, and of hardship realised. Individual circumstances, accidents of time, space, life stage, relationships, coalesced to determine one's position in relation to official divides between worker and relief recipient. But accidents alone constitute no sufficient explanation of the vulnerability of women to poverty. Deeply gendered assumptions regarding women's economic, social and cultural roles both in the workplace and in the domestic sphere structured the meaning and outcomes of those experiences, and revealed entrenched patterns of disadvantage. Indeed, attention to these broader assumptions reveals that the line demarcating poverty for women was in fact not a line, but a fluid zone of experience and meaning influenced by wider discourses on gender, and the regulation of working-class femininity.

To some extent, the historiography of poor relief in nineteenth-century England has done little deconstructive work around the dominant categorisations of the poor employed in contemporary records. Debates about continuities and ruptures in the administration of relief around the pivot of the 1834 legislation focus attention more towards descriptions of practice than to analysis of the deeper assumptions which underlay those practices. Norman McCord's conclusions about the administration of poor relief in the northeast, for example, emphasise the factors which led to continuity in local administration before and after 1834: it was not until mid century, he argues, that poor law machinery was sufficiently well-established to bring the northeast into some degree of conformity with the more stringent and 'professional' administrative system conceived in London. Yet attention to the underlying economic structures and cultural milieu of the poor, and the gendered variants which operated, opens up enquiry also into the more distinct gendered lines of continuity between the experiences of Elizabeth Graham, for example – her social and economic marginality – and other women during the period, and the reasons why, in the face of reform and reconstruction of the Poor Law, these continuities and structures within which women operated remained so secure. Joan Scott's contention regarding the historian's task, not to replicate the 'standard woman worker' from the discourse of the period, but instead to recognise the discourse and subject it to critical scrutiny,[72] can equally be brought to bear in relation to the construction of the 'standard' poor woman in receipt of relief.

---

71 Gladstone Walker, *Wages and pauperism, being a report as to the occupations and earnings of recipients of out-door relief and their dependants*, Report to the Newcastle Board, Nov. 1915.
72 Scott, 'The woman worker', 423.

Conceptualisations of poverty in the nineteenth century provide another useful avenue for understanding the ways in which working-class femininity was actively constructed and perpetuated in policy, as well as in practice.

Dilemmas of definition: women in poor law policy and debate

To rationalise relief, to render its administration uniform across the nation, and simultaneously to achieve a 're-moralisation' of the poor: the objectives of the Poor Law Commissioners appointed in 1832 to investigate relief systems and to make recommendations for change were clearly elucidated in the Commission's report.[73] The report clearly sought to establish morally-organised categories to objectify and control those seeking relief. Of course, categorisations of the poor as 'deserving' and 'undeserving' were by no means new. Mulligan and Richards's discussion of the discourse of poverty in the mid seventeenth century, for example, emphasises the ways in which debates about the poor were 'embedded in fundamental moral imperatives'.[74] However, the recognition and significance of such categories can only be understood as part of the broader patterns and general assumptions which constituted the 'conceptual map by which those people made sense of their world'.[75] Gertrude Himmelfarb has argued that the 'enlarged conception of poverty' which operated in the nineteenth century was underpinned by material advancement: in 1833, de Tocqueville explored the terrain of English poverty and pauperism and identified the 'paradox' that 'the progress of civilisation brought with it . . . an expansion of needs . . . [and] also a determination to alleviate poverty as it had come to be understood'. The task for early nineteenth-century reformers like Nassau Senior was to ensure that relief operated, not as a force for demoralisation 'undermin[ing] the natural, healthy impulses of the "normal type" of English laborer', but as a rational system which would encourage productivity.[76] Like notions of the deserving and undeserving poor which continued to be emphasised in the nineteenth century, conceptions of 'the labourer' gave explicit expression to contemporary assumptions about gender, as well as class and ethnic identities, which shaped the boundaries of the Victorian discursive universe.

The gender assumptions which operated in the overhaul of the poor laws were evident in the 1834 Report, as well as in the subsequent debates and later legislation. The commissioners enunciated the principle of 'less

---

[73] Report from the commissioners for inquiry into the administration and practical operation of the poor laws, PP 1834 [44] xxvii (cited hereinafter as Poor law inquiry, 1834 Report).
[74] Lotte Mulligan and Judith Richards, 'A "radical" problem: the poor and the English reformers in the mid-seventeenth century', Journal of British Studies xxix (1990), 118–46 at p. 128.
[75] Ibid. 145.
[76] G. Himmelfarb, The idea of poverty: England in the early industrial age, London 1985, 148–9, 158.

eligibility' as a means of re-establishing the 'line between the pauper and the independent labourer', without which a country could not 'retain its prosperity, or even its civilisation'. The fundamental principle guiding all future relief, they stated, should be that the recipient's situation should not, through its provision, 'be made really or apparently so eligible as the situation of the independent labourer of the lowest class' who did not receive such support.[77] The 'pauper' – the indigent, able-bodied labourer who it was claimed under existing systems was provided with outdoor relief at some considerable burden to the parish rate-payer – provided an alarming example which could be all too readily emulated. While the primary division between pauper and independent labourer was utilised throughout, the fear was expressed that dangerous blurring would (and did) occur unless 'bona fide claimants . . . are incessantly watched'. Relief paid on the basis of fraudulent settlement claims dictated stricter laws of removal and settlement to regulate the movement of paupers. Only the most intense vigilance could prevent creeping imposture, and this only if local discretion in relief provision was replaced with a uniform, centralised, public control.[78]

In general, as Thane has argued, the 'policy-makers of 1834 identified the unemployed male "able-bodied" worker as the central problem of poverty at that time', and they 'took for granted the universality of the stable two-parent family, primarily dependent upon the father's wage, and the primacy of the family as the source of welfare'.[79] Women were for the most part defined out of the discussions of poverty, its causes and its meanings, both in official literature and later commentary on the poor laws: three years after the Poor Law Amendment Act had been passed, for example, a local supporter of the law, Samuel Donkin, wrote that 'as a Northumbrian I am proud to think that there is not at this time an able-bodied labourer within her [ie. the county's] limits depending upon parochial relief'.[80] His pride rested upon an exclusive definition, of the male labourer. Similarly, in 1850 George Robinson listed the causes of poverty in Newcastle. While he included the impact of unemployment among the causes, he discussed this in relation to men only. Women's poverty, on the other hand, was caused by 'defective sanitary conditions', as through 'the results of preventible disease' they became widows, or ill-paid workers with sick spouses.[81] The emphasis upon the male poor and the relative silence on women in itself attested to the deeply entrenched, 'self-evident' assumptions about the nature and function of the family and women's position within it.

This insistent construction of women as dependants was in some respects

---

77 *Poor law inquiry*, 1834 Report, 126, 127.
78 Ibid. 26, 157.
79 Thane, 'Women and the poor law', 29.
80 Samuel Donkin, *Observations upon the nature of parochial relief and the principles upon which the poor law amendment act is founded*, Newcastle 1837, 45.
81 *Inquiry into the condition of the poor*, 2nd ser., letter ii, 72.

rigidified over the century and exemplified through both formal and informal processes of exclusion. It was also linked to broader visions of progress and Victorian social stability. Gendered prescriptions of public and private spheres, and essential biological definitions of femininity which rendered it a 'natural' force requiring social regulation, made the 'proper' position of women within the family more central to the project of contemporary social reform. The centrality of the family in social life was explained by the Registrar-General in 1851: 'families', he argued, were the elementary communities 'of which larger communities in various degrees of subordination, and ultimately the nation, are constituted', and it was upon marriage and the family that the nation's 'manners, character, happiness and freedom, intimately depend'.[82] In the 1834 Report, in similar vein, the commissioners argued that it was in the localised site of the family that the disruptive effects of pauperism were most keenly experienced; where the curse of Speenhamland had supposedly spread uncontrollably,[83] the disordering havoc which outdoor relief and allowance systems brought to family life was severe:

> Now pauperism seems to be the engine for the purpose of disconnecting each member of a family from all the others; of reducing all to the state of domesticated animals, fed, lodged, and provided for by the parish, without mutual dependence or mutual interest.[84]

In the Northumbrian context, the centrality of the patriarchal family had been cited by Eneas Mackenzie seven years earlier: the non-working woman, in a region where there was steady trade, good education and plenty of coal for heating, served crucially to 'bind the domestic circle'.[85] Contradictions around Mackenzie's visions abounded. His 'steady trade' characterisation was not borne out generally across the century in Newcastle, as downturns in trade, specific industrial slumps, and extended labour disputes brought privation in their wake particularly in the 'hungry forties', the late 1870s, and in the century's final decade. The characterisation also obscured from the outset the almost complete absence of employment for women in the core industries of the region. The 'steady trade' conception, like those of the 'prosperous north' and the 'industrious' and 'independent' labourer, were generalisations whose relevance attested to a masculinised vision of social and economic progress, a vision whose terms relied upon defining women out of the formula, except in roles as dependants and as private persons. The appropriate ordering of domestic and public spaces, and of bodies and identities within them was deemed fundamental, and as both national and regional

---

[82] *1851 Census*, pt i, Registrar General's report, xxviii.
[83] M. Blaug, 'The poor law report re-examined', *Journal of Economic History* xxiv (1964), 229–43 at pp. 229ff.
[84] *Poor law inquiry*, 1834 Report, 53.
[85] Mackenzie, *Descriptive and historical account*, ii. 730–1.

evidence suggests, the home and the patriarchal family lay at the heart of this conception.

Where the gendered variants of the category of 'pauper' were made clear in the evidence presented by the commissioners in 1834, their arguments were set against this normative backdrop of femininity and family life. The male pauper was immoral through his idleness, trading the wages of honest labour for the ease of unearned relief, without conscience. The female pauper, to the extent she appeared, was, first and foremost, exemplified by the figure of the unmarried mother who had used her sexuality actively, and had calculated that the production of children outside marriage would secure a bountiful living upon the parish. She engaged in 'successful bastardy adventures',[86] and evidence from parishes was highlighted in the body of the report which stated that the impetus to 'illicit' intercourse 'has, in almost all cases, originated with the females'.[87]

In his passivity, then, a man was transformed from a state of independence to pauperism. On the other hand, it was in her activity that a woman journeyed, not from 'independence' as it was normatively constructed for men, but from the orbit of socially desirable and constructive private dependence in marriage and motherhood to a disordering public dependence as a pauper. The notion of public dependence in itself was extremely disruptive, almost a contradiction in terms: the loose, financial arrangements between woman and parish under regimes of out-relief were deemed void of any of the crucial moral imperatives which were thought to mark relations of hierarchy and subordination in the more intimate terrain of family life. In this scheme, then, although the female poor and their life styles were not written up as central to the report, the treatment of subjects such as bastardy were not 'detached from . . . the main body of the Poor Law . . . but were closely related' to the overall vision captured in the scheme to revise systems of relief.[88] This elaboration of disordering feminine sexuality provided stark contrasts when set against the image of the well-ordered patriarchal family, that formation which better guaranteed stability and progress.

The report, whose sections and recommendations on bastardy were written by Edwin Chadwick,[89] argued for the complete dismantling of the old system by which putative fathers could be subject to maintenance orders for support of a child (with maintenance often paid direct to the mother by the parish), and could be imprisoned for non-payment. Instead, it envisaged that mothers be made totally responsible for the maintenance of their illegitimate children. The 'shame of the offence' would continue if the automatic income from 'bastardy' would cease, and the norms and practices of the 'labouring classes' themselves were cited in support of such a measure. Working-class

---

86 *Poor law inquiry*, 1834 Report, 95.
87 Ibid. 94.
88 Henriques, 'Bastardy and the new poor law', 103.
89 Ibid. 103 n. 3.

female societies paid no premiums for illegitimate children, but specifically excluded single mothers from benefits.[90] Opponents of the bastardy clauses in the legislation inspired by the report argued, not outside a moral framework, but within one which they expanded to cite the joint responsibility of men and women, and in which they cited disqualification from maintenance as merely exacerbating the disgrace and pain which women had already suffered in such circumstances.[91]

Both the chronology and the defining character of the decisions culminating in the 'workhouse test' in turn, carried different, gendered implications. For men, the decision whether or not to self-regulate one's 'idleness' to avoid the prospect of the workhouse was potentially a decision which could be taken right up to the threshold of the workhouse itself. For poor women, a decision about self-regulation related to that realm of 'private' sexual behaviour which might lead to pregnancy and destitution. Here, there could be no half measures, no gradual 'awakening' tending towards self-regulation. The decision was one which had to be 'lived' at all times as a complete and unbreachable commitment to chastity.[92] That the connection between unregulated female sexual behaviour and pauperism played itself out over the longer term made the connection no less certain: indeed, the qualitatively different gendered forms of behaviour which were envisaged as leading to pauperism made the connection more certain, as any 'wrong' decision could not be later re-negotiated, since women would already be locked into an inescapable, corporeal timetable of pregnancy, birth and 'natural' responsibility for their child once born.

The legislation passed, with modification to the clauses so that actions for affiliation could be brought. But maintenance, payable until a child reached seven years of age, was not to be paid direct to the mother, and a woman's claims regarding the paternity of her child 'had to be corroborated in some material particular'.[93] A woman's own word, in this as in many other aspects of relief decisions, was insufficient.[94] Moreover, the child's settlement, upon which parochial responsibility for relief was established, followed that of its mother until the child reached sixteen years, and relief afforded to the child was deemed to be relief to the mother as well. No more could women claim that it was their children, not they, who received relief, as they had done in the All Saints' applications: by definition under the new act, relief provided to children of a woman unable to support them automatically entailed the woman's classification as an 'able-bodied pauper'.

90 *Poor law inquiry*, 1834 Report, 196–7.
91 *Debates of the House of Commons* (cited hereinafter as *Hansard*), 3rd ser. xxiii. 808 (9 May 1934).
92 '[L]et the woman know the responsibility and the penalty and she would take care not to run the risk of either', argued Hume in the House of Commons during debate on the bastardy clauses of the legislation leading from the report: ibid. xxii. 893 (17 Apr. 1834).
93 Henriques, 'Bastardy and the new poor law', 114.
94 For discussion of the 'need' for investigation to establish veracity, see below, 195.

If, as the radical George Grote maintained, 'the sobriety . . . industry . . . and the independence of the labouring classes are the first of blessings to a country, and the dearest of all objects to every virtuous citizen',[95] what position within the new schemes of relief constructed to achieve such ends was afforded to the other major group of female relief recipients, able-bodied widows and deserted women with children? Compared with the attention given to the subject of bastardy, both the 1834 Report and subsequent parliamentary debates were extremely brief in their handling of the subject. Again, such brief handling attested to women's exclusion from the formula of 'independent labour', and perhaps added weight to the view that the legislation had emerged 'out of the pigeon-hole of some theorist's brain' who had not stopped to consider the 'habits of the people to whom it was meant to be applied'.[96]

Widows and deserted wives were to follow their husbands' settlement, and widows were removable immediately after the husband's death, until the 1846 Poor Removal Act postponed such removal in the first twelve months of their widowhood. Certainly, instances were cited in the report of the misuse of outdoor relief and fraud by women, and a tendency among them to make 'frivolous' application, spurred on by others in their community who saw relief as a right attaching to their status.[97] There was also some slight recognition of the difficult economic circumstances in which widows often found themselves, a situation which could none the less be exploited to the 'benefit' of the system, according to evidence cited by the Commissioners; widows of non-commissioned officers and poor clergymen could superintend poorhouses, since they would be incapable of 'low cunning' and would be 'cheap to the public'.[98] The provision of outdoor relief to 'deserving' women was not to be discontinued under the new legislation: however, the tone of the report, with its emphasis upon the need for constant vigilance to curtail fraud and the incidence of 'hereditary pauperism' among children, lent official weight and a 'progressive', Benthamite rationale to any regimes of localised moral surveillance which were already in evidence.

The informal surveillance and regulation which could influence relief decisions during the period operated more commonly and more particularly with regard to female applicants. As well as the wider contemporary interpretations of different moral standards for women and for men and idealised notions of virtue bound into Victorian visions of femininity, examples of which have already been discussed, the definitions of the female poor which blurred and overlapped along both moral and economic lines found no clear counterpart in discussions of the male poor, whose categorisation under the legislation was more definitive and rested almost exclusively on their obvious

95 George Grote, *Hansard*, 3rd ser. xxiii. 813 (9 May 1834).
96 John Walter, ibid. 830–1.
97 *Poor law inquiry*, 1834 Report, 26.
98 Ibid. 175.

and measurable public employment status. Certainly, while the formulation of 'constructive pauperism' operated to define women and children as automatic dependants of men, it was to some extent a formulation which further entrenched the essentially 'public' and economic quality of a man's poverty, its assessment, and subsequent treatment.

Poor working women occupied a precarious location between public and private spheres, producing in turn a possible double line of scrutiny of the roles and responsibilities they negotiated. A dominant categorisation of woman as 'worker' ran counter to broad assumptions about ideal femininity and domestic life, however, and the path of moral categorisation was perhaps more 'naturally' accessible in that it could draw upon an established and widely understood vocabulary and imagery of 'woman'. To discuss women and their experiences without reference to morality was virtually impossible, since to do so would be to occlude one of the key variables used to construct and to maintain hierarchies of Victorian femininity. Finally, in the specific spatial context, conventions about women's primary responsibility for the care of the aged, the infirm and children both created women's poverty and located experience of it primarily in the private household. Hilary Graham's observations on the gendered nexus between poverty and caring roles is broadly applicable to the nineteenth century as well as to the contemporary period: women's poverty and economic dependence is generally 'not because they need care, but because they give it. . . . For children and for men, it seems, economic dependency is the cost of being cared for; for women, economic dependency is the cost of caring.'[99] Throughout her life, claimed Helen Bosanquet, a woman 'never ceases to be useful to someone', and so lived their poverty more often in the home than in the workhouse.[100] The need for more explicit focus upon classification of the poor, a need expressed in the 1834 Report in arguments about constant and intense 'vigilance', in many cases for women entailed a sustained scrutiny of their poverty in the 'private' world of family life. As the bureaucratic apparatus of poor relief provision expanded along with other forms of city administration across the century,[101] paid officials at the lowest levels of the hierarchy themselves sometimes lived in close proximity to the relief applicants,[102] perhaps contributing to a more sympathetic understanding of living conditions for the poor, but also facilitating procedures of specific local surveillance.

The aim of the new legislation was to produce unprecedented precision in definition and categorisation which would in turn animate policy. The

---

[99] Hilary Graham, 'Women's poverty and caring', in Glendinning and Millar, *Women and poverty in Britain*, 221–40 at p. 223.

[100] Helen Bosanquet, 'The economics of women's work and wages', *The National Liberal Club Political and Economic Circle: Transactions* v (1907), 1–16 at p. 9.

[101] McCord, 'Making of modern Newcastle', 340

[102] In 1841, for example, Relieving Officer William Robins lived with his family in the Sandgate district: census enumerator's returns, St John's parish, Newcastle, TWAS, MF 12, 1841 Census (HO 107/848).

'science' of self-regulation in the management of poverty demanded exactitude and consistency.[103] Only if there was 'a place for everything' could the complex new machinery of poor relief achieve its transformative, progressive goals. In its own discursive terms, there was neither much space for interpretative flexibility, nor scope for the play of traditional local approaches, without jeopardising the key features of the scheme. The dilemmas of definition around the female poor, and the contradiction which becomes evident in relation to the contemporary conceptualisation of poverty – that of a policy framework for poor relief which aimed to provide a complete and certain response to the problem of poverty, yet one which was built from the outset in terms such that the situation of groups of women who were major recipients of relief was neglected – played themselves out not only in official literature. These dilemmas and contradictions were also evident in literature generated by those who sought to criticise the new legislation and its operation. Indeed, the massive conceptual blind spot in policy around the female poor provided an important critical discursive space for those in the north-east (and elsewhere) in their attacks upon the new policies.

The most sustained local attack on the legislation illustrates this process. Robert Blakey, radical mayor of Morpeth, poor relief Guardian, and barrister, published his anti-poor law tract in 1838,[104] substantial portions of which were subsequently republished as part of G. R. Wythen Baxter's nationally distributed *Book of the bastiles* [sic] in 1841.[105] Blakey conceptualised the problem of poverty, as had the commissioners before him, almost entirely around the 'labouring man'. This worker, he wrote, could previously depend upon 'natural' social ties which would ensure his well-being in adversity – a state in which 'genuine patriotism' was secured through recognition of 'binding obligations' and the greater public good. The New Poor Law, by contrast, had acted to distance rich and poor: 'poverty and nakedness [stalk] . . . our streets', he claimed, and

> we find an almost daily account of Coroner's inquests being held on the bodies of men, women, and children, who have died from real starvation . . . [t]he wild Africans are absolutely more wealthy and better provided with the necessaries of life . . . for running wild in the woods would be a more preferable condition on which to ingraft any real social improvement, than such a state of society as we have just now noticed.[106]

Yet while Blakey appealed to some ideal of a 'free-born Englishman', and the 'rights' inhering in a historic conception of the independent male labourer in establishing his framework for discussion of poverty, almost without

---

103 *Poor law inquiry*, 1834 Report, 148.
104 Blakey, *Cottage politics.*
105 G. R. Wythen Baxter, *The book of the bastiles; or, the history of the working of the new poor law*, London 1841.
106 Blakey, *Cottage politics*, 16, 12–13.

exception the case-studies he drew upon to exemplify his argument were those of women's experiences – mainly widows, but also some mothers of illegitimate children.

The history of the Aspin family provided a stark illustration. A 57-year-old widow, Elizabeth Aspin, had been in receipt of relief during illness. The Board had suspended relief after a fortnight, and left Elizabeth 'fast sinking to the grave for want of food'. Elizabeth's three adult daughters, all of whom were the mothers of illegitimate children, lived at home with their mother. Her sister, Jane Aspin, was also a widow and had four children, one of whom was illegitimate. She too was denied relief on the grounds, alleged Blakey, 'that she is not as good as she ought to be. According to [the Board's] notions of public duty, they have a right to starve a human being to death if her morals should not square in with their *own purity*.'[107] Elizabeth's daughter, Mabel, also swore a statement that, in refusing her mother relief, 'the Guardians . . . clearly intimated that I and my sister ought to follow improper practices to obtain my mother a livelihood. . . . I nearly fainted on the Town's Hall stairs.' Her sworn statement was followed by the independent statement of a 'respectable' male who had interviewed Mabel immediately after the incident, to vouch for the objective truthfulness of Mabel's own 'truth'. Blakey added that in relation to the treatment of Mabel, 'I cannot give in writing the precise language used; decency forbids it.'[108]

In the case of the Aspins, assessing the 'truth' of the allegations and counter-allegations surrounding the details of the case is difficult. As one of many of the stock images of the anti-poor law repertoire, the Aspins appear in Blakey's work as one of the 'fragments' which fuelled the perception of cruelty under the poor law, and as Crowther maintains, the proportions of the 'workhouse myth' or official harshness did not necessarily rely upon a basis in fact.[109] Certainly, however, there is evidence from other sources of coercive treatment of women and suspect intervention by local officials.[110] In many respects the Aspin case shored up the generalisations made about the taint of 'hereditary pauperism' as it affected women. In particular, the accused Guardians made clear that, indeed, relief had been refused on moral grounds: Jane Aspin was 'much addicted to habits of intemperance . . . the woman prefers a state of profligacy to the monotony of the workhouse'.[111] Elizabeth, it was decided, would be denied all forms of outdoor relief until she sent her daughters out to service. What would become of her daughters' children was not made clear, and Elizabeth did not apply for relief for her daughters, but only for herself; none the less, the Board of Guardians had 'frequently remon-

---

[107] Ibid. 63, 75.
[108] Ibid. 94.
[109] M. A. Crowther, *The workhouse system 1834–1929: the history of an English social institution*, London 1981, 270.
[110] *Poor law inquiry*, 1834 Report, appendix a, pt i, 126.
[111] George Brummel, Clerk to the Morpeth Union, to *Newcastle Chronicle*, 22 Mar. 1837, in Blakey, *Cottage politics*, 63.

strated with her on the propriety of keeping her daughters at home in indolence and profligacy', and this specific regulation of her adult daughters was the precondition of future assistance.[112] Both Blakey and his opponents, however, began from similar first principles about the central importance of the family, and the male breadwinner within it, and conducted their appraisal of women around the pivot of morality. While Blakey deployed material about women in his attack, presenting vivid and shocking illustrations of the practical weakspots of the legislation by highlighting images of female helplessness, his wider critique did not shift the terms of the debate about female poverty, it causes, and its treatment.

'Although some inconvenience should occasionally arise . . .': the provision of relief to women in Northumberland

While Chadwick, Senior and the other commissioners outlined the major problems to be remedied through legislation, and advanced views about society and about poverty which were heavily laden with assumptions about gender and the economic and moral underpinnings of the labouring family, the application of legislative remedy in the north-east after 1834 was neither instant nor straightforward. Northumberland had been cited both in the report's evidence and in parliamentary debate as exceptional. Reiterating that even-by-then standard article of faith of nineteenth-century northern 'difference', landowner John Wilson began his regional report by citing 'the known superiority in moral and physical well-being of the North of England peasantry over their brethren in the Southern counties'. In the countryside, one could find indications of 'substantial comfort', and at its centre

> the blazing hearth, that keystone of all household and domestic comfort; perhaps the mother and younger children beside it . . . [and] an expression of content in ordinary circumstances, of tranquility and patience in occasional distress, which attests the character of a peasantry not as yet corrupted by precarious gain or intolerable misery.[113]

The 'hinding' system contributed much to prosperity, he said. With the Revd Mr W. S. Gilly, he visited and reported on the houses of 'decent' widows, whose old-age comfort was overseen by caring relatives and local farmers who provided coal and potatoes.

The only disruptions to this rural idyll cited in the evidence, were brought by foreigners, and by disorderly women whose actions interrupted this clear vision of prosperity and comfort. The Irish who came for the harvest, reported Wilson, did not usually become vagrants, although they were riotous

---

112 Ibid.
113 *Poor law inquiry*, 1834 Report, appendix a, pt i, 119. Wilson and Gilly figured consistently when local opinion was canvassed on matters connected with social 'progress'.

and drunken; the Scots, on the other hand were quiet, but inclined to vagrancy and begging. There were anomalies which were worrisome in respect of the removability of Scottish mothers of illegitimate children, and some disquiet was expressed about the inclination of people to remain unmarried until after the birth of children.[114] But beyond these problems, there was nothing within the structures of social and economic life in the north which was believed to underpin poverty and misfortune. Wilson quoted one employer regarding his impoverished employee's family circumstances:

> He said that the . . . condition of the family can only be attributed to general mismanagement and the laziness of his wife. The man being a hind, his wife was bound to the usual work of bondager; her usual mode of proceeding was to perform this work in a slovenly manner in order to attract reproaches, and then walk off the field 'in the sullens'. Here, then, was an instance where a family, placed in circumstances rather more than averagely favourable, simply through defect of conduct and principle, present to a chance visitor an appearance of the utmost misery, while others, much less favourably situated, exert sufficient moral energy to maintain themselves on a decent footing.[115]

In the House of Commons, the reputation of the north was further secured with Robert Slaney, pro-reform MP for Shrewsbury, citing Northumberland as the county where the poor laws were best administered.[116] Himmelfarb has contended that the 1834 legislation was 'obsolete almost from the time of its enactment, the abuses it was meant to correct having become less urgent by 1834',[117] and certainly Northumberland was cast as an exception even before the legislation. As the All Saints' applications suggest, there was continuity between the pre- and post-1834 period in relation to the local application of relief: some local select vestries had already begun to move towards the principle of 'less-eligibility' in broad outline, and exercised discretionary power in the administration of outdoor relief. While there were clear points of continuity in poor relief provision however, in both the urban and rural contexts the changing balance of power between the central administration in London and the local relief bodies produced confusion. In the north-east region under the old poor laws, Rushton's study bears out in a particular context the generalisations advanced by Snell: 'parochial organisation ensured a face to face connection of administrators and the poor', resulting in tailor-made relief in cash and kind, but also 'wide-ranging influence' in social relationships.[118] In the region, while the boundaries of settlement clearly influenced the scope of relief, 'inside the boundaries' personal knowledge of

---

114 Ibid. 126.
115 Ibid. 120–1.
116 Robert Slaney, Hansard, 3rd ser. xxiii. 818 (9 May 1834).
117 Himmelfarb, Idea of poverty, 153.
118 K. Snell, Annals of the labouring poor: social change and agrarian England, 1600–1900, Cambridge 1985, 104–5.

applicants could operate to their advantage. Largely absent from the scene, however, was any broader response to poverty 'wider than the face-to-face relations of everyday life'.[119]

Yet this broader, generalised, national conception underlay the 1834 legislation. As Himmelfarb maintains, reflecting this conceptual gap between the old and the new administrative approach to poverty, the act in operation was subject to 'compromises, exceptions, evasions, and regional variations', elaborated in 'an entire literature . . . demonstrating the gap between the law and its application'.[120] What has not been well-elaborated however, is the extent to which a good deal of this tension crystallised around the different groups of female poor under discussion. Such attention to these groups was perhaps unsurprising, given the discursive tensions around them which have already been identified. Relative silence from London about the status of widows and deserted wives left ample scope for piecemeal local interpretation, which was sometimes then questioned or gainsaid by the central authorities. At the same time, the strikingly clear moral imperatives constructed around the mothers of illegitimate children in official literature could seem rather less clear and less practicable, viewed from within those economic frameworks which underpinned local relief practices.

At local level, the twin concerns to find adequate solutions to poverty and to maintain 'rigid economy in public expenditure' were commonly expressed throughout the period. Rather than consideration of broad policy matters, Boards devoted time to questions about such matters as 'the control of official patronage or whether the workhouse inmates should be allowed beer at Christmas'.[121] Certainly, the sheer volume of paperwork – processing of applications, removals, correspondence, minutes of meetings and statistical returns – suggest that throughout the period much of the working time of many local officials must have been spent in attending to basic administrative requirements.

However, while the imperatives underpinning local action may indeed have led to quick, practical, economic decisions which were far removed from the the more ponderous and theoretically elaborate arena of social policy formation at the centre, these local processes none the less occurred within a broader range of legislative definition and gendered cultural parameters which affected perceptions of what was 'possible', 'desirable' or 'necessary' in that historical context. The spheres of policy-making and practically-driven local decision-making cannot be easily separated. The latter provided the bridge between the policies and the construction and experience of poverty in everyday life. The case of Mary Moralee, the woman whose 'character' as an associate of 'notorious prostitutes' did not bear close

---

119 Rushton, 'The poor law, the parish and the community', 152.
120 Ibid.
121 N. McCord, 'Ratepayers and social policy', in Pat Thane (ed.), *The origins of British social policy*, London 1978, 21–35 at pp. 22, 30.

scrutiny, and to whom the provision of whisky caused such consternation, for example, provides evidence of just such a process.[122] In the case, the rate-payers exerted pressure certainly with an eye to economising, but in so doing cited reasons which were in accord with the moral regulation of paupers envisaged in policy. Attention to the minutiae of local administrative deci-sions and interactions in such cases can provide an important translatory key between broad conceptions of poverty, and the material and cultural meaning of those conceptions for poor people in particular times and spaces. In the local context, women's marginal and uncertain connections to dominant definitions of the 'able-bodied' in policy and in poor law literature were made manifest in the arena of practical application.

Only four months after the Poor Law Amendment Act was passed, for example, the Clerk of Newcastle's Justices wrote to Edwin Chadwick seeking clarification of the powers of magistrates to secure payments for mothers of illegitimate children. The magistrates had been 'plagued . . . [with] complaints against the Overseers of the poor' who, he said, had refused to use their new powers under the act to pursue those maintenance payments which had been ordered previously,[123] and who had refused as well to provide relief to women from the parish. Could the magistrates step into the breach if the select vestries were obstinate in their pursuit of maintenance, since 'in many cases it is extremely hard upon the Mother to bear all the burthen'? Chad-wick responded unequivocally. The overseers were supposed to prevent pauperism. The magistrates could not act, and the law 'must be complied with', although, he added, 'some inconvenience should occasionally arise'.[124] The 'inconvenience' which Chadwick described relating to the conditions of relief and status of poor women in various categories continued to 'plague' the authorities in Newcastle and London, and was a prominent topic around which broader bureaucratic skirmishing over regional autonomy and central enforcement of policy took place.

Inconvenient women – there was no easy category for that femininity which burst out of the normative constructions of female dependence, and presented ongoing dilemmas of definition for officials in London and the north. The contradictions which clustered around working-class femininity, at times apparent in discussion of women's work, their family roles and their position within narratives of progress, appeared in most acute and sustained form in the texts and practices of poor relief. As Thane has argued,[125] the chief conundrum confronting policymakers in the relief area was precisely along which lines were widows and deserted women to be defined – as

---

122 See ch. 2.
123 On maintenance orders see Henriques, 'Bastardy and the new poor law', 104–5.
124 Thomas Turnbull, Clerk of Peace's Office for Northumberland, to Edwin Chadwick, Poor Law Commission, 17 Dec. 1834, PRO, MH 12/9096; Edwin Chadwick to Thomas Turnbull, 19 Dec. 1834, ibid.
125 Thane, 'Women and the poor law', 36.

mothers, or as workers? It was around these dual identities that tensions between economic and moral definitions of femininity came to the fore. As seen in the All Saints' records, women negotiated their identities as 'deserving' recipients of outdoor relief with reference to both categories, and establishing relief credentials was essential for women attempting to avoid removal, or in claiming temporary out-relief. Local peculiarities led to some anomalies: the Glendale Guardians, for example, enquired whether widows and single women employed as 'cottars' – given a rent-free cottage, coals and potatoes, and undertaking to work for wages when needed by a farmer – could gain settlement through their continuous hiring, or whether their settlement would remain linked to birth and marriage. The London commissioners were again unequivocal. Local practices in relation to these women simply lacked 'all essential ingredients of hiring and service',[126] and therefore such women could not be defined according to their work identity.

The problem of primary identity was particularly clear in the Northumberland Unions' correspondence relating to settlement, an activity which took up a great deal of time for local Guardians. The prospect of a widow's removal to the parish of settlement of a deceased husband could sever all ties of friendship and knowledge of local work among women, in favour of confirming sometimes distant patriarchal links. The problem was effectively summarised by the Clerk of the Rothbury Union when he enquired about the status of Jane Hale, a widow who had been removed to Rothbury Union from Durham on the death of her husband, along with two of her three children. The economic impact of removal was severe, he argued, for in Durham the widow and her children could support themselves. In Rothbury, only unfamiliar agricultural work would be possible, if employment were found at all.[127] Certainly there was some local sympathy for the plight of widows. A steady stream of correspondence, particularly from rural areas, enquired as well about the possibility of extending out-relief to non-resident widows who resided with adult children in nearby parishes, where removal to the parish of settlement would prove more costly. Such plans were invariably approved.[128]

Significantly, however, the large Newcastle Union did not participate extensively in these non-resident schemes. In the city, removal regulations were consistently followed, and even after the passage of the Irremovable Poor Act of 1861 which altered the grounds for removal, the Newcastle Union's main removal activity was in relation to neighbouring unions, and the majority of people so removed appear to have been widows and deserted

---

[126] Poor Law Commission to Wooler Board of Guardians, 21 June 1838, Glendale Union correspondence, 1834–45, PRO, MH 12/9020.
[127] Thomas Arkle, Clerk, to Poor Law Commission, 6 May 1842, Rothbury Union correspondence, 1834–45, ibid. MH 12/9145.
[128] On non-resident relief see David Ashforth, 'Settlement and removal in urban areas: Bradford, 1834–71', in Rose, *The poor and the city*, 57–91 at pp. 71–2.

wives.[129] Moreover, where settlement claims were uncertain the union some-times acted to remove the poor none the less. Perhaps the most grimly ironic procedure under settlement removals occurred where deserted women had no claim to relief unless they returned to the parish of settlement of the husband who had in fact left them.[130]

The women more generally subject to automatic removal were those who were the mothers of young illegitimate children. Here, while the dual identi-ties of worker and mother were clearly both still relevant, the weight of judgement fell even more clearly along moral rather than economic lines. In the early period, queries were raised about the possibility of parishes supple-menting the cost of children being nursed in order to allow their mothers to go into service.[131] Questions were also raised about the desirability of mothers remaining outside the workhouse in the care of relatives. The Rothbury Guardians enquired whether Mary Jane Mason, an intellectually disabled woman and mother of a six-week-old baby, could be allowed to continue to reside with her aunt and receive relief. The response from London brought clear instructions not to sanction out-relief, and, evoking the shadow of hereditary pauperism, advised that preventive, restraining forms of relief in this case were clearly in order: she would 'be better in the Workhouse, if only to prevent the chance of her bearing any more children, who would in all probability be imbeciles like herself'.[132]

Ellen Ross contends that in late nineteenth-century London, 'every poor woman had to demonstrate almost continuously . . . that she was not a "low" woman', and that 'her respectability was under perpetual suspicion'.[133] The same was true in Northumberland, and in cases where single women had given birth, the suspicion was realised: the moral 'taint' was paramount in the classifications imposed upon them by the central poor law authorities. Women classified as able-bodied paupers who had entered workhouses to get relief for themselves and their illegitimate children at times seemed locked into a category from which there was little prospect of escape through the conventional de-pauperising avenue of hard work. Lengthy correspondence, for example, took place between officials in the agricultural union of Castle Ward, the assistant regional commissioner, and officials in London, regarding the possibility of women with illegitimate children, who had received relief in the workhouse, leaving the institution during the day or for longer periods

---

[129] See, for example, removal orders, 1857, Newcastle Union, TWAS 359/341/3; removal orders, 1887, Newcastle Union, TWAS 359/342.

[130] Case of Mary Anne Backhouse, ibid.

[131] Robert Salmon to Poor Law Commission, 15 Jan. 1838, Newcastle Union correspon-dence, 1834–40, PRO, MH 12/9096.

[132] Letter from Wooler Board, 4 Feb. 1868, Glendale Union correspondence, 1862–71, ibid. MH 12/9023.

[133] Ellen Ross, ' "Not the sort that would sit on the doorstep": respectability in pre-World War I London neighbourhoods', *International Labor and Working Class History* xxvii (1985), 39–59 at p. 49.

in order to undertake paid work when it was available. The Guardians of the union had claimed

> That it is very difficult to parry satisfactorily the question 'are women who have been tested by the Workhouse and have shewn by their continued residence therein that they cannot maintain themselves and bastards out of it, never to be permitted to make another endeavour to gain an honest livelihood'?[134]

The response from the assistant regional commissioner was again unequivocal, and the rationale provided indicated the strong moral control (although expressed with confusing haste) which it was hoped the workhouse regime would provide:

> an insuperable objection [to outside employment]. . . . The adoption of the scheme imagined by [?] parishes in the Castleward [sic] Union would at once destroy the moral power of your workhouse system . . . [which] depends upon the continuous maintenance of those *restraints* by which the [?] comforts of a workhouse residence – especially to females – be counterbalanced . . . it should be recollected that the peculiar cause for which ablebodied women usually become inmates of the workhouse adds, as regards them, very seriously to the impropriety of adopting the resolution.[135]

Certainly, the conditions of relief for women varied within the region, and across time. Sparse population and considerable distances in rural areas often made out-relief a more practical alternative, and certainly in the early period before workhouses were built in outlying areas out-relief was provided, if reluctantly on the advice of London, to any women who could not be removed. In the small hamlet of Ewart, for example, when Elizabeth Arnot became pregnant with an illegitimate child in 1836 she insisted 'upon having a house found her by the Overseers . . . she has no father or mother or Grandfather or Grandmother living, but is a stout ablebodied woman'. Since the new Wooler workhouse had been planned but not yet built, relief was afforded to Elizabeth on these terms.[136]

While relief patterns varied depending upon local differences in employment and seasonal factors, and while alterations in provisions occurred due to policy changes over the century,[137] there were consistent lines of dependence upon the union which were observable across regions and which operated beyond the boundaries of immediate employment conditions, seasonal or trade fluctuations. As well as the broadly recognised links between poverty

---

134 Memorandum on departure from Prohibitory Orders in the Castle Ward Union, Castle Ward Union correspondence, 1836–41, PRO, MH 12/9002.

135 Sir John Walsham to Castle Ward Union, 5 Sept. 1841, ibid.

136 Wooler overseers to Poor Law Commission, 1836, Glendale Union correspondence, 1834–45, ibid. MH 12/9020.

137 For a survey of policy trends in relief of the able-bodied see J. H. Treble, *Urban poverty in Britain 1830–1914*, London 1979, ch. iii.

and production, there was also the important 'knot' between poverty and reproduction which 'gender was central in structuring', and which vitally conditioned the type and circumstances of women's paid employment.[138] Life circumstances for the aged, infirm, widows, deserted women, the mothers of illegitimate children and children themselves coalesced to ensure that, regardless of the focus upon the 'independent labourer', these groups were always the major recipients of relief. That a significant number of women who were dependent upon relief were also able-bodied, led inevitably to complications and tensions arising from a clash between moral and economic definitions of femininity which remained unresolved during the period,[139] and many women in their everyday experience of relief systems were materially affected by these shifting definitions and uncertainties around their status.

Local practice with regard to these women often focused on attempts to resolve these uncertainties, within a complicated, triangular process of negotiation and interpretation. Poor women occupied a disordered and disordering position, because the material effects of their poverty forced them to negotiate their subjectivity across boundaries of constructed 'female dependence', and the realities of their independence. The local authorities themselves were located on the boundaries, between a discourse of general policy imperatives, and consideration of the provision of relief in specific cases under local conditions. They were confronted at times by the determination of women before them to assert their own subjectivity, yet were charged with implementing laws which did not recognise women's self-definition. That local officials sometimes attempted to give some voice to the women's own views about themselves and their positions, by appealing to the central authorities, is testament in part to the agency of those women, and in part to the officials' own consideration of local economic imperatives. The women asking for relief sought to negotiate a position for themselves which both answered the need to present themselves as 'deserving' of relief, and which evaded capitulation to the regulatory imperatives embodied in policy where possible. That their attempts were not always successful suggests the power of the ordering impulses embodied in the poor law. Through its objectifying categories, the fluidity of women's subjectivities would be reshaped within a structure of fixed categories. Yet the evidence from the north suggests that the process of 'fixing' identities of poor women, and categorising them in certain pre-set terms, was awkward.

For some poor women who had not been able to meet the economic

---

138 Rose, *Limited livelihoods*, 101.
139 In Newcastle as late as 1915, Gladstone Walker, Clerk to the Newcastle Union, stated that 'we are inclined to agree that a woman's place is at home to look after her children', but for widows and deserted wives part of their obligation was 'to make a personal effort' to work and 'not throw the onus of maintenance on to the public': Walker, *Wages and pauperism*, 5.

demands and moral standards expected of them as women, as workers, as mothers, and who with reference to their circumstances were automatically cast as 'undeserving', the cost of relief was more onerous, requiring submission to workhouse systems in the region. Although workhouse relief was the experience of a minority of the poor throughout the period,[140] attention to these specific local sites provides another point for examination of the relationship between policy and practice, and between broader cultural assumptions about the poor, and the material consequences of these assumptions for women in the north-east. In the space of the workhouse, the experience of the female poor was structured more explicitly by regimes of control and surveillance. Significantly, the workhouse was also the place where the very poor recipients of relief were often superintended by other women who were themselves quite consistently subject to the scrutiny of a masculine bureaucracy.[141] The workhouse, therefore, provides another spatially and historically-specific context in which to examine the fluidity of definitions of femininity, and the intersection of these with views about and experiences of poverty for women.

Femininity and poverty: constructing institutional boundaries

In a rash of construction in Northumberland in the late 1830s, new workhouses were established and older poorhouse networks were rationalised. By the early 1840s Wooler had its new workhouse, although perhaps giving material expression to the marginalisation of women in conceptions of poverty, as well as in policy and planning in relation to the poor, within a decade the Clerk of the Glendale Union was writing to London requesting that the workhouse be extended 'to give additional accommodation to the Female department, which owing to the great disproportion of the sexes is not so well provided for emergencies as that of males'.[142] By 1840 in Newcastle, the four inner-parish poorhouses in Newcastle had been replaced in their function by one large workhouse with accommodation for over 300 people in the less central location of Arthur's Hill to the north-west of the city. Even many Chartists, the Clerk of the Union informed the London Board, had visited the institution '(by permission of course)' and expressed

---

[140] The proportion of relief recipients inside the workhouse stood at about 7% of all receiving relief in 1848, although it increased gradually over the next two decades: Poor Law Inspectors' returns, 1848–69, TWAS 359/300–1.

[141] There were no female Guardians of the poor due to the property-based qualification for election to the office, which was reduced in 1892 and then abolished in 1894: Pat Thane, *The foundations of the welfare state*, London 1982, 33.

[142] Clerk to the Poor Law Board, 15 Jan. 1853, Glendale Union correspondence, 1853–61, PRO, MH 12/9022.

gratitude and surprise at its good management, while the 'happiness, contentment and comfort' of its inmates bore testimony to its fine administration.[143]

The 1834 commissioners' report had portrayed the role of the workhouse as one of deterrence for the pauper, and of providing necessary shelter and relief to the aged and infirm. For the able-bodied who did enter the workhouse, it was suggested that through work and personal regulation it would provide a place of 'wholesome restraint'. Chadwick argued that 'suitable employment' would contribute to the 'amendment' of the pauper. The specific programmes tailored around each group could function without interference or 'evil consequences' of mixing categories of the poor through rigorous spatial separation.[144] Evidence was also cited in the report of the usefulness of institutional uniforms, of women's hair braided and hidden under caps – a clear marker of appropriately contained femininity. Uniforms not only saved money, but in the instance cited, ensured that if women left the house, 'they were known and liable to observation'.[145]

In the Northumbrian workhouses such separation and strict superintendence was pursued if possible, although here as elsewhere the general rule applied that 'the smaller the union, the less likely it was to have special provision for any class of pauper, except perhaps the children'.[146] While the Newcastle Union workhouse was comparatively large, Gateshead was too small to allow rigorous classification and separation within the building, a factor cited as contributing to two women becoming pregnant within the workhouse in 1874.[147] The separation deemed necessary to secure propriety among the poor extended beyond sleeping quarters. Work spaces and dining areas, it was envisaged in the report, should be similarly segregated,[148] ensuring that the clearly designated function of each space was maintained physically as well as morally, and not subject to transgression. Certainly local evidence indicates that spatial boundaries were not recognised by 'disorderly' inmates who used the sometime-privacy of workrooms for prohibited activities. In Newcastle, in the old poorhouse of St Nicholas's parish, an eighteen-year-old pauper, Elizabeth Atkinson, was interrogated on two occasions about having sexual relations with two male paupers. On both occasions the men involved were discharged from the house, and Elizabeth was confined to a strongroom and fed bread and water.[149]

The duties assigned to officials in the workhouses again suggest that

143 Clerk to Poor Law Commissioners, 3 Oct. 1840, Newcastle Union correspondence, 1834–40, ibid. MH 12/9096.
144 *Poor law inquiry*, 1834 Report, 175, 173.
145 Ibid. 174.
146 M. A. Crowther, 'The later years of the workhouse', in Thane, *Origins of British social policy*, 36–55 at p. 38.
147 F. W. D. Manders, *A history of Gateshead*, Gateshead 1973, 225.
148 *Poor law inquiry*, 1834 Report, 172.
149 Workhouse Visitors' Book, St Nicholas's parish, 12 Feb. 1828, 11 Oct. 1829, NRO, EP 86/124.

scrutiny of female able-bodied paupers was particularly pronounced. In the Bellingham workhouse, for example, papers on the respective duties of master and matron show that the former was in charge of accounts, and the employ- ment and supervision of men, while the latter attended to housekeeping matters and the work and supervision of women and children. Yet while the tasks outlined were roughly equivalent, no mention was made of the moral superintendence of the males. The matron, however, was ordered explicitly to 'pay attention to the Moral conduct and orderly behaviour of the female paupers and pauper children, to see that they are clean and decent in their dress and persons and to train them up in such employment as will best fit them for service'.[150] The conflation of domesticity with femininity in the workhouse was entrenched with the assignment of sewing, mending and laundering to the old and infirm women as well as to mothers of young chil- dren. That ubiquitous symbol of female working-class labour, the mangle, was found as readily in the workhouse and the Pauper Lunatic Asylum,[151] as in the homes of poor women who laboured to remain outside the institution.

As the meticulous construction of spaces and strictly ordered routines within the workhouse proceeded, so the bodies of the poor were constructed as more specifically or potentially disordered. This opposition of order and disorder constituted a discursive regime in which the more that individual women's bodies were the objects of discipline and surveillance, thus making them 'fit' for relief, the more that, in general terms, 'woman' connoted disorder. Through regimes of work, prayer and close regulation of activities, self-regulation would be promoted, containing the 'excessive' behaviour which was deemed to contribute to pauperism. Once in the workhouse, the rules within the institution subjected inmates to a new and further process of labelling, where potentially they could become 'offenders' if they broke those rules. And pending any self-regulatory transformation, the workhouse offi- cials could impose punishments such as those meted out to Elizabeth Atkinson, which were enacted upon and through the body by controlling movement beyond the workhouse for periods of up to six months, and denying food apart from bread and water. These forms of discipline, which re-established strict boundaries of order, were standard institutional fare in the nineteenth century. Yet their meaning here was in some ways overwritten by the particular conceptions upon which the regime of the workhouse was founded. Within the workhouse, punishment not only brought immediate control within the space of the institution, but could be linked to a broader attempt to inculcate habits of self-regulation: whether through work, rules or punishments in the workhouse, the production of docile, well-contained

---

[150] 'Duties of the matron', article 20, Bellingham Union correspondence, 1840, PRO, MH 12/8964.
[151] Report of Workhouse Committee to Guardians, 30 Aug. 1861, Poor Law Guardians' minute book, 1860–2, TWAS 359/1/14; Newcastle upon Tyne Borough Pauper Lunatic Asylum Report, 1865, TWAS 359/371, 8.

bodies and moral behaviour would be secured. The transformatory power of the institution lay in its role in effecting such successful self-regulatiory impulses that they would operate outside the space of the institution itself, once individuals had left and returned to an unregulated cultural milieu. It is important that punishments in the workhouse required the 'compliance' of the offender in order for them be carried out. The master or matron had no power to direct punishment unless an inmate 'chose' to remain in the institution, highlighting again the self-regulatory underpinnings of such regimes.

As well as punishments for the introduction of alcohol and opium into the workhouse, both forbidden items, the Guardians' minute book for Newcastle reveals that in a number of cases, general unspecified charges of 'disorderliness' were frequently levelled against women.[152] Apart from instances where women disregarded the spatial codes and regimes of disciplined behaviour in the workhouse thereby transgressing the boundaries constructed between orderliness and disorderliness, the most common infringements which led to formal prosecution outside the workhouse system itself were petty theft, usually accompanied by women absconding from the house. Jane Johnston and Margaret Robertson from Berwick were both sentenced to three months' hard labour for 'scaling the walls of the establishment' late one night with (unspecified) Union property in tow.[153] Disorderly behaviour resulting in damage to property led similarly to legal prosecution. Mary Dunn of the same Union had attempted to diminish her sewing work by secretly throwing material out of the window of the workroom. When discovered, she was 'very insolent', and she was denied a portion of her supper. Dunn then 'commenced an assault', throwing the little supper she had out of the window as well, and then smashing sixteen panes of glass in the workhouse.[154]

The lines of resistance which women followed in the workhouses were usually less specific. General 'bad' behaviour, rudeness, smuggling in prohibited goods and reluctance to work were common expressions of resentment against the physical and moral restraints of workhouse life, particularly, but not exclusively, among younger women.[155] The regulatory mechanisms within the institution appeared to be subject to quite constant challenge and subversion, suggesting that the 'transformatory' power of workhouse experience was secondary to the power of surveillance and correction as a means of securing orderliness. Yet in considering such modes of correction and surveillance, and in particular the ways in which these operated for women, some interesting issues emerge from the evidence which warrant consideration.

---

152 For example, Poor Law Guardians' minute book entries, 30 Aug. 1861, 20 Sept. 1861, TWAS 359/1/14.
153 *Berwick Advertiser*, 29 Apr. 1843, 5.
154 Ibid. 6 May 1843, 4.
155 In 1892 Margaret Henderson who was thought to be about 70 years old was locked up for 11 hours with bread and water for refusing to work: correspondence and newspaper report on Margaret Henderson, Aug. 1892, Newcastle Union correspondence, Jun.–Dec. 1892, PRO, MH 12/9192.

The first and most obvious issue relates to the ways in which surveillance was conducted. Who oversaw the maintenance of 'appropriate' feminine behaviour in the workhouse? While the matrons were charged with the task as part of their work, at times it emerges that other women who were inmates were involved in the regulation of behavioural standards. In Elizabeth Atkinson's case, for example, it was not the matron, but other female inmates and a young servant who variously observed her in the company of men, followed her, and reprimanded one of the men involved before the offences became known to officials.[156] While it is impossible to determine the motivations of these women, given Atkinson's 'weak-mindedness' it may have been seen as action taken to protect the young woman from persistent sexual advances. Whatever the particular motivation however, to perceive surveillance in the workhouse and the imposition of moral control as being imposed from above upon a uniformly reluctant population of female paupers would be to miss some of the more interesting insights which the material suggests about the complicated relationship between power, resistance and constructions of femininity within that location.

Among the more routine accounts of disorderly conduct and boisterous activity among the female inmates of the workhouses, a second theme emerges: that of the behaviour and morality of workhouse officials and employees chosen by respective boards to supervise and contribute to workhouses as orderly, clean and respectable establishments. Again, beyond any imperatives within poor law policy which were predicated on the construction of strict distinctions between 'deserving' and 'undeserving' poor, in practice the focus upon the conduct of employees illustrates that women who were paid for their labour in the workhouse, no less than those officially designated as female paupers, negotiated the discursive boundaries of orderly and disorderly femininity.

The hierarchy of female labour within the workhouse extended from the matron and schoolmistress in larger workhouses, to general servants. While the matron and schoolmistress earned relatively good wages, and often had lodgings and food provided, pay for more junior staff and servants was generally low and resulted in a high rate of staff changes. In the Glendale Union in particular, officials bemoaned the incidence of young female servants leaving to work for private families for apparently 'no reason other than the desire for change'. The region's broader agricultural hiring practices and culture of 'flitting', it was believed, contributed to patterns of unreliability and over-mobility among indoor servants as well: for female servants 'as a class to stay longer than twelve months in one situation is quite the exception'.[157]

Employees inside the workhouses in the region were dismissed for 'failings'

---

[156] Workhouse Visitors' Book, St Nicholas's parish, 14 Oct. 1829, NRO, EP 86/124.

[157] William Wightman to Poor Law Board, 30 Apr. 1859, Glendale Union correspondence, 1853–61, PRO, MH 12/9022; William Wightman to Poor Law Board, 19 Nov. 1866, Glendale Union correspondence, 1862–71, ibid. MH 12/9023.

associated more commonly with the paupers themselves.[158] The influence of employees upon inmates as well was closely scrutinised. In some cases those given the responsibility of regulating paupers were in fact accused of promoting behaviour among them which was defined as 'disorderly', recruiting relief recipients in schemes of minor peculation and other activities which brought the employees financial rewards. Mrs Armstrong had her appointment as schoolmistress terminated when she 'induced . . . two child inmates to abscond' under promise of getting them situations, and deliberately circumvented the bureaucratic procedures through which pauper children were placed in outside employment.[159]

For women employed in the workhouse, surveillance as to their character and consistent propriety was certainly in evidence, and again situates them clearly within broader discourses about feminine morality. Soon after the appointment of Mary Fitzpatrick as schoolmistress in 1856, allegations about her moral standing were raised by one of the Guardians. She had 'com[e] under a moral cloud' in relation to her marital status and other aspects of her personal history (she had left her husband). Fitzpatrick's response to the allegations in a letter to the Board showed that she felt keenly the assumptions of immorality which were commonly made about women in her position:

> I felt it to be my duty to leave [my husband] rather than to comply with his orders that I do that which was revolting to my feelings and at variance with morality and virtue. As to my character since I have been a wife, I hope and believe that the worst that can be said of me is that I have been in poverty but that I have been honest and virtuous and I am proud and thankful to think that there are respectable parties who can testify as to my moral character from the time that I was married up to the present hour. . . .[160]

Fitzpatrick supported her character with marriage documents and birth certificates for her two children, and no action was taken. In her letter, she enunciates quite explicitly the difficulties of negotiating the duties of wife and of preserving feminine virtue: while these duties were usually construed as being complementary, the clash which had arisen for Fitzpatrick between the two and her determination to deal with the problem in a particular way, did not effect a complete resolution, but created a space in which later suspicions about her morality could be fuelled. And characteristic of many women of her class, Fitzpatrick herself showed an awareness of how commonplace was the elision of economic status with moral character, through her specific denial of the connection: she was in poverty, but honest and virtuous none the less.

158 Poor Law Guardians' minute book, 21 Dec. 1855, TWAS 359/1/11; Clerk to Poor Law Commission, 8 Oct. 1838, South Shields Union correspondence, 1834–40, PRO, MH 12/3201.
159 Ibid. May 8 1856.
160 Mary Fitzpatrick to Thomas Ridley, 25 July 1856, Poor Law Guardians' minute book, 1854–6, TWAS 359/1/11.

The scrutiny of lesser employees by senior employees to ensure conformity to specific moral standards was at times woven with even more coercive and tragic elements. Dinah Armstrong, a servant in the Glendale Union workhouse, was becoming 'so stout' that Matron Margaret Hall suspected she was pregnant, and sacked her. Dinah's mother went to the workhouse with Dinah to take issue with Hall, who admitted that she had never seen Dinah with a man. Dinah's mother flew into a rage and left, whereupon the matron called for a doctor to examine Dinah Armstrong. 'The poor thing cried bitterly', wrote her father to the commissioners in London, 'and said no if I am to go before a Doctor I will go home and have my Mother with me.' The internal examination was conducted against Dinah's wishes none the less, and revealed that she was not pregnant. Afterwards, Dinah went home 'and compleatly brock [sic] down and said she could not go and we could not advise her back. . . . In my Humble opinion, gentlemen, my daughter has been badly used'.[161] The Clerk of the Union agreed that the action of the matron had been 'unjustifiable . . . involving serious loss of character to the Servant', and wrote that the local committee of inquiry had duly expressed 'their disapprobation of the Matron's conduct'.[162] However, while the matron was not dismissed, the following year the Clerk reported that she had resigned: 'she has never done well after the fracas about the Medical examination of the Servant Girl', and the stress of the case culminated for Hall in an attempt to 'commit suicide by cutting her throat and also one of her arms'.[163]

For Margaret Hall, the pressures of moral scrutiny were exerted in different directions, as she occupied a dual position as both the subject and object of surveillance. Her necessarily 'scrupulous' standards were measured not only in relation to her personal conduct, but were to be reflected as well in her ability to ensure the proper conduct and demeanour of her employees. While both Margaret Hall and Dinah Armstrong bore the obvious physical and mental burdens of Hall's misjudgements, more generally and perhaps less immediately, the cost of 'proving' respectability for poor women both within and outside the workhouse was considerable. Hints of the cost borne by some women was given in the records of the Newcastle Pauper Lunatic Asylum, another institutional arm of the poor law which housed as patients those paupers whose mental illnesses and behaviour rendered them 'unmanageable' in the context of the Union workhouse. The medical superintendent of the asylum in 1865 argued that in Northumberland inmates were particularly turbulent, owing perhaps, he believed, to 'the sturdy independence of the northern labourer [which] still lives in the darkened intellect'.[164]

Diagnoses of women in the asylum showed that, characteristically, female

---

[161] William Armstrong to Poor Law Commission, 1 June 1864, Glendale Union correspondence 1862–71, PRO, MH 12/9023.

[162] William Wightman to Poor Law Commission, 18 June 1864, ibid.

[163] William Wightman to N. E. Hunt, Poor Law Inspector, 19 Mar. 1865, ibid.

[164] Newcastle upon Tyne Borough Pauper Lunatic Asylum annual report, 1865, TWAS 359/371, 13–14.

insanity was linked to specifically female biology. As well as these constructions, however, there was some recognition of the role of poverty causing stress and mental illness. The 1867 Asylum report declared that 'the condition of semi-starvation in which many of the poorer classes of our large towns must live', was a potent contributor to lunacy.[165] While acknowledging that lunacy is 'a tangled area brambled with problems of causation, perception, and evidence', John Walton has commented upon a more general pattern of poverty causing mental illnesses, a pattern particularly evident in contemporary patient records relating to 'hard-pressed working-class wives and mothers'.[166]

Certainly, the notes compiled on Newcastle patients when they were admitted reveal that the theme of poverty loomed in the women's own accounts and concerns about their lives. Sarah Greener was admitted after her husband deserted, and she was discovered wandering the streets 'in a destitute and near naked condition'. Jane Clark was admitted because of suicidal depression 'from anxiety about money matters'. The physical conditions of crowded urban living, lack of privacy and high infant mortality in the slums were also reference points for patients. Catherine Russell spoke constantly of her acute sadness over the loss of her young children one of whom as a baby, she alleged, she had 'killed' in Manchester (although there was no evidence to support a record of infanticide): 'I am a bad woman, I have many things on my mind. . . . I am sometimes haunted by the thought of my three dead children.'[167]

In general, constant vigilance had to be met with constant proofs of propriety and self-regulatory behaviour, and where such was not achieved, women could and did fall prey to an array of general assumptions about the low moral standards of working-class women at work, at home and in their poverty. In the workhouse, the avenues of resistance available to women were few, with more explicit resistance resulting in punishment or formal prosecution. For those who absconded or left the house voluntarily, the freedom from institutional control meant a return to conditions which, none the less, were shot through with similar, broader contradictions and tensions which clustered around women's economic and moral identities. For employees within the workhouse, there were also clear economic disincentives to engaging in actual modes of behaviour which ran counter to dominant constructions of docility and orderliness for women: even the suspicion of disorderliness was sufficient at times to see employment terminated.

The 'stigma' of workhouse life carried with it particular meanings for the female poor. Crowther has argued in relation to a later period that the stigma

---

165 Ibid. 1867, 15.
166 John Walton, 'Poverty and lunacy: some thoughts on directions for future research', *Society for the Social History of Medicine* xxviii (1986), 64–7 at p. 65.
167 These cases appear in orders for the reception of pauper patients, TWAS 490, cases 114, 145, and medical certificates of examination of lunatics at police courts and recommendations for detention, 1883, TWAS 359/358, case nos 114, 98, 55, 43, 8, 46.

of the workhouse varied depending upon the specialisation of institutional functions: that less stigma was attached, for example, to the use of a union's hospital facilities than to seeking relief in the workhouse proper. McCord maintains that in the earlier nineteenth century, a sense of disgrace attaching to workhouse residence in the region was not keenly felt, and Crowther cites oral evidence that at the Newcastle workhouse by the twentieth century, 'they were queueing up to get in',[168] although she states that the impressions gained from oral sources vary considerably. While arguing that the stigma of workhouse life was sufficient to keep people from seeking much-needed relief, however, she concludes that in many respects, the stigma of the workhouse was not peculiar, but was one which has been attached to, and felt within, a range of modern institutions.[169] Lynn Hollen Lees has argued persuasively in her study of London as well, that in assessing 'stigma', historians should be aware of the possibility of strategic exploitation of poor relief services by poor women, mainly outside the workhouse, but at times also within it.[170] In Northumberland, just as Hollen Lees found in her study of London, there is evidence of women, for example, using the workhouse at times to house their children while they sought or undertook paid employment outside the house.[171] The north-eastern evidence would support Hollen Lees's argument that avoidance of poor relief negotiations for many women was impossible, and the task before them was to gain much-needed resources through 'the more desirable forms of aid' such as out-relief where possible.[172]

Yet the evidence regarding the stigma of the workhouse is rather more blurred. Against any positive, strategic use of the workhouse by women for childcare and temporary shelter, uses which at times were resisted by poor law officials, there is more ample evidence of a sense of fear and avoidance attaching to the workhouse. Such fear is evidenced in the applications to All Saints' parish in the 1820s and 1830s, as well as in individual recollections, such as that of a woman who had worked as a bondager over the border and who was so ashamed of the time she spent in the workhouse that she was unwilling to speak of it to her interviewer.[173] The workhouse was also at times the site where women were confronted with close reminders of the costs, not merely of poverty, but of the existing poor conditions for women outside the house, as some with specific work-related illnesses sought indoor relief. It was

[168] N. McCord, 'The implementation of the 1834 Poor Law Amendment Act on Tyneside', *International Review of Social History* xiv (1969), 90–108 at p. 105; Crowther, 'Later years of the workhouse', 53. The oral evidence Crowther cites however, as she points out, is scanty and is drawn mainly from visitors and workers in the workhouses, rather than from inmates themselves.

[169] Ibid.

[170] Lynn Hollen Lees, 'The survival of the unfit: welfare policies and family maintenance in nineteenth-century London', in Peter Mandler (ed.), *The uses of charity: the poor on relief in the nineteenth-century metropolis*, Philadelphia 1990, 68–91 at p. 85.

[171] Poor Law Guardians' minute book, 16 Feb. 1855, TWAS 359/1/11.

[172] Hollen Lees, 'Survival of the unfit', 88.

[173] Taylor, 'Days of the bondager', 8.

to the Newcastle workhouse for example, that Elizabeth Ryan went, suffering from acute lead poisoning, to suffer her last days and then die.[174]

The evidence across the nineteenth century, when positioned within the broader context of gender meanings and experiences, would also support an alternative interpretation of the stigma of the workhouse in relation to other forms of institutional regimentation than that suggested by Crowther. The inextricable links between economic and moral failure which were constructed around the younger and able-bodied female paupers, the assumption of unfettered sexuality or the suspicion of such which was given ample airing, as was well-known by both inmates and employees, and for which there was no direct equivalent for the male pauper, meant that the workhouse carried a more particular gendered stigma for some women. It was a site where traces of discourse about femininity, disordered sexuality and poverty were anchored and given material expression, and within which the strands connecting these categories were woven more tightly.

Certainly, the 'taint' of pauperism and the risk of exposure to pernicious influences in the workhouse continued to preoccupy officials in the region throughout the century. While Chadwick in 1834 had enunciated some transformative mission for the workhouse, increasingly the solution forged by poor law officials in the north, as elsewhere, was one of ever-increasing specialisation and separation to ensure, not the 'transformation' of single mothers and the indigent, but the 'rescue' of children from a future of pauperism ordained by heredity. After the passage of the General Education Act in 1870 in particular, a measure which a supporter had claimed (with that sweeping rhetoric perhaps reserved for political speech-making) would ensure that 'no child in the country should henceforth be allowed to grow up in gross ignorance',[175] regional relief officials at the Poor Law Conference in 1872 discussed the means by which pauper children could be best educated. Theirs was a vision which again reflected the different underpinnings of poverty relief for males and females. While boys, argued Charles Bosanquet, could be catered for in larger reformatories and training schools, 'yet it was not enough for girls'. As well as systematic training, girls required 'home life'. A Cumbrian delegate maintained that the particular stain of the workhouse for girls was so clear that 'it can need little to be said', and then went on to elaborate in detail the processes of degradation where their natural female affection and tenderness, having 'no outlet', burst out instead in the certain direction of shame and ruination.[176]

While specialised training was harder to organise in small towns, in Newcastle prior to 1872 the training of pauper children had occurred both

---

174 Sherard, *Cry of the poor*, 144.
175 D. Main, 'Reformatory schools and the Elementary Education Act of 1870', *Proceedings of the National Association for the Promotion of the Social Sciences (Newcastle)* (1870), 289.
176 'The boarding-out system', *Conference on poor law administration*, 1872, 18, 16, 11 (NCL, DY 56, no. 9).

within the workhouse, and through private charitable organisations such as the Girls' Ragged and Industrial School. Such enterprises in the region confirm the more general relevance of Ellen Ross's findings in London: 'the distinction between private philanthropic and state or municipal welfare measures' is at times difficult to draw, since there was substantial overlap between both the activities of the agencies, and the personnel involved in them.[177] Both the (private) Ragged School and the Workhouse Visiting Committee trained and placed girls as domestic servants, although the results of the activity were questioned at times by the female volunteer workers themselves. The Workhouse Visiting Committee in 1874, for example, expressed grave concern that 'accounts of the Girls leaving the House . . . have not been so satisfactory as they desire . . . [they] believe the reason greatly to lie in the circumstance that no control is exercised over the Girls immediately they leave the house', and that no formal avenue for ongoing regulation of their conditions existed. Boys who were apprenticed out to trades were checked annually, and such a system should be extended to the girls. Those householders who employed the girls should be compelled to enter an agreement to oversee the girls' moral, as well as domestic, training in the course of their employment.[178]

The girls from the Ragged School were subject to close monitoring by a staff of matron and teachers, as well as philanthropic volunteers such as Elizabeth Spence Watson, who concerned themselves with the minute organisation of training, clothing and feeding the girls, and the emigration of a few of them.[179] While specialised schooling was increasingly provided, the vision of separate living for pauper children was achieved more slowly. It was not until 1901, for example, that the first separate cottages for poor children were opened in the region, by poor law authorities in Gateshead,[180] while the vision remained beyond the means of the smaller outlying unions.

None the less, the gradual shift in focus to the children of the poor from about 1870 onwards attested to a growing concern that 'progress' should be measurable in part with reference to physical and moral 'improvement' across successive generations. While the objects of these specific forms of relief were children and adolescents, the posited natural links – moral, spiritual, physical – between women and their children inevitably drew poor mothers into discourses of generational advance and transformation. Attempts to regulate children therefore, also implicitly or explicitly involved the definition of boundaries around the 'good' and 'bad' mother. Just as women in the lead works in the 1890s faced exclusion, not merely on the basis of their

[177] Ellen Ross, 'Hungry children: housewives and London charity, 1870–1918', in Mandler, Uses of charity, 161–96 at p. 188.
[178] Report of the Workhouse Visiting Committee, Poor Law Guardians' minute book, 5 June 1874, TWAS 359/1/20.
[179] Thirty-fourth annual report of the Girls' Ragged and Industrial Schools, n.p. 1881 (NCL, DY 56/13).
[180] Manders, History of Gateshead, 226.

individual position, but because of the responsibilities their female biology 'necessarily' implied for future generations, so it was that poor women were seen as literally and metaphorically embodying the hopes and fears of reformers in the arena of poor relief directed at children. And again, in Northumberland as elsewhere, it was mothers, 'despite their anomalous civic status . . . who were the "heads" of families when children were the issue, and they would be the ones to conduct the family's public business' in the main,[181] with poor law and other public officials, thereby being subject to further scrutiny of their personal moral standards and character.

The scope for visions of 'proper' and 'improper' femininity to influence local relief decisions throughout the period which operated clearly in relation to poor women in the region was considerable. While in many respects the legislation of 1834 neglected to consider the variety of circumstances of the poor woman, and was built upon the foundation of the 'independent male labourer', it drew upon stereotypes of immorality among the female poor which were constantly invoked throughout the century, and which in some important ways determined the discursive dimensions of the negotiating field within which women sought relief. The Northumbrian poor relief material suggests that tensions between local and central officials around the issue of poor women arose quite frequently, but the dilemmas which sprang from their multiple (and in contemporary terms, sharply conflicting) identities as mothers and workers were never resolved. Further, the 'solutions' to confusion about the poor, their classification, and their treatment envisaged both in the 1834 Report and certainly by later reformers – of constant and detailed scrutiny of the poor themselves, in tandem with the introduction of more 'scientific' and systematic regimes of poverty-management – provided no simple solution, but instead encouraged conditions where the many variations in circumstances and needs of the poor if anything rendered more obvious the clumsy inadequacies of the dichotomy of the deserving/undeserving poor.

While poor relief services provided a range of basic resources to the very poor, it was argued by some social commentators and philanthropists that the individual needs and circumstances of the poor required more specialised individual treatment and intervention than relief officials or relief policy could provide. Concerns about the conditions and inappropriate treatment of women in the workhouses, and particularly in the casual wards, were also fuelled by a rash of investigative reports from the 1860s onwards.[182] Certainly, as McCord and Rushton have argued, the readiness of parishioners and ratepayers to finance relief provision was always limited.[183] Perhaps more important, however, than long-existing economic pressures upon public

---

181 Ross, 'Hungry children', 185.
182 Vorspan, 'Vagrancy and the new poor law', 66–8.
183 McCord, 'Ratepayers and social policy', 30; Rushton, 'The poor law, the parish and the community', 149–50.

authorities was that in the specific context of the later nineteenth century, the discourse of poverty had shifted, in line with broader conceptions of progress and its achievement in Britain. The moral imperatives of the Victorian bourgeoisie, the increasing concern with 'respectability' among sections of the working class itself,[184] and towards the turn of the century the predominance of discourses of 'scientific' management of race and generation, home and family, all coalesced to ensure that private charitable institutions remained centrally important in the arena of relief provision, and women's experiences of poverty.

David Thomson contends that in the nineteenth century, and indeed in other periods, there was never one single debate about poverty and its relief. Rather, 'society in effect conducts many welfare debates simultaneously, one for each of a wide range of possible welfare claimants. The degree of collective commitment to the welfare of individuals depends critically upon the characteristics of the people in question.' For poor women, appraisal of their characteristics proceeded not merely with reference to some general view of poverty, nor with reference to a general view of femininity which was deemed applicable to all women. If, as Thomson maintains, debate about poor relief was at its core 'more of a multi-stranded cable than a thick wire',[185] then the strands of both class and gender were critically interwoven in discourses about the female poor. Poor women in many ways experienced a distinctive kind of poverty, the 'poverty' not only of their class but of their gender, a poverty inscribed with meaning around the pivot of their sexuality. Poverty for women, no less than work or domestic life, was a material and cultural experience which was understood, negotiated and at times resisted through the site of their gendered bodies and identities. Moreover, discussion of relief for women was, crucially, a debate which both reflected and reinforced broader conceptions of the female poor, in the context of workplace and home, as much as in the context of the relief office and workhouse.

To separate poor law policy and experience, or poor relief provision from other aspects of working-class life for women, is to ignore the multiple connections and interactions between these areas of discourse and experience. The notion of gendered identity being simultaneously constructed and actively negotiated in particular sites and in the realm of particular experience is also evident, at times perhaps even more clearly, in the records of Newcastle's charitable institutions. The following chapter considers philanthropic activity in Newcastle in the second half of the nineteenth century, and explores the relationship between this activity and the visions of femininity which underpinned so much philanthropic initiative. The study of charities reveals, however, that the area was not without its own tensions and

---

184 See Ross, 'Not the sort that would sit on the doorstep', 39–59; Brian Harrison, 'Class and gender in modern British labour history', *Past and Present* cxxiv (1989), 121–58 at pp. 128–9.
185 Thomson, 'Welfare in the past', 23.

contradictions, as the committees and central organising bodies of institutions sought to develop 'successful' techniques in the management of the female poor in particular, and attempted to 'remoralise' and 'reorder' the bodies and identities of working-class women and girls. Further, while many such enterprises were fundamentally concerned with the project of 're-making' poor women, the material shows that at times for women themselves, the concern was certainly not to acquiesce passively in these processes, but was rather to interact with them with reference to their own set of economic priorities and cultural practices in nineteenth-century Northumberland. The strategies and tactics adopted by poor women themselves as they tried to 'make do', therefore, constitute the second, interrelated theme of the chapter.

6

Being 'Re-Made' and 'Making Do': Working-Class Women and Philanthropy

While the commemorative monument to Stephenson stood prominently for public viewing in central Newcastle, its pedestal flanked by four figures representing the prosperity and progress of industry upon which the region's reputation was built, another more private and shadowy symbol of the end of the Victorian period was evoked in the work of Jack Common. Born in 1902 and growing up in working-class Newcastle, experiencing a family life where his mother scraped and pinched to make ends meet and often drank to excess after a painful accident which left her semi-crippled, Common later wrote about the bed of conception and childbirth where his own life began. This more intimate Newcastle 'monument' was encircled by four sinister imaginary figures which promised, not progress and prosperity, but a future of struggle and hardship. One figure, certainly, was a labourer, but was no glorious symbol of the dignity and independence of employment: he was 'four-belted as a ghostly navvy', and 'swung his pick in promise of future hard work' – but just hard work. As for the others

> One, somewhat like a tramp, chalked upon the bedstead the sign which means 'No hand-outs here' . . . a blear-eyed one, faintly lit up, lifted the bottle; and one looking like a magistrate, made a bitter mouth over the syllables of an unspoken 'Borstal'.

These 'bad fairies' of physical toil, want, drunkenness and criminality loomed over the yet-to-be-born child of poor parents. While Common conceded that there were possibilities for unknown 'blessings' to come to the child, yet 'you can count on the sad probabilities of its likely fate as you count its toes – and the piggy gets none'. From the beginning, Common 'at once came under the minus-sign which society had already placed upon my parents'. Reminiscent of the fictional Tullivers, they were people, he wrote, who were 'of no account'.[1]

As the sites where family relations unfolded and where negotiations of gender, class and experiences of poverty took place, the physical space of urban households like the one in which Common lived as a boy may have been fixed, but the meanings and images constructed around and within them were not. The divisions between public and private which

[1] Jack Common, *Kiddar's luck*, London 1951, repr. Gateshead 1975, 6.

predominated in the ordered Victorian worlds of work and domestic life, divisions which were related in turn to notions of progress and morality, saw the households of the poor occupy a curious and ambiguous status. Generally, 'home' was a territory of potentials, whose material and cultural significance was wrought by the people occupying it, and no-one was more central to this process of forging meaning than the adult female – whether as single woman, wife, mother, widow, or even as an absent figure. It was in relation to the status and behaviour of the woman that the 'essential' character of the household was most readily understood by those outside it, and possibly those within it as well. In an ideally-ordered bourgeois family, the domestic responsibilities of wife and mother should, it was held, operate to ensure that the household provided both a private refuge for male breadwinners and a meticulously well-organised gendered training ground for children. Women in this idealised conception were instrumental in maintaining respectability, independence and individual morality across generations, and the household was the place where these critical traits were created and nourished. It was a place of privacy from the external world, its overall form subject to scrutiny, but its daily functions ideally free from 'rude' incursions from the public sphere.

Yet while homes could be nurseries of Victorian values, with women acting as both explicit and exemplary overseers, so too could they be 'nurseries of vice',[2] perversely inverted in their function by women whose femininity was 'disordered', and in turn disordering. In this guise, the healthy privacy of the household could be distorted to become instead a dangerous secrecy, the home itself the presumed locus of immorality and indigence, an occluded space secreting its vices against scrutiny. Paul Johnson has argued, citing Brian Harrison, that 'respectability' was 'a process, a dialogue with oneself and one's fellows, never a fixed position . . .'.[3] Johnson further maintains that 'respectability was not a concrete attribute, a tangible thing'.[4] While the autobiographical accounts of Common and of Catherine Cookson, and the historical work of Ellen Ross in particular[5] attest to the constant and often subtle work of forging and maintaining respectability in support of Harrison's formulation, these sources also suggest that in both the Victorian and Edwardian periods 'respectability' often was tangible. As Barret-Ducrocq suggests, it was measured 'by a set of easily seen qualities' such as sobriety and modesty which were materially coded through clothing and household facades. Moreover, an equivalent system of behavioural and material codes betrayed the presumed prevalence of 'counter-values' among

---

2   Mr J. Price, *NDG*, 1885, 280.
3   Brian Harrison, 'Traditions of respectability in British labour history', in *Peaceable kingdom: stability and change in modern Britain*, Oxford 1982, 161, and cited in Johnson, *Saving and spending*, 161.
4   Ibid.
5   Common, *Kiddar's luck*; Catherine Cookson, *Our Kate*, London 1969; Ross, 'Not the sort that would sit on the doorstep', 39–59.

the working class: to many bourgeois observers, their 'outward appearance, the manners, customs, and culture of the people were unequivocal signs of their immorality'.[6] The nuances of respectability within the working class could be lost upon reformers positioned on the margins who peered fleetingly into the overcrowded streets of the slums, and too readily drew conclusions based upon an overall first appearance which was 'identified with essence'.[7]

The 'secrets' of life in poor working-class households, especially in the first half of the nineteenth century, were more often deemed to be all-too-readily imaginable, than ones requiring minute exploration. The assumption that 'external appearance was an exact reflection of internal reality'[8] shored up undifferentiated visions of 'the poor' and their life styles. Even by the end of the century, the influential Charity Organisation Society worker Helen Bosanquet noted the insensitivity among outsiders to the 'manifold gradations' and experiences within the working class. In its attitude towards the poor, the 'rest of the community . . . is somewhat in the position of the spectators of a melodrama: it varies between the wildest sympathy with wrongs which are largely imaginary and righteous indignation against sins which are hardly less so'. She counselled social workers and reformers on the need for more 'patient study' of the objects of relief.[9]

Bosanquet's reference to melodrama in this context provides a useful exploratory framework as the historian considers visions of the poor and their households in nineteenth-century Northumberland, and the frameworks of relief provision erected around these visions by private charitable organisations in the region. Martha Vicinus suggests that Victorian melodrama can be viewed, in its representation of the 'clash between good and evil . . . [as] the means for exploring social and political issues in personal terms', and, in particular, can be read in relation to 'contemporary concerns about class and gender'. Combining 'mythic belief' with historically-specific conditions, melodrama saw the playing out in a popular cultural form of those tensions and contradictions brought by industrialisation and social change. Although some characters engaged in rebellion and resistance, melodrama's essentially conservative resolutions reinforced the centrality of the patriarchal family and traditional social and moral values.[10]

While melodrama was enjoyed by working-class audiences, and women in

---

[6] Françoise Barret-Ducrocq, Love in the time of Victoria: sexuality, class, and gender in Victorian London, trans. John Howe, London 1991, 8–9.

[7] Ibid. 8.

[8] Ibid.

[9] Helen Bosanquet, Rich and poor, London 1896, 4, and The strength of the people, 2nd edn, London 1903, 313, cited in R. I. McKibbin, 'Social class and social observation in Edwardian England', Transactions of the Royal Historical Society 5th ser. xxviii (1978), 175–99 at p. 185.

[10] Martha Vicinus, ' "Helpless and unfriended": nineteenth-century domestic melodrama', New Literary History xiii (1981), 127–43 at pp. 128, 141. Judith Walkowitz also exploits the concept of Victorian melodrama around different texts: City of dreadful delight, 85–102.

particular, the 'melodrama' of charitable activity in nineteenth-century Northumberland was for the most part a characteristically bourgeois pastime, although none the less a similarly feminised one. The ways in which the charities operated, the conceptions of poverty, femininity and social progress which they embodied, the combination of stereotype and particular circumstance which animated charitable activity and the conservative visions of women and the family underlying these projects, bore many of the hallmarks outlined by Vicinus. In some respects, reading the records of charities as 'melodramatic' texts can afford interesting insights into the preoccupations of these charities' benefactors and their (almost exclusively female) volunteer workers, although the metaphor in other respects functions only partially. The records of the charities themselves attest to the constant struggle to encourage poor women to 'correctly' perform in the charitable scripts written for them. While a bourgeois audience may have expected certain resolutions, the poor women who were most centrally involved as participants stepped off charity's carefully-constructed stage (or at least ad libbed and shifted the props), as they negotiated or resisted the roles which they were expected to assume.

'Performing' penitence and re-casting femininity: philanthropy and the mission of transformation

In 1849, a year before the *Newcastle Chronicle* published its *Inquiry into the condition of the poor*, Henry Mayhew interviewed a needlewoman in London about her poverty, and the causes of prostitution among that group of workers. The woman, a widow and occasional prostitute, bemoaned the general lack of understanding of the work conditions of very poor women: 'no-one knows the temptations of us poor girls in want. Gentlefolks can never understand it.' In a way which suggested a preordained pattern of life determined by birth, not dissimilar to that written about by Jack Common, she added significantly, 'If I had been born a lady it wouldn't have been very hard to have acted like one.'[11]

While the opportunity to 'act like a lady' was not celebrated in comedic fantasy until *Pygmalion* was first performed in 1916, before then it belonged in the realm of (unnamed) fantasy none the less. While the adoption of some of the trappings of 'genteel' display through dress by some working-class women was noted, it was a mimicry consistently condemned by urban social reformers as gaudy, inappropriate, and out of place in the environments of working-class life. Yet the notion of 'acting like a lady', the performance of identity appropriate to one's class and gender, attests however fleetingly to an awareness that 'identity', like 'respectability', was forged from a combination

11 E. P. Thompson and Eileen Yeo (eds), *The unknown Mayhew*, Harmondsworth 1973, 177.

of material circumstance, self-definition, and the expectations and assumptions of those with whom one came in contact. It was a combination which was no less relevant to the ways in which the identities of poor working-class women were constructed. The ways in which one 'performed' poverty, and 'acted' a version of working-class femininity in which one displayed individual 'penitence' for the course it had taken so far,[12] were crucial in determining both access to relief, and the manner in which assistance was provided. While the categories of 'deserving' and 'undeserving' poor within legislation and official relief structures were elaborated in a gender/class-based context, so too the activities of private charities and women's negotiations with them were fundamentally influenced by such factors.

What, then, was the character of this private philanthropic and charitable work? In the nineteenth century, general charity – 'the gift of the rich to the poor'[13] – gave way to philanthropic work which was increasingly directed by middle-class women, and was considered by them as a serious vocation.[14] While certain charities such as the Charity for Poor Married Women were recorded by Mackenzie in the 1820s as being 'chiefly supported by the ladies',[15] it was from mid century onwards that female philanthropy expanded considerably. Such philanthropic work aimed to secure well-defined outcomes, including establishing closer relations between those who were assisted and those who provided assistance. In the 1830s, an annual report of one of the older charitable concerns in Newcastle lamented the 'profligacy of manners and disrespect to rank among many of the lower orders' which had supposedly arisen since the beginning of the century; in relation to charity, it was observed, just as 'the objects relieved do not always exhibit external expressions of gratitude to the benefactors, neither do the beneficent and charitable so cheerfully diffuse their wealth as formerly'. Public charity was in a 'critical condition'.[16] The more 'active benevolence'[17] directed towards a particular mission which characterised later charitable endeavour could be viewed partly as a response to this condition.

For the middle-class women who undertook such work, philanthropy could be managed without substantial disruption to their own domestic role (indeed it was portrayed as a 'natural' extension of it), while it provided an opportunity for them to 'take initiative' and broaden bourgeois 'maternal influence' beyond the home.[18] Those domestic roles frequently entailed the

---

[12] 'Performance' here follows the conception developed by Butler, *Gender trouble*, 140–1.

[13] P. Mandler, 'Poverty and charity: an introduction', in Mandler, *Uses of charity*, 1–37 at p.1.

[14] F. Prochaska, *Women and philanthropy in nineteenth-century England*, Oxford 1980, 5–7.

[15] Mackenzie, *Descriptive and historical account*, ii. 521.

[16] Report of the state of the Institution for the Cure and Prevention of Contagious Fever in Newcastle and Gateshead, 1838, TWAS 1547/10, 4.

[17] Ibid. 6.

[18] Martha Vicinus, *Independent women: work and community for single women, 1850–1920*, London 1985, 22.

management and direction of servants who performed housework, and the step from this to the wider management of poor working-class women was a short one indeed. Again, that bourgeois women were so involved immediately renders untenable any simplistic analysis based upon notions of gender oppression: rather, the historian is again alerted to those complex intersections where practices and discourses are structured simultaneously by class formations and gender identities. Bourgeois philanthropists themselves negotiated their identities along gender lines; while from 1892, for example, women acted as Poor Law Guardians in the area, and some involved in charitable work such as Elizabeth Spence Watson both fulfilled this role and continued private work,[19] for other women the more completely feminised environment of some private charitable organisations may have appeared more attractive than the official Boards of Guardians or their associated visiting committees. One member of a ladies' visiting committee complained at the Northern District Poor Law Conference in 1893, for example, that 'Gentlemen . . . were inclined to treat suggestions made by ladies in a facetious way, which did not encourage ladies on the committees.'[20]

The sheer volume of philanthropic work in Newcastle and to a lesser extent in the countryside in the second half of the nineteenth century was remarkable. Norman McCord has claimed that in the region, in terms of relief distributed and funds raised for various ventures, 'it is very clear that unofficial [philanthropy] far outweighed official exertion' from poor law agencies during the period.[21] As well as funds for the provision of 'exceptional' relief during bad weather and trade slumps, and for medical care, the most notable cluster of charities from the 1860s onwards developed around the task of 'rescuing' women labelled as immoral. While the occupation of home-visiting among charity workers was long established in England,[22] it was this work of 'rescue' and training of young women in particular which marked philanthropy and took it to 'new heights'.[23] The 1888 guide to homes and refuges for women in England listed twelve institutions in Newcastle devoted to either a general moral and preventive programme for young women, or more specific training for women who were prostitutes or who were thought to be 'at risk'.[24] Some were attached to major churches. The

19 Elizabeth Spence Watson stood for election as Guardian in Gateshead in 1892. As well as her work with the Ragged School, in the 1880s she became part of a small, influential group which advocated the case work approach of the Charity Organisation Society: Gregson, 'Poor Law and organized charity', 113.
20 'Ladies' Visiting Committees', 22nd Annual Poor Law Conference on Local Government Administration for the Northern District, July 1893, NCL, DY 100/13.
21 Norman McCord, 'The poor law and philanthropy', in Derek Fraser (ed.), *The new poor law in the nineteenth century*, London 1976, 87–110 at p. 97.
22 Prochaska, *Women and philanthropy*, 97.
23 Jane Rendall, *The origins of modern feminism: women in Britain, France and the United States, 1780–1860*, London 1985, 272.
24 *Guide to schools, homes and refuges in England for the benefit of girls and women*, London 1888.

Anglican, Catholic and Jewish communities in the city engaged in specific rescue and training work, while others were non-denominational.

Underlying this activity was what Jane Lewis describes as a type of 'social maternalism', which undoubtedly placed middle-class women in a position to acquire organising skills and to put to use their housekeeping expertise, but which, Jane Rendall has argued, was none the less generally based upon 'a notion of superiority, of class, of education, perhaps of race'.[25] A sense of this superiority, of the mission to transform poor working women through education, and of that group's assumed difference, was conveyed by Elizabeth Spence Watson. Writing to her daughter about the latest round of admissions to the Ragged School, she stated that 'it is really dreadful to see how some people live, and what an utterly different standard of right and wrong they have to those we hold by. . . . How favoured you, dear children & we are compared with many of those around us. It is a great responsibility.'[26] Although motherhood and household experience were the attributes cited as providing a uniquely appropriate training, it was not some generalised celebration of expertise which attached to all women. While late in the century the Mother's Union of the Anglican Church waxed lyrical about 'rich and poor meet[ing] on the common ground of "Motherhood" ', in practice that organisation itself held separate meetings designed for 'educated members and associates', and others to 'appeal more to mothers of the industrial class'.[27] It was the specific bourgeois versions of motherhood and domesticity which were deemed praiseworthy, while the working-class version was deemed to be qualitatively inferior.

Again, the spectre of 'disorder' was invoked in a gender/class-based dichotomy in which bourgeois domesticity was discursively constituted through control, order and cleanliness (although often materially achieved through the labour of working-class employees). The logical trap of bourgeois discourse was that to indicate and establish their own orderliness in the vanguard of progress and civilisation necessarily entailed the assertion of working-class disorderliness, the anchor-point against which that order and stability could be measured. While 'exceptions' and 'gradations' of disorderliness were sometimes specified, and comparisons made between individual working-class households in case studies of the poor, resort to generalisation even among those who studied the internal workings of poor households was commonplace; the problem with the working class, wrote Helen Bosanquet, 'is how to bring them to regard life as anything but a huge chaos. The confusion which reigns in their minds is reflected in their worlds.'[28] And at the

---

[25] Jane Lewis, *Women in England 1870–1950: sexual divisions and social change*, Brighton 1984, 92; Rendall, *Origins of modern feminism*, 262.

[26] Elizabeth Spence Watson to Mabel Watson, 12 Mar. 1884, TWAS 213/173.

[27] *NDG*, Oct. 1902, 149.

[28] Bosanquet, *Rich and poor*, 60, cited in Jane Lewis, 'The working-class wife and mother and state intervention, 1870–1918', in Lewis, *Labour and love*, 99–120 at p. 99.

core of those worlds were families within which women were seen as the guardians both of internal behaviour, and crucial transactions with the wider community which established the measure of its 'respectability', cleanliness, and 'proper' parenting.

Throughout the period, generalisations about inadequate working-class parenting abounded, and the results of this, middle-class reformers feared, could be measured in the numbers of prostitutes and 'uncontrolled' girls in the city. If young women had been made immoral and ignorant, the task of re-education through refuges was clear. As late as 1905 at a monthly meeting of the Diocesan Society for the Protection of Women and Girls, a volunteer worker, Mrs Creighton, outlined the philosophy, aims and progress of the society's charitable work within its two urban refuges for the city's 'sad' and 'suffering' class of women. There were, she said, two aims in the work of the society: 'one was to raise the fallen, and the other was to safeguard those who had not fallen but were in more or less danger of falling'. The themes of danger, evil and temptation loomed large in Creighton's speech as she detailed the deep-rooted and widespread 'cancer' of prostitution, alcoholism and indigence which the society sought to remedy in its charitable mission, and she outlined the relevance of the problems not merely to their immediate 'victims', but to the whole foundation of the family and society.[29] Above all, she reminded her audience,

> Let it be remembered, that the girls dealt with, have been indulged by foolish parents, brought up without discipline or control. There has been no cultivation of the better nature. There is no love of work. Such girls have to be re-made, and such work cannot be done in a hurry. . . . It was a work which affected the nation's life, and it was not only important to carry on the work for the sake of the girls of the country, but for the good of the whole community. . . . In dealing with the girls, light is thrown upon other evils and we must all . . . courageously and unflinchingly do battle with the common evil, for the common good.[30]

While Mrs Creighton spoke in this instance of parents, the more frequent and specific image of the 'common evil' was constructed around the figure of the 'bad' mother, a stock figure in the melodrama of Victorian rescue work. It was the results of her 'perverted' handiwork in the construction of femininity which had then to be 're-made'. The 'bad' mother could be such through sins of both omission and commission: working women who were away from the household could not oversee their daughters' behaviour, and so left untutored they became 'wild'. Alternatively, the problem revolved around a poor woman not working, but instead training her children to public dependence and the rewards of laziness and vice. The exact permutations were varied, but the discursive links between women's work and disordered female sexuality

---

[29] Ibid. 31–2.
[30] *NDG*, Mar. 1905, 32. The emphasis appears in the original source.

were consistently present. That alongside the figure of the mother stood the 'sorrowful' victim, the young woman at the mercy of her surroundings and her own lamentable ignorance, provided the melodramatic symmetry which infused contemporary accounts of rescue missions. As well as conditioning, her very biology seemed to condemn her to a future of vice: as a child, 'the germs of passion [she] will have to contend with are in [her] already'.[31] Separating bad from good, and meticulously setting the stage where the dream-sequence of feminine transformation could occur, became the abiding imperatives of a wide range of philanthropic institutions and individuals.

Significantly, the young 'victim', as Creighton and many others conceived of her, could be either prostitute or an 'almost-prostitute': their conception of the deeply entrenched immorality of lower working-class life indeed positioned prostitutes on a firm continuum with other poor women. In the 1842 annual report of the Asylum for Female Penitents, it was claimed, for example, that 'the definition of a prostitute' was a 'general application' for those who had had sexual relations in a variety of circumstances. While poverty was mentioned as the condition into which these women could expect to 'become involved' after their 'fall', the definition itself excluded any economic component.[32] And here lies one of the crucial disjunctures of definition which is interspersed throughout the sources on rescue work: while poor working women at times viewed homes and rescue agencies as a source of economic provision and shelter, to the bourgeois rescuers themselves, 'rescue' was never a mere synonym for relief, and the 'moral' space of their homes was conceived as much more than a convenient alternative to sleeping in the streets or 'low' lodging houses. The differences not only played themselves out around the physical space of the homes and their meanings, but also in temporal perspectives: while women usually sought short-term solutions, reformers structured their schemes around a commitment to long-term residence.

The construction of definitions used by the homes raises important general issues about the 'prostitute' and her function within discourse. Philippa Levine argues persuasively that nineteenth-century commentaries on prostitution 'demonstrate the contradictions which arise out of [the] need for taxonomic identification, of labelling to construct simultaneously the deviant and the essential woman'. While there was reference to external circumstances, argues Levine, such as neglect, 'seduction' and low wages (although I would argue that in the Newcastle material, the economic argument is frequently submerged) which together 'allowed the new category of feminine, dependent, asexual, helpless "Woman" to stand firm', there was also reference to 'inherent female peccadilloes', an essentialism which was

---

[31] Mrs Sumner, 'The responsibilities of mothers', in Angela Burdett-Coutts (ed.), Woman's mission, London 1893, 67.
[32] Eleventh annual report of the Asylum for Female Penitents, 1842, TWAS 586/1, 5–6.

based apparently outside frameworks of class and economic circumstance.[33] Certainly, as has been argued in a previous chapter, the hint of essentialism was evident in discussions of prostitution in Newcastle, and remained throughout the century. However, I would argue further that any too-simple essentialist model yielded contradictions which were more and more difficult to sustain as bourgeois women themselves became more involved in rescue work. Increasingly, the force of essentialist arguments either had to be abandoned (which they were not), or demanded the simultaneous establishment of the essential 'difference' of identity based in class. If a proclivity to immorality was located within a 'natural' femininity, then that 'natural' or essential femininity had to be discursively distanced by constructing the poor working-class woman as part of a 'race apart' from her female bourgeois 'rescuers'. As Littlewood and Mahood point out too, while many of the discourses around prostitution were defined on the basis of femininity and sexuality and occluded economic definitions, producing 'apparently non-class based characters', the 'way in which they were mobilized was class specific'.[34]

The longest-established home in Newcastle was the Asylum for Female Penitents which opened in 1831 and which continued its work throughout the century. It provided a model of the growth of philanthropy and increasingly regional and national networks of charitable work. Its committee, about a dozen people in 1842, had grown to number over fifty women and men serving on a central Newcastle committee and organised into regional sub-committees by the 1880s. And here, particularly in its early reports, the sense that the project was not a response to poverty was conveyed very clearly. Here was no haven of relief for society's female 'detritus', 'the miserable remains of decayed and inveterate prostitution'. Women who were admitted first had to exhibit a 'temper of genuine penitence', to fit themselves to the models of identity generated by the asylum's bourgeois committee. Just as Littlewood and Mahood found for Glasgow, the asylum and other homes in Newcastle throughout the period were 'not so much selecting from a pre-existing population of "prostitutes" in the city, as much as they were *creating* candidates for their programme'.[35] Moreover, the home was no mere shelter, but a space where 'strict discipline' was to be enforced, where restraint and obedience were 'imperatively demanded', and which, significantly, would ensure that women were 'confined from public observation'.[36] The absolute requirement of strict discipline was echoed repeatedly through the century by other agencies and individuals; with regard to slum-dwellers and their culture in general, stated one reformer in 1885, 'depraved minds only practise virtue under compulsion'.[37]

33 Levine, 'Prostitution, law, and the social historian', 270–1.
34 Littlewood and Mahood, 'Prostitutes, magdalenes, and wayward girls', 171.
35 Ibid. 170.
36 Eleventh annual report of the Asylum for Female Penitents, 1842, TWAS 586/1, 4, 7.
37 Price, *NDG*, 1885, 280.

After eleven years of operation, the asylum's report summarised its work in a statement headed 'the total number of objects who have been received, and how disposed of'. The home had 'disposed' of 125 women in the period, sixty-four of whom had absconded, been sent to home parishes or had requested that their 'confinement' end. Another seven women had died, although six 'of this number gave pleasing Testimony that they were converted to God' on their death-beds.[38] Little or nothing was written about the women themselves; although they were required to constitute themselves as 'proper' subjects prior to entry, once within the asylum their primary function within the discourse was as objects. In this and in other respects the asylum's reports and organisation were broadly representative of the institutions which followed with similar objectives from the 1860s onwards. While there were subtle variations in perspectives on, and treatment of, 'inmates' in these establishments, some key features and problems were common to most. First, institutional committees had to determine the basis upon which 'rescue' would be carried out; second, the recruitment of staff and female inmates had to be undertaken; and finally, committees had to ensure that the programmes they oversaw fulfilled the primary requirement of moral 'cleansing', but remained economically viable. The experience of those engaged in the administration of one such institution referred to previously, the Brandling Home, illustrates the context of problems and dilemmas within which charitable enterprises functioned.

The Brandling Place Home for Penitent Women was established in the 1860s and, although non-denominational, the committee overseeing the home included representatives from Evangelical churches and notable local philanthropists.[39] Situated in Strawberry Place, outside the area of the slums, the home was close to the 'respectable' heart of the city. Initially, it was intended as a temporary refuge for women who had engaged in prostitution, rather than as a training centre. This early emphasis upon the provision of shelter, with apparently no undertaking on behalf of the women with regard to the duration of their stay, was combined with an active missionary role. In early 1871 a Mrs Holland was engaged to spend three half-days a week seeking out the 'fallen young women of the town'. However, the committee's initial enthusiasm for the venture soon waned. By December Mrs Holland had visited

> the houses of ill-fame in upwards of thirty different streets. She has also paid 16 visits to the Infirmary. She has spent altogether about 137 hours. . . . Only one girl appears to have found her way to the Home as yet, as a direct result of her labours.[40]

---

[38] Eleventh annual report of the Asylum for Female Penitents, 1842, TWAS 586/1, 13.
[39] Brandling Place Home for Penitent Women, General Committee minutes (cited hereinafter as Brandling, GCM), 1863–78, TWAS 584/1/1.
[40] Brandling, GCM, 6 Dec. 1871, ibid.

In a similar vein, and meeting with the same spectacular lack of success, the committee organised night-time meetings with free refreshments in order to contact women. One such meeting held in 1872 saw upwards of thirty women attend and take refreshment, but none could be persuaded to go to the home.[41] After the failure of such measures, Lady Armstrong suggested to the Brandling committee in 1872 that, rather than accommodating women on a short-term basis, the home should turn to the work of providing more permanent shelter and training to counteract the 'disorderly' character of these women, and organise their placement as servants. Again, this focus on service was not only based upon economic considerations of the state of the local market for female labour: the training of servants was one of the primary fields of bourgeois women's 'expertise', while lodging ex-prostitutes in well-run households where they would submit to disciplined work regimes as servants provided a clear contribution to the bourgeois project of creating moral order through the regulation of bodies as well as public and private space.

This redirection of the home's work was in part due to the failure of its early recruitment schemes. The population of the home stood at around twenty women in the 1870s although more could be accommodated, and by the mid 1890s when the function of the home had changed, an average of only ten women stayed in the home at any one time.[42] In the face of declining numbers and economic pressures the home was finally closed in 1896. The closure was not due to lack of zeal for the project. The history of its decline in the records, however, presents a picture of the growing disjunction between the abstract moral 'rescue' imperatives of the committee, and the economic and social 'relief' imperatives of women targeted by the home.

The first practical problem faced by the committee was economic: inmates were required to work during their stay, and the home took in laundry from surrounding areas to provide income. Laundry work was the standard occupation within rescue homes throughout England. Ellice Hopkins, a leading figure in the rescue movement and a regular contributor to its various newspapers and journals, explained the suitability of the work among 'fallen' women: 'As a rule, it stands to reason that the wild restlessness, the lawlessness, the animal passions and excitement of the old street life are best worked off by muscular exertion, and laundry work is on the whole the best and most profitable.'[43] At Brandling, a laundress was employed to oversee the operation, but a very high turnover of staff was reported. Drunkenness and inefficiency of employed staff were compounded by the allegedly thieving propensities of the inmates. The women's conditions of work perhaps contributed to poor work standards and theft. It is impossible to gauge from

41 Ibid. 20 Mar. 1872.
42 Brandling register and diary, 1894–6, TWAS 584/3.
43 Ellice Hopkins quoted in *All the World*, Feb. 1885, 27, cited in Jenty Fairbank, *Booth's boots: social service beginnings in the Salvation Army*, London 1983, 18.

the records the extent to which theft was general, or whether the actions of a few were taken as confirmation of the assumed 'riotous and disorderly' propensities of the class of 'fallen' women as a whole.[44]

Laundering was carried out each day from 7 a.m. to 7 p.m. or later, and women complained that their work was 'burdensome and exhausting'.[45] The volume of the work was subject to fluctuation too, depending upon conditions in the local economy. In the mid 1880s, for example, a period of economic slump and widespread unemployment in the area, both Brandling Home officials and those from other homes complained of the noticeable drop in available laundry work. At such times, the proliferation of agencies relying upon laundry work receipts created intense competition for a shrinking market, not only between homes, but between them and the outside labour force of women who sought to secure their living in the trade.[46] Moreover, the 'cleansing' and 'taming' rituals of laundry work envisaged by Hopkins stand in stark contrast to the women's own views, and those of other Victorian working-class women. In another area, Kathleen Woodward recalled her mother's work as a laundress, in similar terms of exhaustion: 'Out of the steam comes mother's face – pinkish-purple, sweating . . . hands unnaturally crinkled, bleached from the stinging soda water. "Wash, wash, wash; it's like washing your guts away." '[47] Apart from food and lodging, women were not paid for the laundry work they performed in the Home.

Other aspects of life in the home may have accounted for young women's reluctance to remain there. Rules of orderliness and locked doors at night were viewed, perhaps, as unacceptable restraints. By the 1880s new residence requirements for inmates – a minimum eighteen-month stay in order better to train and regulate their behaviour – would have provided further disincentive. Institutional uniforms had been introduced from the outset as an important means of regulating and 'elevating' the women, although by 1884 the committee was considering the introduction of more 'varied dress with (possibly) a gradation according to merit' as a means of further 'raising their self-respect'.[48] As a means of inculcating personal responsibility, recouping costs, and perhaps as an encouragement to women to invest in the material signs of their newly-forged identity, those who were provided with uniforms for service from 1879 onwards were 'encouraged to repay a portion of the cost of their outfit'.[49] The measure may also have been viewed as a guard against the frivolous disposal of the service livery once outside the home; some years later

---

[44] Brandling, GCM, 10 Feb. 1866, TWAS 584/1/1.
[45] Brandling, GCM, 2 Aug. 1893, TWAS 584/1/2.
[46] Fifty-third annual report of the Asylum for Female Penitents, 1885, TWAS 586/1, 9.
[47] Kathleen Woodward, cited in Patricia Malcolmson, 'Laundresses and the laundry trade in Victorian England', *Victorian Studies* xxiv (1980–1), 439–62 at p. 439.
[48] Brandling, GCM, 6 Nov. 1884, TWAS 584/1/2.
[49] Brandling, GCM, 4 Jun. 1879, TWAS 584/1/1.

another charity reported an instance of a young woman being encouraged to pawn her newly-acquired servant's clothing.[50]

The second major failure of the home was in fulfilling the goals of secure, 'respectable' positions for its inmates. Concern that women should not return to the streets saw the committee become involved in emigration and placement schemes. In 1879, for example, there were negotiations with a Mr Craster for the removal of women through emigration to 'proper' homes in Canada as servants. Craster portrayed the destination in terms almost irresistible to a committee concerned about female morality: '[T]he tone of morality [is] much higher than in this Country: there is less open profligacy . . . [Craster] never saw a drunken woman, nor did he see a woman ever entering a drinking Saloon.'[51] Two women were duly dispatched as a result of these negotiations. One was sent to be a nursemaid in Toronto, and her subsequent history is unknown. Another, Jane Walker, had fits on the voyage and ended her trip in a Montreal hospital.[52]

The destination of other inmates varied. Some were recorded as having returned to relatives outside Newcastle, perhaps suggesting that the women had travelled from home in Sunderland or Edinburgh in search of work and had become stranded in the city. Relatively few women were sent to service – many more were sent on to other institutions, either to the workhouse, or to private concerns. The committee recorded that their efforts to contain and regiment the women met with overt resistance – the majority of inmates absconded, or were discharged for misconduct or having a 'bad influence' upon the other inmates. Jane Ward, for example, was sent home to an aunt in Sunderland in 1894 after she tried to persuade two others to leave the home with her. The secretary and matron that night '[p]rayed specially . . . that it might please God to arrest her in her downward progress'.[53] How such 'bad influence' was manifested is not made clear. Certainly, given the confines of the home, the conditions of constant surveillance which prevailed, and the expectation that women would readily conform to the processes envisaged and would mould themselves to the pre-formed categories defined to effect their 're-making', there was considerable scope for much pre-home style activity to be cast as resistance, however much that activity had been a regular and entrenched part of the women's own culture. Despite the careful consultations the committee engaged in about emigration schemes, and their careful formulation of residence rules, even after the introduction of the eighteen-month training programme most women only remained for a few months.

In the records of the Brandling Home, the preparedness to generalise

50 Newcastle and Gateshead Poor Children's Holiday Association and Rescue Agency, annual report 1901, DU Archives 234/8, 16.
51 Brandling, GCM, 19 Feb. 1879, TWAS 584/1/1.
52 Ibid. 4 June 1879.
53 Brandling register and diary, 4 Oct. 1894, TWAS 584/3.

about the immorality of working-class girls and women and the blurring between actual and potential prostitution occurred alongside an almost complete silence about the women's broader economic and social circumstances. Little direct reference is made in the records to poverty, for example, although clearly the women were poor. That some were sent on to workhouses in itself suggests their economic marginality. The reality of their poverty, however, was secondary to the moral task the committee took upon itself. And yet it was belief in a primary moral mission, and adherence to the observance and promotion of 'correct' feminine behaviour among inmates, however fervently subscribed to by the home's administators, which perhaps helped to ensure the demise of the project. The home did not meet the needs of women, and perhaps too directly and completely challenged the women's desire for self-identity. It could not recruit and keep inmates, and therefore found it difficult to function economically. What may strike the historian (but not the contemporary observer) as ironic was that the home trained women in the very occupations from which prostitutes were most likely to be drawn, and imposed a regime and constructed a future for inmates from which most fled. By 1893, the matron complained that the newer charitable homes in Newcastle, such as that established by the Salvation Army which did not impose such rigorous restrictions, 'had drained off the supply of women'.[54] Poor working-class women in Newcastle sought shelter elsewhere, and by the 1890s were perhaps better placed to secure relief in a form which accorded more closely with their own needs and priorities.

Although the Brandling Place Home for Penitent Women closed, there were many others which continued and ran along very similar lines, but which enjoyed more extensive institutional and economic support from, for example, the Anglican Church. The Diocesan House of Mercy opened in 1889 under the auspices of the local Society for the Protection of Women and Children, with the purpose of caring for women who 'had to be restrained from a life of vice'. The home used the services of both religious and laywomen to oversee the ubiquitous cleansing and rescuing laundry work, and to recruit young women. Sister Agatha from the home regularly visited workhouses in the region, looking for candidates for training,[55] while other members of the diocese acted as police court agents, recruiting women with the assistance of magistrates' clerks from the ranks of those prosecuted for a variety of minor offences. While the workhouses may have provided shelter, and the courts represented a space in which the regulatory regimes of authority operated only in a transitory fashion, the home represented a space of stability, continuity and personal growth. After one year in the Diocesan House, it was claimed, women from the court who had once been 'mere bundles of wretchedness . . . slaves to their own thirsts and lusts' had been

[54] Brandling, GCM, 2 Aug. 1893, TWAS 584/1/2.
[55] Minute book, 12 Mar. 1889, Diocesan Society for the Protection of Women and Children, NRO 3435.

transformed into 'bright, happy girls'.[56] There were occasions when the women in the home had some respite from laundry work taking organised day-trips to Whitley and elsewhere; but while on the whole official reports in the *Diocesan Gazette* tended to emphasise the success stories of the home, occasionally there was an admission there too that some cases 'have been very difficult and discouraging to deal with'.[57]

The records for the Diocesan House itself are very sparse, and again focus very little upon the women residing there, but some indication of the 'failures' the home's staff experienced are conveyed none the less. As at Brandling, women absconded. Some women simply refused to work and so were discharged. For one woman, the confines of the home proved insufficient to contain her 'temptations', and so she was sent to a home in Leicester 'to remove her from her former companions'. Another left the home abruptly because she was not allowed to smoke there.[58] Women exhibited different levels of acceptance of the behaviour required of them, different degrees of readiness to 'perform' appropriately penitent roles. For some, a pipe was the simple prop which threatened the orderly symmetry of the charitable stage, and they chose to leave entirely rather than give it up. For others, the demands of 'performance' were more clearly consonant with their own needs and views of themselves, and so merged into their identities in ways which ensured that the 'rescue' sequence was triumphantly resolved.

Pervading the Victorian melodrama of rescue, then, was the image of the 'gaudy' woman, the woman who required restraint and extended scrutiny to be 're-made' and both figuratively and literally re-clothed to conform to the more comfortable, sepia tones of the ideal bourgeois stage set. It was a mission which drew discursively upon powerful symbols of disordered womanhood – the 'evil' mother, the 'wild' young woman whose sexuality was uncontrolled – as well as powerful constructions of cultural transformation in the name of progress, civilisation and secure identity for family and nation. It was transformative work which was seen as increasingly urgent in the second half of the century: given the overwhelming association of prostitution with the allegedly immoral or 'at risk' status of poor women generally, no adequate solution lay in the simple 'containment' of prostitutes as had been attempted earlier in the century. As previously argued, the actual transition to more extensive programmes which sought transformation of 'prostitutes' and general concern about the impact of 'uncontrolled' female sexuality cannot be located simply in changing material conditions. Rather, it was the contemporary interpretation of these conditions, and the increasingly influential, connected and fundamentally gendered discourses of progress, domesticity and moral elevation which rose in the second half of the century, which

---

56 *NDG*, Oct. 1899, 154.
57 Ibid. Aug. 1901, 117.
58 Minute book, 14 Apr. 1892, Diocesan Society for the Protection of Women and Children, NRO 3435.

provided the context. The formulation of 'ideal femininity' through these discourses saw the prostitute in turn 'constructed *through* resistance. A prostitute woman was one who by definition lived in defiance, in resistance – of the proper sphere of Woman, of the male order, of respectability.'[59] And in many respects the discursive construction of poor women in the texts of charities perpetuated, perhaps relied upon, such clear melodramatic dichotomies. Transformative work held the promise of converting the 'animal' woman, the prostitute and her 'almost-cousin', from being a drunken 'creature, whose face has lost all human resemblance',[60] into a more 'acceptable' form of Victorian womanhood. If women and households lay at the heart of society, this mission had more significance than that of assistance to individuals: it locked into wider discourses about moral regeneration as a key underpinning the country's visible 'progress'.

Barret-Ducrocq states that it is a vast over-simplification for historians 'to imagine the nineteenth-century in primary colours' in which the 'gaudy' woman appears in a position of 'perpetual subjection',[61] operating in a bifurcated environment of either gross exploitation (the streets) or gross oppression (the homes). Similarly, through the pathologising of the prostitute in contemporary literature, the varieties of women's own experiences and the subtleties of meaning which surrounded them were obscured. Although the responses of women themselves to such 'rescue' regimes are almost entirely absent throughout contemporary literature however, except through negative constructions of churlishness and 'misbehaviour', one further body of source material makes those responses a little clearer, provides some glimpses into women's perspectives and some indication of the ways in which these overlapped with, or diverged from, the preoccupations of those who viewed poor women through the lens of the philanthropic committee.

'God's relieving officers' and the battle for female souls: the Salvation Army in Newcastle and Wooler

The Salvation Army Rescue Home's records for Newcastle are more comprehensive than most, and move beyond the 'gloss' of annual reports, or the carefully constructed diaries and meeting minutes generated by other institutions, sources which reflect a great deal about the structure and imperatives of relief provision and assistance, but relatively little about the recipients themselves. Furthermore, the Salvation Army's general work in the city was periodically described in *The Deliverer* magazine, which featured stories of slum rescue work throughout England. The Salvation Army opened its home in 1891 after moving its rescue activities from Middlesbrough to Newcastle,

---

59 Levine, 'Prostitution, law and the social historian', 278.
60 *NDG*, Sept. 1899, 35.
61 Barret-Ducrocq, *Love in the time of Victoria*, 183.

since it was deemed that the need for services in the latter city was more urgent. While the move to Newcastle coincided with a major coal strike which the Army believed would undermine the short-term financial security of its project, since residents would be less likely to make donations at its open-air meetings, 'the need of the [rescue] work is as great as ever'.[62] The practical organisation of the Army's rescue work in some respects mirrored that of Brandling and other homes in the area; the Salvation Army's Rescue Home with its accommodation for thirty women was 'substantial and charming . . . situated on high ground in the bright and cheerful Parade, sufficiently removed from the back of the town, where temptation is strongest for the girls'.[63]

Yet in other important ways, the philosophy behind the Salvation Army's work constituted a considerable departure from that underlying Newcastle's established philanthropic ventures. First, the Salvation Army's basis for action was not a selective philanthropic model which was based upon individualistic notions like those enunciated by Charity Organisation Society writer and reformer Charles Loch, who claimed that economic need in society was infinite since society itself was characterised by 'a restless movement' of people 'continually falling lower, [and] others continually . . . climbing higher'.[64] The Salvation Army promoted, not welfare but 'warfare' against economic and social conditions which contributed to 'a perfect quagmire of human strife', warfare fuelled by religious enthusiasm for the Salvationist doctrine. While the solution which founder William Booth envisaged was individually based – rescue through personal religious enlightenment – there was considerable attention paid to the general circumstances of life and poverty which were thought to generate the immorality and misery which blocked religious feeling. Certainly, the other rescue agencies in the city portrayed themselves as 'total' services, where the transformation of both body and soul was envisaged.[65] The difference lay not so much in rhetoric, as in the respective motivations and processes through which the transforming work was presumed to occur. For Salvationists, the emphasis upon the 'salvability' of every soul above all else, meant that the task of 'remoralising' the poor was always secondary – an important accompaniment to the evangelical aim, but never the primary goal. 'In many modern schemes of social regeneration', wrote William Booth, 'it is forgotten that it takes a soul to move a body.'[66] If neglect of the spiritual dimension of welfare marked the

---

62 Adeline Lampard, 'Reconnoitering in Newcastle-on-Tyne', *The Deliverer*, May 1892, 191; Mrs Bramwell Booth, 'Personal notes', ibid. 184.
63 Mrs Bramwell Booth, 'Personal notes', ibid. June 1892, 200.
64 C. S. Loch, *An examination of 'General' Booth's social scheme*, London 1890, 94.
65 NDG, Sept. 1899, 35.
66 William Booth, *In darkest England and the way out*, London 1890, cited in Fairbank, *Booth's boots*, 93, 141.

work of poor law and other agencies, wrote another evangelist, the Army would act as 'God's relieving officers' to redress the problem.[67]

The Salvation Army's emphasis upon spiritual transformation, a transformation which could occur at any time, cut across the more commonly held opinion that it would be only via careful, prolonged and precise regimes of physical and moral education that a woman would be 'saved' from prostitution or the presumed pernicious influences of working-class culture. In the Brandling Home and the Diocesan House of Mercy signs of spiritual transformation were to be found in the form of outward observances such as participation in regular prayer sessions; in this respect, spiritual transformation appeared as another outcome of regular training. While the Salvation Army did include religious meetings in its homes, there was no necessary connection seen between training and spirituality. Further, the evangelical impulse and the Army's belief that with patience, 'salvation' could occur for anybody, meant that there was more scope within its philosophy for the fairly ready accommodation of recidivists. 'Hating the sin but not the sinner' and so accepting consistent 'transgressors' in rescue work, again cut across predominant notions of individual responsibility and self-help, and rendered meaningless the dominant dichotomies which had been commonly employed to classify the 'deserving' and 'undeserving' poor.

Significantly too, the female officers involved in the work with poor women conceived of themselves in different terms than, for example, a philanthropist like Elizabeth Spence Watson. The Army's active recruitment of working-class women and their assignment to duties as rescue workers in some cases turned 'the saved into the saviours of the class to which they formerly belonged'.[68] The expressed Army sentiment that workers were no different from the women they sought to assist (since all were 'sinners'), meant that overt identification with the women, rather than 'rescue' across a gulf of class and social status and effected through a chain of paid functionaries, provided the basis for the Army's activities. Florence Booth wrote that 'one of the first duties of the rescue officers is to take a stand firmly against the position that women guilty of immorality are *worse* than other transgressors'.[69]

The founders of the Salvation Army's Women's Social Work section were explicit in their rejection of many of the standard practices of rescue agencies and their homes. Women were not to be made to feel 'confined' in the homes. If anyone wished to leave, they should be allowed to leave freely, but received again if they chose to return. Florence Booth was convinced that the prison-like regimes and surroundings in many homes undermined their avowed purpose.[70] Similarly, laundry work was regarded, at least in the 1880s,

---

67 Ibid. 6.
68 William Booth, *The War Cry*, 23 June 1888, cited in Fairbank, *Booth's boots*, 20.
69 Mrs Bramwell Booth, *A brief review of the first year's work*, n.p. 1891, cited ibid. 21.
70 *The Sunday Circle*, 18 Mar. 1933, cited ibid. 16.

as an unfitting occupational backdrop to the more important task of saving the soul: 'we keep *off* the laundry work because we wish opportunity for more personal influence over the girls'.[71]

The Salvation Army operated within a framework which prized close contact and personal communication within the terrain of the streets and poor working-class districts, and this approach characterised its Newcastle venture. Army officers immediately toured Newcastle at night, 'looking over the worst quarter of the city, familiarising ourselves with all the houses of ill-fame',[72] constructing a mental map of the geography of vice in the area. The night-time forays of the corps in other areas were fraught with danger.[73] In Newcastle in stark contrast, at least in the official version of events described in the Army's newspapers, the reception of the corps was uniformly hospitable. Carol-singing in Sandgate was met with 'deep attention' as the appreciative householders came and filled the alleyways;[74] a later visit to Wooler by William Booth himself attracted a spontaneously-gathered crowd which was put at between 200 and 300 people in a matter of moments, who reportedly stood awe-struck in the general's presence, keenly absorbing his religious message.[75] Indeed from 1902 in Wooler, the date at which 'the Hallelujah bonnets' first arrived in the area, it was reported that 'the natives were highly delighted' at the Army's presence, and a Sunday School for local children was well attended.[76]

The records of the home itself, and some other sources, suggest in fact that the relations forged between the Salvation Army and the women they sought to assist were not always entirely cordial. Despite the stated philosophy which underpinned the rescue work and which was couched in terms which were less severely judgemental and less generalised in respect of 'disorderly' poor women than that of other organisations, those officers 'on the spot' at times none the less operated within familiar discourses about immorality and the 'undeserving' poor. One Salvation Army worker described for Sherard the 'inner' life of poor women as one of almost universal drinking, fighting and depravity. The fights were especially fierce on Saturday nights, as she recalled one instance of a woman struggling for ten minutes on the ground with a police officer before he was able to gain assistance; another occurred the following night when a woman in Silver Street had had all her clothes torn off. The women of the slums, she told Sherard, were 'extremely idle', and did

---

71 *The War Cry*, Feb. 1886, cited ibid. 18.
72 Lampard, 'Reconnoitering in Newcastle', 191.
73 Prochaska, *Women and philanthropy*, 193. See also Walkowitz, *City of dreadful delight*, 75; Rebecca Jarrett, manuscript autobiography, 32–3, held at SAA. Jarrett (1846–1928) was a brothel-keeper turned Salvationist whose role in the W. T. Stead case has been well-documented: A. Sebestyen, 'Two women from two worlds', *Spare Rib*, June 1985, 21–4; Walkowitz, *City of dreadful delight*, 106–20.
74 Hollins, 'In the slums', 167.
75 'The General's motor ride', *The Deliverer*, Oct. 1904, 61.
76 'What she could', ibid. Aug. 1904, 20.

little except smoke, drink and bet. And stepping outside the usual vocabulary of the Army, she claimed that she could think of only two cases of 'deserving' poor women in the immediate district.[77]

In the home itself over a period of six years, 241 women had their case histories recorded by the Salvation Army officers.[78] Again, while some had been prostitutes, many of the women had not engaged in prostitution but were seen to be in severe 'moral danger' none the less. These case statements reveal the occupational and family backgrounds of the women, the circumstances of their 'first fall', and their personal 'moral' record in relation to crime and drunkenness. The statements also contain valuable information about the women's previous experience of charities and workhouses. While the evidence even of these Statement Books appears quantitatively slim, they contain a rare, longer-term perspective on the poverty and the strategies of individual women. What do the records reveal?

Most women in the Rescue Home were young: 41 per cent were in their teens, and a further 44 per cent were in their twenties.[79] Occupationally, the vast majority – 60 per cent – were drawn from the ranks of servants. While women in public workplaces drew sustained attention of reformers and moralists, it remained the 'private' space of employment in households and the traditional life styles of domestic service which surrounded it, which generated the largest number of women who were recruited into the categories of 'immorality' established by the discourse of 'rescue'. Significantly, only 9 per cent of the women who went to the home actually identified their occupation as prostitution. For the most part, women who worked on the streets or in brothels did so casually, or clandestinely, while they were employed elsewhere.[80]

Records of the 'reason for the first fall' of the women compiled by the Salvation Army officers are fraught with interpretative difficulty. A little over one quarter of the women had been first 'seduced' by male friends, with those women sometimes specifying that they had had sexual relations only under promise of marriage. Promises of marriage, and the life changes which women made as a result, could prove very costly. Josephine Boyce left her job in a Dundee mill to follow her fiancé to Newcastle, selling shoe laces on the way as she tramped through the countryside. Three weeks after she arrived in the city, the man broke the engagement.[81] Generally, the contemporary vocabulary of 'seduction' is notoriously difficult to untangle, blurring as it does issues of consent and coercion, and tending to throw the focus of attention upon an individual woman's sexuality and behaviour, rather than upon the

---

[77] Ibid. 155–6.
[78] SAA Girls' statement books, vols ii–vi. The relevant volumes in this series are numbered as follows: vol. ii, 1890–2 (Newcastle cases recorded from 1891 only); vol. iii, 1892–4; vol. iv, 1894–5; vol. v, 1895–7. Hereinafter references are to volume numbers only.
[79] Calculated from SAA Girls' statement books, vols ii–v.
[80] Ibid. vol. iii, case 207.
[81] Ibid. vol. iv, cases 47, 240.

constellation of economic and social factors which structured women's vulnerability to sexual advances in the home and in the workplace.[82]

11 per cent of women were allegedly 'seduced' by an employer, an employer's relative, a family relative or had been procured for prostitution by a member of their own family. In some cases, elements of coercion and violence involved in these events are very clear. Annie Hunt had been raped by her father and borne a child, and the father was sent to gaol for seven years for his crime.[83] Sarah Sykes at sixteen recalled that she had 'been ruined by her own brother when she was little more than a baby', and had run away from home in Wakefield when she was able, only to face destitution in Newcastle.[84] Appalling violence and coercion underlay some of the histories, and contemporaries railed against evil relatives – especially mothers – involving their daughters in prostitution. However, in other cases daughters themselves sometimes saw other determinants operating. Rebecca Jarrett, perhaps the best known convert to the Salvationist cause, related her introduction to prostitution in London's Cremorne Gardens by her mother; yet Jarrett in writing about her experiences issued a poignant plea to her audience:

> Some of you will say as read this what a *bad Mother* she must have had but *Please don't* she was a good Mother it was my wretched Father doing[.] He left her several times and lived with other woman [sic] my poor Mother was left with 8 children I was the baby . . . she took to the drink it was the trouble that drove her to it she had to work.[85]

Similarly in Newcastle, although Mary Quinn's mother before her death had not been involved in Mary's prostitution, Mary was at pains to reassure the officers that she had been a good parent, struggling in difficult circumstances, although her father was allegedly a drunk.[86]

Two further categories of 'reason for first fall' were recorded which warrant examination. The largest category was one where definitions were further blurred. The category could be (and was) summarised as 'falling under bad influences' – of companions or alcohol, a 'wild' temperament, or a plain 'choice' to turn to sex for profit or to supplement income. More than one-third of the women were so described, although clearly the designation covered a multitude of circumstances. While in two particular cases women's poverty was explicitly cited as the reason for their prostitution, in many cases in this category poverty was a strong motivation for turning to sex work. The final category of women in the home were there, not because they had 'fallen', but as a 'preventive' measure. Over one-quarter of those in the home,

---

82 See Anna K. Clark, 'Rape or seduction?: a controversy over sexual violence in the nineteenth century', in London Feminist History Group, *The sexual dynamics of history*, London 1983, 13–27.
83 Annie Hunt, SAA Girls' statement book, vol. iii, case 268.
84 Ibid. case 235.
85 Jarrett manuscript, 3.
86 SAA Girls' statement book, vol. v, case 88.

especially the very young women and girls, spent time there for this reason. Some, like Isabella Hallett, had been sent by relatives anxious about the young woman's behaviour. Mary Donald, a sixteen-year-old servant, was sent by her father for more serious 'regulation' after she had spent a term in gaol for stealing and putting poison in her employer's teapot, and then bartering all her father's goods upon her release.[87] Some older women had been sent by husbands as a remedy for their alleged drunkenness. Elizabeth Crozier, whose husband worked at Armstrong's, was sent to the home by him for drunkenness. Her husband took away her two children to live with their grandparents, and had previously sent Elizabeth to the Brandling Home for two years. Elizabeth left the Salvation Army Home one morning, the officers commenting that 'the race week was just coming on; this probably influenced her in her temptation'.[88]

While in some cases there is little doubt that 'preventive' measures for alcohol dependence were not without some foundation – Mary Stockley, for example, had been imprisoned thirty times on charges of drunkenness[89] – two themes emerge from these cases which underscore the regulatory regimes which women experienced in their daily lives both within and outside their households. The image of the drunken woman in public was linked firmly with that of the prostitute, whether or not such a link was borne out for individual women; and the degree of control exercised by husbands over the movements and activities of their wives and children was considerable. As well as the cases of Kirkpatrick and Crozier, other women attested to their husbands' domination of family life. Phillis Stewart was sent to the home as a 'preventive case'. At fifteen, with mother and father out all day, Phillis's Sunday School teacher recommended her to the home, a measure with which her mother appeared to agree – perhaps to remove the girl from an abusive household. When her father found that Phillis had been sent away, 'he got very angry and drunk and gave the mother no peace till she came and fetched Phillis away'.[90]

For women who were not 'rescued' but were there for other reasons, the home was often a useful and important stopgap or refuge. Women like Elizabeth Lamb turned to the home to avoid the abuse of a drunken spouse. Louisa Watson left her husband and came to the home when he attempted to coerce her into prostitution.[91] The home also acted as an agency, getting employment for women and providing shelter in times of urgent need. Catherine Martin, at twenty-one, had given birth to a child three months previously. The father, Henry Porter, was a miner, whose parents had cared for Catherine during her pregnancy. During a hard winter, however, there had

[87] Ibid. vol. iv, cases 464, 426.
[88] Ibid. vol. iv, case 214; vol. iii, case 11.
[89] Ibid. vol. v, case 329.
[90] Ibid. vol. iv, case 463.
[91] Ibid. vol. iii, cases 213, 428.

been no work 'and poverty stared them in the face'. Henry wanted to marry Catherine when he was able, and in the meantime his parents were prepared to care for the child if the Salvation Army were able to get the woman a situation, which it duly did.[92]

The Salvation Army records and associated literature in many ways read differently to the records from other charitable organisations. At one level the material consistently emphasises some of the major general preoccupations constructed around prostitution and female sexuality during the period. Although in practical operation the Salvation Army appeared more sensitive to the links between poverty and prostitution, and displayed an awareness of the incidence of violence and abuse in the lives of some women, the records are shot through with many of the predominant motifs of disordered femininity which arose in other contexts. The figure of the 'bad' mother loomed large, as did the figure of the drunkard. The view expressed by Jarrett, that women drank 'to deaden . . . feeling, to meet the men if you were not bright they would not come again',[93] was borne out in some respects in the Newcastle records in accounts of women drinking as an accompaniment to their 'wretched lives'. Much more often, drinking was characterised by officers in their concluding appraisals of women in the statements as a personal failing. Certain public spaces received special attention as dangerous zones for 'reckless' young women – lodging houses where young women lived independent of parental control were portrayed as self-evident dens of vice, and the lure of theatres, travelling shows, fairs and pantomimes in particular was cited as well.[94] The 'bad' influence of the factory environment for women also figured.[95] A 'natural' fondness for public display and excitement, and a restlessness which militated against the construction of a sober, private, virtuous life also featured in the reports. The concern about the 'public' woman again came to the fore, and included, but was by no means confined to, women who were actually engaged in prostitution. Notably absent from the Army material, however, were explicit statements that women's biology, in tandem with their class position, somehow predisposed them to vice. The transgressions of femininity which the Salvation Army sought to combat in its battle for souls were seen as transgressions borne of circumstance and conditioning, not of heredity.

The sheer volume of information about the individuals contained in them presents abundant evidence of the fragility of these women's position, and the very real material consequences which faced them and the cultural constructions forged around them. Mary Turley worked for a while in a factory, but when there was no work, pawned all her good clothes. Once these were gone,

---

92 Ibid. vol. iv, case 349.
93 Jarrett manuscript, 4.
94 SAA Girls' statement book, vol. iii, case 314.
95 Ibid. vol. ii, case 340.

she could not get work, and she turned to prostitution instead.[96] Ellen Buttery, the mother of an illegitimate child, worked hard to try to support herself. Coming from an obviously 'disordered' home, since not only were her parents lazy but her brother 'minds a baby!!!', Ellen simply could not make ends meet despite her best endeavours.[97] These vicious circles of economic need and cultural constructions of immorality abounded, and were inextricably joined. The threads of respectability and individual responsibilty were both materially and culturally conditioned, often hard to grasp, and perhaps harder still to hang on to.

Women who had lived as prostitutes for some time, were also perhaps subject to a different pressure in the form of the public gaze and surveillance of their activities, but one which none the less could affect their capacity to earn a livelihood. At eighteen, Margaret Hooper had made a living as a prostitute for three years. She came to the home after she 'had been brutally kicked and injured in a brothel in N[orth] Shields'. A police officer had come to Margaret's assistance, and he too had been attacked. The assailant was imprisoned for three months, but as a result of the incident Margaret lost her job; the owner of the house 'refused to have Margaret in again as the case brought her house into notice' by the police and other authorities. Even those defined by contemporaries as the most 'public' women were expected to observe boundaries of discretion and silence in their work by their employers.[98] Brothel and lodging-house keepers, themselves usually women, faced the constant risk of prosecution.[99]

Greater detail in the statements provides a better sense of these women as agents, holding their own views about the boundaries of respectability, and of the leisure and work available to them. While official accounts invariably highlighted the 'success' stories of the Army, where a spiritual transformation was claimed and women had like 'waterlilies . . . ris[en] from the muddy past, through the "Cleansing stream" to show all around the white flower of a blameless life',[100] reading against the grain about the 'failures' takes the historian closer to the priorities of women themselves. Although choice was often severely circumscribed, women none the less negotiated their way through the patterns of constraints and opportunities which did exist. No easy generalisation can be made about the women's own responses to prostitution and its connection to poverty. While many turned to prostitution through sheer need, some young women expressed some positive views about the advantages of sex work over other areas of employment. Margaret Harrison had been a hawker, was 'very independent', and 'never really [had]

---

96 Ibid. vol. v, case 182.
97 Ibid. case 10.
98 Ibid. vol. iii, case 338.
99 See, for example, the case of Ann Young, 28 Oct. 1853, Alnwick House of Correction journal and order book, NRO, NC 12/25, 2180.
100 'Over a cup of coffee: a Newcastle secretary's reflections', The Deliverer, Apr. 1895, 149.

any desire to give up' prostitution. Annie Armitage, aged twenty, was a tailoress, but ran away from very stern grandparents. '[T]he girl was giddy and fond of theatres', and so joined Laurence's Travelling Show where she formed a liaison with her employer's nephew and then turned to prostitution. Others saw sex work as more profitable than, and preferable to, 'the drudgery of service' and its low pay. By contrast, when Elizabeth Dodds 'fell' after being turned out of home when she was seventeen, she earned 5s. for her first night's work.[101] The issue of morality as it was defined by their 'rescuers' appeared to have little meaning for some women. Jane Mayne, it was claimed by a Salvation Army officer, 'never really seemed to realise her sin as we desired she should'.[102] In this respect, as Littlewood and Mahood contend in their work on a Glasgow home's records, such 'failure' can be read 'as resistance [by women] . . . not only to the Institution's regime, but also to its account of them as "fallen women" or "sinners". . . ., an index of the "real" subjects' struggles against their incorporation into the "ideal" subject statuses held out to them'.[103]

Where the trace of women's own voices can be detected, the different perspectives which informed their decisions are clearer. By situating prostitution in a fuller context which at times identified the other work which women undertook, or the pattern of their family circumstances, it becomes possible to understand something of that logic which led a 'girl' who was giddy and fond of theatres to reject other options and turn to sex work. There is some sense also that poor women resented the images of 'good women' held up to them to which they were supposed to aspire, and were aware that those who did so simply did not recognise their circumscribed options. One prostitute, approached by Salvation Army rescuers late at night on the street, was asked if she was 'not wary of her sin'. She replied with a certain weariness, 'I am sick of it. I sometimes think you people believe we enjoy our life, but I tell you we are wretched.'[104] Further antagonism over rigid models and categories of female behaviour may have been experienced by other poor women who worked in different trades which took them out at night to occupy the 'dangerous' spaces of Sandgate and elsewhere and who were regularly approached by 'rescuers' who assumed too simply that 'no-one is to be seen abroad at such an hour but [prostitutes], their accomplices, [and] a few policemen'. The blurring of categories of actual prostitution and general 'immoral' life styles was expressed by the officers reporting an encounter with a young woman in the theatre district late at night. She had been employed in the theatre for years, she said, and was emphatic in her protest that, despite her

---

101 SAA Girls' statement book, vol. ii, case 414; vol. iii, case 311; vol. ii, case 177; vol. iii, case 440.
102 Ibid. vol. v, case 115.
103 Littlewood and Mahood, 'Prostitutes, magdalenes, and wayward girls', 169.
104 Lampard, 'Reconnoitering in Newcastle upon Tyne', 191.

admission that 'she lives in an immoral house [and] her companions are all bad', she did not belong 'to their class'.[105]

The records of poor women in the home and prior to their reception there also provide evidence of the ways in which charity was positioned as one of a broader range of strategies used to survive. Just as the matron at the Brandling Home had intimated, a number of the women had come to the Salvation Army after receiving assistance from other homes and charities. Five women who had been at Brandling made their way to the Salvation Army Home later, and another twenty-one had formerly been residents at the Wansbeck Home, the Diocesan House of Mercy and other institutions. Some of these women, and others besides, had also spent part of their lives in the workhouse – some indeed had been born there – or in the Union Infirmary during their confinements. A few women were labelled as being 'cynical' charity-dependants, moving from one place to another. In a four-year period Margaret Graham had lived at the Brandling Home, the Wansbeck Home, the Newcastle Infirmary, the Workhouse Hospital, the Newcastle Workhouse and the Salvation Army Home. Annie Paddock was reported to have 'lived for years on various societies and benevolent people', but in the context of the Army Home made a great strategic error of mocking 'our services and openly sa[ying] she would never serve God', and so (quite unusually) was dismissed from the home outright.[106]

The suspicion of abuse of services was widespread in charity circles throughout the century, and Ellen Ross contends that then, as now, 'charity mongers' were 'stock literary figures' and received 'considerable sensational-ized attention in the press'. She points out that in London 'working charities as a way of life . . . required considerable dramatic skill, information, and luck. Individuals who supported themselves in this way were rare'.[107] The adoption of 'charity mongering' as a long-term survival strategy was probably even less tenable in the smaller city of Newcastle, and certainly no strict equation can be made about the frequency of a woman's institutional residence, and her 'abuse' of services. Indeed, the whole framework of abuse/not abuse merely replicates a contemporary moral stereotype, rather than providing any further insight into the circumstances of women's lives. Overwhelmingly, the records indicate that women who sought charity sometimes found themselves moving between a network of homes through sheer need. Mary Ruddy, for example, at seventeen, had spent the previous year living in three work-houses, the House of the Good Shepherd in Gosforth and the Salvation Army Rescue Home. She had been turned out of home by her father when she bore an illegitimate child, and was simply unable to provide for herself and her baby.[108]

105 Ibid.
106 SAA Girls' statement book, vol. v, case 85; vol. ii, case 449.
107 Ross, 'Hungry children', 173.
108 SAA Girls' statement book, vol. iii, case 366.

For most women seeking institutional relief, the Salvation Army's regimes may have appeared in certain respects better than most. While uniforms were worn, the home did not emphasise strict confinement, nor did it impose a minimum residential term (although women were encouraged to stay long enough to better ensure their 'salvation'). It also accepted women whose circumstances precluded their admission elsewhere. Recidivists and those with children were accepted, at least in the short term, while the Army's country home in Wooler took children as full-time residents with their mothers. Another important attraction in Newcastle was that the city home did not require the women to perform laundry work. Sewing was the order of the day, interspersed with 'three short bright meetings' to enliven the 'busy hive'.[109]

Although Florence Booth had early insisted that laundry work should not be a regular part of Rescue Home life, many Salvation Army Homes by the 1890s had in fact introduced it as a measure of economy. In Newcastle, however, it appears that laundry work was never introduced. Laundry work was done in the region, but only at the country home opened in Wooler in 1902. The Wooler venture was promoted as a bucolic destination for those for whom more complete separation from the city was deemed desirable, for long-term residents, and for those who were 'suited' to laundry work. Although the village clergy of the Established Church and other reformers saw rural towns as having their own particular perils for unwary young women, the Army viewed Wooler as a safe haven. As well as the beauty of the countryside, the 'beauty' of the work performed there was extolled: 'we could have spent a day watching the happy, neat, and deft-fingered women and girls ironing, folding and sorting', wrote one visitor.[110] (The sentiments of the women so observed were not recorded.) The establishment was run by an Ensign who sat in her glass-house office near the front door, 'in the centre of which she can sit enthroned and view the laundry operations on all three sides'. But as if anticipating an historical interpretation of creeping panopticism, reassurances were provided that the residents were not only happily and fully occupied, but actually 'love rules'. The Wooler Laundry was presented to Salvation Army readers as a stroke of good fortune. Local philanthropist Lady Tankerville had had the laundry built in 1900, its profits to be devoted 'to missionary purposes'. The venture became inconvenient for her to maintain, however, and so 'it passed into the hands of Mrs. Bramwell Booth'.[111] It also proved to be very profitable. While the Newcastle home was running at a clear loss in 1904, the considerable income from Wooler not only covered this shortfall in the region and its own costs, but generated a modest surplus for the Army.[112]

---

109 Hilda Copeland, 'Our north country rescue home', *The Deliverer*, Aug. 1893, 2.
110 'A Salvation Army laundry up amongst the Cheviot hills', ibid. July 1904, 7.
111 Ibid.
112 The annual report of the women's social and rescue work of the Salvation Army, 1904, SAA.

Assessing the significance of the Salvation Army's work in the region and its impact upon poor women immediately highlights certain tensions and ambiguities. In its own terms, the Army's 'success' was mixed. While some women professed to have received religious enlightenment, for many more silence about their spiritual state suggests that the impact of the Army was more material than spiritual. Certainly, the philosophy underlying assistance and the regimes in the Army's home would have made possible the strategic use of its services, without professed conversion. Barring a clear public outburst of complete non-belief, the women were not denied assistance for want of religious feeling.

The Army's 'success' in redirecting women's lives and occupations, too, is a little unclear. While the majority of women in the home were found places in service, and this at a higher rate than at the Brandling Home, the more fluid residential requirements of the home meant that those who drifted in and out over a short period were less likely to have their cases detailed. There was no real category of 'failure' as such set up within its records, as it was in those of the Brandling Home where officers were concerned to document those women who 'absconded'.[113] The sources show that the Salvation Army certainly seemed more alert to the intersection of poverty, prostitution and employment than many other organisations. Clara Ozanne wrote in *The Deliverer* on the poverty of working women, and located it in the gap between social assumptions – that men would provide for women – and economic and social realities which ensured that this arrangement was not commonplace, but 'too often exceptional . . . Eve's daughters find themselves compelled to take a large share of the curse pronounced upon the grand old gardener and his wife.'[114] It was an alertness to conditions which materially benefited poor women in need, and translated into sympathetic views of individual women. While Harriet Atkinson came to the home at twenty-eight as a 'very sullen and discontented woman', what else could be expected, mused an officer, from one who had so 'very much to fight against' in her daily life?[115] In broader terms, however, the group none the less operated within and contributed to a gender discourse which continued to connect prostitution to general issues of working-class sexuality and 'immoral' life styles.

---

[113] The Brandling Home and Diocesan House of Mercy were funded through local public subscription and thus subject to public accountability. The different funding basis of the Salvation Army created no such imperative to quantify its successes and failures.
[114] Clara Ozanne, 'Woman's side of the labour question', *The Deliverer*, Aug. 1891, 26.
[115] SAA Girls' statement book, vol. iii, case 114.

From rescue work to case work:
the Charity Organisation Society in Newcastle

In relation to other charitable schemes in Newcastle, the Salvation Army was uncomfortably positioned. While there is evidence of co-operation between the Army and other charity workers like Lady Tankerville, opposition to the Army's work sprang from sources beyond the homes which vied with the Army for rescue cases. To Charles Bosanquet and other similarly COS-minded reformers in the area who sought to systematise and individualise private relief provision, the Salvation Army was deemed not only religiously suspect, but destructively broad and indiscriminate in its work. In particular, the Army's schemes for rescue homes and other shelters for women, the *Charity Organisation Review* stated in 1889, were disastrous:

> It is stated [by William Booth] that many women are tempted or driven to prostitution by poverty, and it is proposed to establish a rate in aid of virtue by multiplying shelters and homes. Nothing could be kinder in intention, nothing could be designed more likely in practice to renew and intensify the evil. Mr. Booth, in fact, proposes to get rid of vice by smoothing its path and mitigating its consequences.[116]

Fear of the abuse of services provided by such enterprises as the Army's Rescue Home was growing, with stories and case histories of women cited to illustrate that even the best laid plans to alleviate suffering could be taken and, redrawn by poor women, turned into blueprints for harm. 'Within the last month one worker has told me she overheard a bad girl in the street say, "If I get into trouble, Mrs. ___ will help me out of it".'[117] By the early 1890s, after the opening of the Salvation Army Rescue Home, the COS's expressed misgivings about the Army's 'indiscriminate' aid were further supported in the editorials of the *Newcastle Journal*.[118]

Undoubtedly the influence of COS thinking grew considerably in some charitable circles in Northumberland from the 1870s. As well as the proliferation of local societies which corresponded with the COS in London, and the emergence of local groups which firmly adhered to the philosophy of the COS such as that in Gateshead, some of the most notable identities within the London COS had strong links to the north-east. Charles Bosanquet, the paid secretary of the COS in London from 1870 to 1875, and Charles Trevelyan, another prominent figure in the society's work, both had extensive economic, social and family ties in the region,[119] while the duke of Northumberland acted as a vice-president for the London group in the 1890s. For both local and national COS adherents, the simultaneous assumption of roles in

116 *Charity Organisation Review* v (Jan. 1889), 22.
117 'Leaves from a lady visitor's notebook', ibid. 19.
118 See Gregson, 'Poor law and organized charity', 102.
119 Ibid. 113, 104.

charities and poor law bodies outside the COS provided further scope for the advocacy of the society's ideas. The most important aspect of its philosophy was a belief that charity should not be haphazard, but 'a partner . . . in the work of thrift', which should always contribute to self-dependence. Although the individual should be trained to responsibility through active charity, consideration of the circumstances of an individual's overall family structure should be routinely undertaken, 'otherwise the strongest social bond will be weakened' by undermining 'natural' familial obligations. In tandem with material assistance, charity should provide aid through instruction, and should foster the 'personal influence and control' of the giver over the recipients of charity. Overall, the idea of treating 'individual cases on a definite plan' would require 'thorough knowledge' of all applicants to charity. This was a '*sine qua non* in beneficial almsgiving'.[120]

In relation to groups of the female poor, the COS's 'self-support' formula again acted automatically to exclude some from assistance. Charles Loch's 1883 handbook, for example, specifically excluded deserted wives from assistance, for fear that benevolence to them might encourage 'other persons to follow a pernicious example' and abandon their wives and families; mothers of illegitimate children similarly should not be assisted except by the most 'careful personal charity', and with 'a quality of sternness to the charity . . . [in order] to stamp out vice'. Widows as well, it was held, should be dealt with cautiously. The chief problem here lay in example once again, with the COS loathe to provide any incentive to men not to prepare adequately for death by providing for their families via insurance, or to women to simply 'squander' money received when they first became widows 'with a most perverse disregard of the future'.[121] Overall moral goals and the reformation of society over-rode any short-term aims of simply helping the poor to cope with misfortune. In such a situation, the poor woman became less of a real person and more of a cultural figure utilised in a moral script.

Gregson argues that in many respects the COS in its Newcastle operations co-operated closely with poor law agencies, the latter recommending cases to the COS for investigation.[122] The regional leader of the Poor Law Administration Conference held in 1874, a conference at which Charles Bosanquet was in attendance, claimed that 'poverty . . . is to be sought out in secret places . . . by agencies beyond and outside of our extensive poor law machinery'.[123] In its co-operation with poor relief officials, Newcastle COS was the exceptional case for the region. Other local societies such as that at Sunderland remained more distant from the poor law agencies. It was, wrote the

---

[120] C. S. Loch, *How to help cases of distress: a handy reference book for almoners, almsgivers and others*, London 1883, facsimile edn, Plymouth 1977, 8–9.
[121] Ibid. 36, 53.
[122] Gregson, 'Poor law and organized charity', 104.
[123] Lord Eslington's address, *Conference on poor law administration held at Newcastle upon Tyne*, Newcastle upon Tyne 1874, 6.

editor of the *Newcastle Journal*, 'thoroughly experienced men acquainted with the seamy side of charity' like those in the COS who were best able to distribute charity to the benefit of both the recipient and society.[124] The Newcastle COS indeed mustered a significant roll-call of prominent urban men. Its patrons included Lord Armstrong, the industrialist husband of Lady Armstrong (whose work figured prominently in the Brandling project), and its physician was Dr Oliver, whose medical and parliamentary committee contributions to the examination of women's labour in the white-lead industry were to become nationally recognised.

The emphasis in the work of the COS was clearly upon the households of the poor rather than the generation of projects which sought to separate poor people into charitable establishments. The theme of revelation through case work was standard fare in the society and within similar charities in the city. Sometimes the revelation of distress, neglect, and its 'proper' solution were visually underscored later in the century with increasing use of before and after photographs of relief recipients, in particular of young people who had been assisted by clothing charities,[125] whereby subscribers could see at a glance that their funds had been applied economically and appropriately, and through which the material markers of 'respectability' and its opposite were again elaborated and further entrenched. Just as Edgar Lee provided through his photographs an opportunity for a 'respectable' audience to inspect the slums at a safe distance, so too these photographs enabled reformers not only to engage in a kind of voyeuristic spectatorship of disorder, but marvel as well at the instantaneous transformation suggested by the photographic medium.

Proceeding systematically, removing the layers which separated the 'legitimate' from the 'fraudulent' claimant, examining the veracity of begging letters, and the minute dissection of personal and family circumstances, all contributed to the construction of the COS as an organisation which was progressive and scientific in its outlook. Despite the views expressed by the regional leader in 1874 about men investigating the 'seamy' side of poverty, moreover, many of the people who assumed these investigative roles were women, although there was evidence that some philanthropic women in the area still adhered to an idea of their passive role in the society, rather than the more active personal involvement in assessment procedures which the society's philosophy demanded. A London visitor to the Sunderland COS reported, with some exasperation, that some philanthropic women in the local society failed to understand the principles of close, personal investigation of cases which characterised the COS: 'One lady on the Committee Miss Nelson . . . seemed amazed at the idea of visiting the poor herself, [and] asked,

124 *Newcastle Journal*, 16 Nov. 1892, cited in Gregson, 'Poor law and organized charity', 102.
125 See, for example, annual reports of the Newcastle-upon-Tyne Police-Aided Association for the Clothing of Destitute Children, NRO, NL/6/5.

what her Agent was for?'[126] The articulation of class differences in the context of case work was not exclusive to bourgeois women either. Some years later, another London visitor was told by the local paid agent of the COS that she 'considers as a working woman herself she can enter into the [circumstances?] of the applicants better than "gentlefolks" could'.[127]

Most of the work of the COS revolved around providing temporary loans for the 'deserving' cases which came to its attention, and acting in a consultative fashion with regard to the provision of relief in the city during periods of 'exceptional distress' – periods which arose frequently in the last three decades of the century. Its annual reports contained 'specimen cases' of assistance although, significantly, the lists of those who were exposed as undeserving and fraudulent were usually twice as long as those which were deemed satisfactory, since 'we wish our friends to see the various methods adopted for extracting money from the unwary and large-hearted, though too often misguided public'.[128] The need for constant, minute surveillance via a more systematic and personal approach and a preoccupation with the adoption of strategies to expose the misuse of relief were imperatives, and permeated many of the texts of Newcastle charities in the second half of the century.

Ellen Ross has found for London that charity was never put to the uses it was intended. Utilising the image of the 'deformation of the gift' elaborated in the work of Gareth Stedman Jones, Ross maintains that while reformers sometimes optimistically viewed the charitable gift as a means of bridging class differences, it was 'invariably distorted as it travelled from one side to the other'.[129] Examples of this 'deformation' were to be found in Newcastle. The Lord Mayor's Relief Committee, for example, regularly dispensed soup in the streets for the needy, usually upon production of a ticket provided to them by respectable philanthropists. In January 1867 nearly 3,000 gallons of soup were dispensed in this way from a shop front in the dingy arched underbelly of Stephenson's celebrated High Level Bridge.[130] Even at this early date, fears were expressed that a market in tickets had been developed to secure a small profit for their holders. By the 1890s, when COS advisers played a role in the soup kitchen, the system was revised so that soup was directly dispensed by relieving officers, experienced charity workers and others with a specific local knowledge of the poor. Allegations had been made by the mayor that under the ticket system, 'people at the bottom of Pilgrim Street [i.e. the slums] had for weeks kept their lodgers with the soup from the soup

[126] Mrs C. T. Streatfield to Mr Masterman, 24 Sept. 1893, Provincial COS files, Sunderland 1892–1913, GLRO, A/FWA/C/F7/1.
[127] Mrs C. T. Streatfield to Mr Masterman, 2 Dec. 1906, ibid.
[128] *Newcastle-on-Tyne Society for the Organisation of Charitable Relief and Repressing Mendicity*, annual report 1885, Newcastle upon Tyne 1885.
[129] Ross, 'Hungry children', 173–4; Stedman Jones, *Outcast London*, ch. xiii.
[130] Committee minutes, 18 Jan. 1867, General Soup Kitchen minute book, 1862–8, TWAS 595/72.

kitchen'.[131] Concern was evinced in the previous year that, while 'suffering families are not responsible for the indolence of the paternal breadwinners', those who staffed the kitchen should exercise a 'wise discretion' to ensure that no encouragement were given to the 'sluggard' to cease providing for his family.[132]

Similar concerns were expressed by the organisers of 'exceptional' relief in the city in the 1880s, when extraordinarily severe weather had curtailed employment. Men (and it would appear only men were defined here as 'workers') were provided with the opportunity to participate in public works on the Town Moor. Public dinners were held to feed the hungry, and were usually accompanied by an educational speech from a local dignitary. At one such dinner, despite the later claim that women and children were not to be punished for their husband's sluggardliness, the gendered text of the accompanying speech implicated women and their overseeing of the household in the maintenance of a man's respectability: the speaker advised the women present that in such hard times their task was 'to make their homes as bright and cheerful as possible as some inducement to their husbands to stay indoors, and as a counter attraction to those places [i.e. pubs] where money was spent in such a manner as to deprive many families of the comforts of life'.[133] But against the possibility that women might take those goods – blankets, clogs and clothing – provided by the Relief Fund to make households more 'comfortable', and subvert their intended purpose by pawning them, the Town Clerk reported that the Pawnbrokers' Association had 'issued a special circular warning their members to be careful and not to take in any goods bearing our stamp'.[134]

The shift to case work and the systematic investigation of relief applicants thus exposed in greater detail the uses to which poor women themselves put charitable assistance. The ways in which case work was presented in the reports of the COS fuelled a discourse of suspicion in the realm of charity which in some respects carried echoes of Chadwick, Senior and the other 'system-builders' of 1834. That poor women once more, through the greater use of more 'scientific' management of charity, were frequently excluded from the outset by the definitions used by the COS in its approach to the (male) worker, or alternatively cast in stereotypically dichotomous terms of 'deserving' or 'undeserving' with all of its gendered variants, is evident from the source material. Against the definitions of the 'ideal' thrifty and respectable woman of the working class, the identity of the poor woman was often constructed as incomplete, disordering, and always still-to-be-worked-upon, to be 'improved', to be 're-made'.

131 Newsclipping, 11 Mar. 1892 (unidentified newspaper), in the General Soup Kitchen minute book, 1879–1900, TWAS 595/74.
132 Newsclipping, 31 Jan. 1891 (unidentified newspaper), ibid.
133 *Daily Chronicle*, 1 Mar. 1886, news cutting in Newcastle Relief Fund, extracts from newspapers, 1885–6, TWAS, L361/30227.
134 *Daily Chronicle*, Jan. 21 1886, news cutting ibid.

Yet the constructions of femininity within the texts of charity, and within the texts of poor relief, should not obscure the element of negotiation which occurred between providers and recipients. Certainly, the evidence from Newcastle would support Ross's contention that 'working-class people knew that middle-class probing demanded circumspection'.[135] While the respective power of each group was certainly unequal, and the opportunities available to women in their negotiations occurred within an overarching framework of spatial, temporal and behavioural constraints which may have prompted them to 'perform' both their poverty and their femininity in ways which better matched the categories devised by reformers, there were negotiations, and evidence of women's agency throughout. Although women were constructed discursively within the categorising constraints of the charitable text, there was more to their history and experience in the homes than the mere exemplification or simple passive ventriloquism of dominant images generated by a reforming, philanthropic bourgeoisie. Further, while the extensive material generated by charities and relief bodies present a dichotomised view of working-class life in Victorian Northumberland – of a world divided between those in receipt, and those not in receipt, of charity – which was informed by numerous stereotypes and symbolic images of poverty and progress in the region, charitable and poor law agencies provided only one set of sites and texts contributing to the construction of meanings around the female poor. To focus exclusively on the terrain of charity and poor relief, on the relations between and respective expectations of provider and recipient, is perhaps to create the false impression that outside these constraints, outside these specific sites, women enjoyed considerable freedom to constitute their own identities, and these were identities somehow at odds only with the views of bourgeois reformers.

Yet women were engaged in constant processes of negotiation. Previous discussion has highlighted the importance of the workplace, for example, its changing meanings, and the implications of these changes for women. It has been suggested in those contexts that in both urban and rural Northumberland, the workplace was a primary site in which gender identities were actively elaborated. At work that process was by no means confined to negotiations between employers and employees, but also between male and female workers. While many of the tensions around feminine identity and the experiences of poor women were elaborated most obviously and most dramatically when they intersected with class differences as well, the scanty evidence from court records, newspapers and memoirs attests to similar tensions arising within working-class culture. Leading from this discussion of charitable and philanthropic work, then, with its overwhelming reliance upon moral definitions of poor women, the following section explores the strategies for survival which women engaged in, their patterns of life, and the construction of their gendered identities within the terrain of working-class culture. In some

---

[135] Ross, 'Hungry children', 168.

respects a paucity of literature in this area renders the section more speculative than others, yet this quality itself may prompt the historian to reflect upon the significance of the gaps, silences and omissions which make the 'conversations' of poor women from within, and about, their own culture the 'coldest' and most inaccessible of all.

'The best kept secret': women's survival strategies and the negotiation of working-class cultures

Discussion of prostitution and related issues in Newcastle was not confined to the arena of middle-class philanthropy. The dialect poet James Horsley, for example, wrote a direct appeal to the working women of Newcastle around 1880 which sold as a halfpenny ballad sheet in the city:

> O, lasses, remember yor feythers at hyem,
> An' yor muthers, whe's hearts ye are breakin',
> An' the bruthors an' sisters yor bringin' te shyem,
> An' the awful-like future yor myekin;
> Divvent hanker for plissure nor dresses se fine,
> Nor be tempted bi fashin' an' beauty;
> Think twice ere ye start on that dreadful decline
> That leads ye fre' virtue and duty.
> Remember, yor sumboddy's bairn.[136]

This address, directed at a working-class audience in the authentic language of its culture, serves as a timely reminder to the historian that, as well as dominant middle-class discourses about female working-class sexuality expressed through the records of institutions such as the Brandling Home, there existed other discourses in which the meanings of sexuality were explored. Horsley's poem drew on long conventions of ballad and folk-poetry writing in the area, and its cautionary tone around issues of sexuality replicated one of the themes so frequently found within them. 'Blue-eyed Mary', for example, told the standard tale of seduction leading to prostitution and poverty, and incorporated the key symbols by which degradation could be readily measured:

> Pale want now approaches – the pawnbroker's near,
> And her trinkets and clothes, – one by one disappear;
> Till at length sorely pinched and quite desperate grown,
> The poor blue ey'd Mary is forc'd on the town.
> In a brothel next see her, trick'd out to allure,
> And all ages, all humours – compell'd to endure.[137]

---

136 James Horsley, *She's sumboddy's bairn*, Newcastle c. 1880 (TWAS 1074/228).
137 'Blue eyed Mary', n.d., BL, MS Bell 11621.i.2., vol. ii.

As well as sentimental cautionary ballads around the figure of the prostitute, the other dominant image of women which emerged was that of the notorious, 'disreputable woman' – the scold, the fishwife, the raucous street-seller, the 'vulgar vendor void of shame'.[138] Frequently, the subject was constructed from a disparaging masculine perspective and relied upon that tired combination of hostility and sexual goading which marked patriarchal ribaldry, although occasionally complaints about specific incidents were aired from a 'female' point of view. For example, the authorities' decisions to relocate market-women early in the century as the steady work of urban improvement and the rationalisation of city spaces took place were marked in protest ballads which complained of unequal treatment of different categories of sellers, or bemoaned women's removal from more traditional expansive selling spaces to confined and regulated locations: 'Ye've cram'd us in a Dandy Cage/ Like yellow yowlies, bears and monkies', ran one such ballad after Sandgate fishwives were moved to the New Fish Market in 1826.[139]

While the ballads and folksongs were usually written by men, they none the less convey some sense of alternative dimensions and spaces of identity construction, where the figures in the broadsheets were not 'mere ornaments', but were drawn from and contributed to 'living elements in the popular imagination'.[140] While it is impossible to gauge the extent of broadside and popular literature in the city, much less its influence, bourgeois contemporaries expressed particular alarm at the circulation of 'vulgar' material and 'prints' which were allegedly 'doing more to demoralize and pollute the minds of the rising generation than any other agency in existence'.[141] At street-level in Sandgate, Quayside and elsewhere, modes of behaviour and cultural 'rules' may have set men and women 'apart from the dominant code of morality' of bourgeois society,[142] and overlapped with it at other times, but none the less there were codes and rules and they were strongly gendered in their formulation.

How did poor women experience working-class culture? As Marion Glastonbury observes, the ways in which working-class women live and what they know in twentieth-century culture constitute the 'best-kept secret[s]' of all. Her perspectives are similarly relevant for the nineteenth century in Newcastle. Her reflections on the status of working-class women's experience are worth quoting at length:

> The mass of women . . . [are] bound to activities so irredeemable that they scarcely merit the name of experience. By definition, experience is part of a bargain in the minds of articulate people; time, your allotted span of consciousness, is exchanged for your impression of the world. . . . Experience is

138 J. Holling, 'Mustaches; or, the C___l and the fish wench', n.d., ibid. vol. i.
139 R. Emery, 'The fishwives' complaint', c. 1826, ibid. vol.ii.
140 V. de Sola Pinto and A. E. Rodway (eds), *The common muse*, Harmondsworth 1965, 27.
141 *Inquiry into the condition of the poor*, 1st ser., letter vii, 57.
142 Barret-Ducrocq, *Love in the time of Victoria*, 180.

that residue of existence that counts as an asset because its validity is acknowledged by others; its acquisition entitles us to speak. . . . Working-class women,
literate or illiterate, play virtually no part in these transactions since their preoccupations are not convertible into the accepted currency of truth. Their
days yield no lessons, stimulate no ideas, confer no distinctions, take no recog-
nizable shape. What happens to them and what they make of it is by common
consent devoid of interest and goes unrecorded, unless the overflow of their
lives threatens to block our drains.[143]

As previously discussed, the 'currency of truth' was always at issue where poor
women did speak in nineteenth-century Northumberland, and certainly
much investigation into the conditions of life for women occurred within a
context of 'dangerous' encroachment and overflow. Glastonbury's plumbing
metaphor is reminiscent of the strong images of contagion and disorder of
working-class culture drawn by the *Newcastle Chronicle* reporter in 1850
interviewing a street-seller in her home next to a Sandgate soapery, a soapery
whose drains were so frailly constructed that, ominously, 'the filthy stream had
burst through' again and again.[144]

Working within the available body of sources makes generalisation about
women's experience both inevitable and dangerous. In Newcastle, virtually
the only fragments of poor women's experience are 'embedded in the literary
testimony of others'.[145] The sources can trap the historian within the discursive structures of meaning which first produced those sources. It can reproduce those acts of generalisation which, for example, nineteenth-century
discourses of relief and rescue necessarily relied upon to transform individual
women's experiences into a few distinct objective categories. Yet it is essential at least to attempt to assess where working-class women's understandings
of themselves were distinct from bourgeois constructions of their experiences;
to indicate that, for these women, establishing identity and location within
society and culture was an exercise constituted through multiple, overlapping
and conflicting discourses. It is also important to assess the degree to which
women's behaviour represented a 'chameleon strategy',[146] a sort of cultural
surrender of the self, the tactical concealment of personal priorities to secure
– however temporarily – social and economic survival. Such assessments
operate in the margins: in the search for those faultlines in the contemporary
literature which attest to the negotiations and contests of gendered working-
class subjectivities, what is most usually revealed are indeed not radical
fissures, but more subtle ripples, shadows and hairline cracks. Diffuse and at
times contradictory source material which relates to the constant process of
'making do' and the gendered parameters of daily life for poor women none

---

143 Marion Glastonbury, 'The best kept secret: how working-class women live and what
they know', *Women's Studies International Quarterly* ii (1979), 171–81 at p. 172.
144 *Inquiry into the condition of the poor*, 1st ser., letter ii, 13.
145 Glastonbury, 'The best kept secret', 172.
146 Ibid. 173.

the less again suggests that they were never wholly constructed objects, nor fully active constructing subjects.

Beyond the formal chronologies and texts of charities and poor relief, there are no ready ordering principles through which poor women's experiences may be analysed. In relation to Northumberland, however, three recurring images of poor women's daily life appear throughout the century, all of which locked into broader dichotomies of virtuous/dangerous, clean/unclean femininity, which are useful for the purposes of this discussion. Some of the most frequently cited measures of feminine identity and respectability applied both to and within working-class culture were sexual conduct, thrift (or lack of it) and sobriety. Each of these measures at times shaded almost imperceptibly into the others, which is not surprising because all were elaborations upon a discourse of excess. Their application in practice often illustrated the constant spatial and discursive interactions which blurred the edges of demarcation between the contemporary bourgeois impetus to 'remake' the working-class, and the working-class's own regimes of regulation.

The maintenance of respectability for working-class women was a continuous process. While there was perhaps some scope for negotiation in certain areas of behaviour, some observation of appropriate sexual behaviour was fundamental to forging a respectable identity. While references relating to pawning, criminality and public disorder are scattered, sources which provide some insight into working-class views on sexuality are virtually non-existent. Clearly, as relief applications and rescue records demonstrate, the reforming middle class were quite fixed in a view that illicit sexual relations underpinned much of the misery which poor women experienced. How far this conception was actually shared by women themselves remains unclear. Catherine Cookson writes that when her mother 'had to come home from "her place" and say she was going to have a baby, The Fathar [Cookson's grandfather] as he was always called, was for killing her – she had committed the unforgivable sin'.[147] On the other hand, the willingness of kin to support mothers of illegitimate children and the matter-of-fact attitudes evinced in rural Northumberland around the issue perhaps attest to different sensibilities.

Beyond these impressionistic sources, much of the history of working-class sexuality is bound up in the records as accounts of those moments where 'life went wrong', where that history of female sexuality is expressed through records of criminal proceedings for abortion and infanticide. These may tell the historian something of the material conditions in which tragedy occurred, and much about bourgeois readings of those conditions, but shed little light upon either women's perspectives of these experiences, or, indeed, the perspectives of working-class men. The standard constructions of working-class sexuality in bourgeois sources were sensationalised, presented

[147] Cookson, *Our Kate*, 150.

in terms which underscored a sense of distance between working-class and bourgeois sensibilities, or merely reduced to a discussion of bodily excess where any affective context was redundant or characterised in broad, 'self-evident' categories of ignorance, naivety or brutishness. The medical details of Elizabeth Hall's botched abortion which led to her death were described in graphic detail in the local press, for example, so that a readership learned about the coroner's findings concerning the state of her reproductive organs, but Hall's life circumstances were only sketchily presented. A 24-year-old servant, she had become pregnant by the married organist of a local church. She was sent by her mother to Durham to sit out the pregnancy at her aunt's, but twice secretly travelled back to the city to meet her lover, who arranged for the abortion which eventually led to her death.[148] Like Elizabeth Graham, Hall appeared fragmented in death, the sum of her bodily parts. The motivations of Hall, her mother, and her lover – whether they acted through moral or economic reasons or both – are just one case where sexuality and its outcomes for working-class women remained perhaps the 'best kept secret' of all.

Infanticide records are similarly difficult to interpret. While contemporary commentaries on infanticide often stressed the incidence of the crime as further proof of the brutality of poor women, any too-ready classification of it as a 'strategy' utilised by poor women can both obscure the complexities of each story, and unwittingly perpetuate contemporary stereotypes of maternal indifference. That infants were abandoned in the city in particular is clear from contemporary accounts; concealment of birth or infanticide were activities perhaps harder to keep secret in the closer face-to-face communities of the rural north. The depositions of witnesses gathered at the assizes, where infanticide cases were tried, again certainly attest to the context of poverty in which the death of an infant occurred. For example, Margaret Allison spent eight days in Alnwick gaol immediately after giving birth, arrested on a coroner's warrant on suspicion of murdering her newborn son. She was acquitted at the inquest where the coroner reported his findings, but Allison in fact requested to remain another night in the cells since she had no home to return to.[149] In another case illustrating the connections between poverty and suspicion of infanticide, Eleanor Thompson's husband had died suddenly, and she had then been forced to remove her infant from the care of a nurse to whom she had paid 3s. 6d. per week for the child in order that she could continue herself to work in service. No longer able to afford the nurse while she herself worked, Eleanor took the child into her own care where it had died, she said, from convulsions.[150] The economic circumstances of

148 *Morpeth Herald*, 12 Feb. 1859, 5. The Salvation Army reported cases of unsuccessful abortion attempts: SAA Girls' statement book, vol. v, cases, 1, 8.
149 Alnwick House of Correction journal and order book, 9, 17 Nov. 1853, 1853–64, NRO NC/12/25 2180.
150 Deposition of Eleanor Thompson, 30 Oct. 1839, Northumberland, Depositions, PRO (Chancery), ASSI 45/65.

Eleanor and other women were referred to in proceedings, seen as a motive for wrongdoing, and a construction of which women themselves were aware. In the case of Ann Hudson, whose child she said was stillborn, the woman had protested to an overseer of the poor when the infant's body was discovered and suspicions of infanticide were first aired, that although she was poor 'she was not without feeling, for if her child had lived, she would not have troubled the overseers, but, would have rather taken it upon her back and gone a begging'.[151] Poor women were deemed suspect if their babies died, their poverty rendering them vulnerable to contemporary prejudice about the ready dispensability of life in poor working-class families. If they had sought to conceal their pregnancy for either reasons of preserving reputation, or to ensure that employment was not jeopardised, that suspicion grew enormously.

If sexuality and its position within contemporary discourses appear problematic, gender negotiations within households often appear in the record, again, only where tragedy, violence or sensation brought them into the public domain, and it is therefore difficult to generalise about the quality of working-class relationships. While unhappy marriages and the violence depicted in the sources may not have been representative, it is interesting none the less to consider the role of marriage in women's strategies and experiences. For some, like Cookson's grandmother, marriage was indeed represented as a possible economic strategy. Despite Cookson's accounts of the husband as a cruel and loathsome individual, her grandmother perhaps married him to allow her to stop working at the Puddling Mills at Jarrow, 'where the owners supplied milk or beer at break to keep the women going', and where 'death met you early'.[152]

The economic desirability of marriage, at least for certain periods in a woman's life cycle, was clear from countless records which attested to the utter destitution women faced when spouses suddenly died or deserted. The economic significance of marriage was legally coded in many ways, and at times in Northumberland women's recourse to law illustrated further their own perception of marriage as an economically-important step, beyond any (invariably unrecorded) appreciation of affective and other bonds which it may have provided. Annie Smith, a 31-year-old servant in Hexham, had been engaged to Thomas Woster for ten years when he broke the engagement, and Annie sued for breach of promise. The jury in the case was specifically instructed that 'the plaintiff was undoubtedly entitled to compensation. The amount ought to be something substantial for loss of the improved prospects a marriage with the defendant had held out.'[153] Annie was awarded £150 by the jury. Odd glimpses into women's sturdy defence of the economic functions of the family also appear in records of industrial protest. While

---

[151] Deposition of Edward Watson, 26 Sept. 1834, ibid. ASSI 45/64.
[152] Cookson, *Our Kate*, 13.
[153] *Hexham Courant*, 12 Mar. 1892, 2.

women had for so long been excluded from mining in the region, and where in mining villages women's work appeared to revolve almost exclusively around the constant maintenance of the men and boys who performed mining labour, Richard Fynes's accounts of the strikes and the accompanying evictions of miners' families provide the only space in his narrative where women appear. Attempted evictions by 'candymen' employed by mining bosses in the 1860s, protected in their work by police, met with fierce resistance from neighbourhood women. After an incident in which a candyman had emptied slops on a woman's head, another group met the evicters with pieces of sheet iron 'used as blasts to draw up the fire – and, accompanying their shrill treble yelling with an incessant and discordant banging on these iron plates, they created a perfect panic. The terrified horses of the policemen plunged and kicked'. The men joined the fight, a riot began and the evictions were suspended.[154]

While discourses on sexuality in the Victorian period frequently deployed images of bodily and affective 'thrift' against which the role of working-class women was frequently portrayed as transgressive, the imagery of excess and lack of control was also deployed consistently in relation to the family economy.[155] There was no more central sign of the instabilities and excesses of life among the poor than the practice of pawning. The extent of pawn-broking as a measure of working-class thriftlessness was almost universally cited by charity workers and other reformers. Although Helen Bosanquet revealed some sensitivity to the logic of pawning in the minute workings of a family economy,[156] most middle-class observers were scathing in their condemnation of this widespread activity. At mid century, there were twenty-six 'official' pawnbrokers listed in a local directory, four of whom were women.[157] Many more acted as small scale money-lenders, and some pawn-brokers lived among the very poor themselves.[158] A woman's responsibility for the family budget took her into a world 'entirely separate from that of her husband . . . encompass[ing] a thriving sub-culture of credit activities', maintains Melanie Tebbutt.[159] In 1854 Rewcastle characterised it as 'particularly a female vice', whereby men's homes were stripped of furniture and 'robbed of all comforts', and where children were left 'starved, naked and neglected'.[160]

---

154 R. Fynes, *The miners of Northumberland and Durham: a history of their social and political progress*, Blyth 1873, repr. Newcastle 1986, 250.

155 See Sally Shuttleworth, 'Female circulation: medical discourse and popular advertising in the mid-Victorian era', in Mary Jacobus, Evelyn Fox Keller and Sally Shuttleworth (eds), *Body/politics: women and the discourses of science*, London 1990, 47–68 at pp. 55–7.

156 H. Bosanquet, *The standard of life*, London 1906, 68, cited in McKibbin, 'Social class and social observation', 180–1.

157 Whellan, *History, topography, and directory*, 356.

158 For example, Ann Stamp, a sixty-year-old pawnbroker, lived in Silver Street in the Sandgate area: 1841 Census, Silver Street, District 5, TWAS HO 107/848.

159 Tebbutt, *Making ends meet*, 38.

160 J. Rewcastle, *Newcastle as it is; reviewed in its moral aspects, social state and sanitary condition*, Newcastle 1854, 22.

Certainly, as the poor relief applications from All Saints illustrated in the previous chapter, women relied upon pawning when faced with destitution, making difficult decisions about the goods which could or could not be relinquished. Other sources attest to the more creative use of pawning to finance leisure: while ratting provided the favourite sport in the area for men, for women horse-racing attracted attention, and Mondays – after pawning – was usually the time when bets were laid. The bookmakers would make house to house calls after husbands had gone to work, to induce women 'to put their bit on'.[161] Most women, though, looked to pawning to fill the perpetual weekly gap between one week's earnings and the next. Catherine Cookson's mother Kate recalled the joy she felt when she was given boots by a charity, but 'her delight . . . was shortlived because her mother immediately took them to the "In and Out" '.[162] Jack Common remembered his mother preparing her Monday bundle with purpose and efficiency, taking care to wash and brush her hair for the trip, and spending a morning enjoying the sociability after a pawnshop visit, meeting and talking with 'Ma This and Ma That'. In Common's account, the elaboration of respectability operated clearly even within pawning: women like his mother 'took a wholesome pride in themselves' because they always paid the interest on their pledges. Other women, however, were disparaged as 'pledge-swipers', prevailing upon women in the neighbourhood to provide them with goods to pawn when their own goods had all been 'popped'.[163]

Although Tebbutt's contention that pawning activities constituted a subculture is borne out in relation to the transaction itself, the separation of the worlds of men and women could collapse into gender tensions when the results of the transaction did not proceed smoothly. Tebbutt cites a Newcastle street ballad composed after a pawnshop burned down in 1849, which warned that 'mony a wife will rue the day/she put her husband's things away'.[164] In the Common household, his father was always bad-tempered when confronted with 'a kaleidoscope of household property in which objects appear and disappear at the whim of the pawnshop poltergeist'.[165] In the miniature economies in which women managed their families' poverty, the financial transactions of pawning also created some scope for disagreement and allegations of peculation between women. In the Mayor's Chamber in the late 1820s, a number of cases heard involved disputes about the ownership of property which had been pawned. Margaret Bennett was charged with pawning a shirt which was not her own; Elizabeth Johnson had pawned items for Jane Davison one Monday morning, but had allegedly retained 2s. from

161 Sherard, Cry of the poor, 152.
162 Cookson, Our Kate, 150.
163 Common, Kiddar's luck, 119–20.
164 Tebbutt, Making ends meet, 49.
165 Common, Kiddar's luck, 122.

the pawn herself.[166] The pawnbrokers themselves, although relying upon the straitened economic circumstances of poor women to maintain the cycles of their trade, appeared as informants in cases where theft was suspected, although on one occasion a pawnbroker who had gone out of business was herself brought up on charges of disposing of all the goods she held in pledge at that time.[167]

That some women turned to illegal activities is made abundantly clear in the newspaper accounts of the period. Certainly there are numerous accounts of petty theft, with frequent hints as well of the poverty which underlay them. Boots, those relatively expensive but absolutely necessary items, featured commonly in such cases. Elizabeth Short stole two pairs of boots, kept one pair for her own use and sold the other for 5s. When she appeared in court, she pleaded poverty as an extenuating circumstance.[168] Ann Johnson, an Irish woman supporting six children enlisted their aid to steal boots which she hid temporarily in a manure heap outside the premises from which she had stolen them; Isabella Richardson, aged fifteen, was charged with stealing her own stepmother's clothes after she determined to run away from home, but had no resources.[169] Occasionally, an instance of female criminality was considered so audacious that it elicited praise. The *Morpeth Herald* reported a case from the Yorkshire Assizes where a woman had attended an execution and claimed to be the prisoner's mother. Pleading poverty, she was provided with money by local charities, and it was only after her departure that it was discovered that she did not know the deceased prisoner. It was, concluded the Morpeth reporter, 'one of the most extraordinary pieces of imposture we have heard of, and one which shows the greatest amount of tact and ingenuity'.[170]

Other women, their identity as known pickpockets brought constantly before the authorities, saw their notoriety celebrated in nicknames: 'Shepherdess Speedy', for example, figured in the proceedings in the Mayor's Chamber in 1829 and 1830, along with numerous other women charged with stealing, often in the context of prostitution.[171] Late in the century 'Old Sal' was known around Sandgate for her regular 'run ins' with the police for fighting in the street, where she was the 'popular favourite' of those who bet on the outcome.[172] The use of nicknames for the notorious woman is an interesting link between the negotiations of everyday life, and the collective images of disorderly femininity which were generated in the popular imagination. 'Old Sal' and 'Shepherdess Speedy' appear as quintessential 'bad' women, almost caricatures of feminine disorder and a part of its mythologising in working-class cultural forms. But for other women as well, daily life in the Sandgate

---

166 Mitchell, *Proceedings in the mayor's chamber*, 126, 25.
167 Ibid. 22, 142.
168 *Morpeth Herald*, 20 Nov. 1858, 8.
169 Ibid. 9 Apr. 1859, 5.
170 Ibid. 19 Feb. 1859, 5.
171 Mitchell, *Proceedings in the mayor's chamber*, 18, 14.
172 Sherard, *Cry of the poor*, 155.

area was punctuated with regular confrontations and negotiations with authorities. Two Hannahs – Rickaby and Lickley – were brought before the court eleven times between them in a two-year period early in the century, on charges of drunkenness and sleeping in the streets. The occupation of public spaces for some women made their surveillance and arrest more or less constant, and could generate suspicion of their involvement in or knowledge about the violence and crime which occurred around them. Rickaby, for example, as a known 'common prostitute' was detained in connection with a murder in the area, but was later released.[173] In 1886, based on figures presented by the Chief Constable in Newcastle, 'known unfortunates' in the city were on average arrested 2.4 times per year, chiefly for loitering and disorderly conduct.[174] As the city's police force mushroomed from the 1830s,[175] and the identification of 'disordered' parts of the city proceeded rapidly, so the likelihood that women's public behaviour would be scrutinised increased, and with it the possibility that women would have to deal with figures of authority.

Women's involvement in a more constant series of transactions between householders and public authorities came as a consequence, not just of a growing police force, but also of the proliferation of other government and charitable agencies whose employees moved about the terrain of the poor working-class population to conduct their business. Indeed, negotiations of the conditions of daily life both within households and with public officials were fairly constant, and as Ross has found in London, it was women who usually conducted a family's business with debt collectors and local authorites who came to the doors of households.[176] Jack Common's father was called to his school only on the serious issue of Jack's truancy; his mother attended to all usual matters of liaison between school and home.[177] Thomas Callaghan recalls women who enlisted children in doorstop 'skirmishes' with collectors of various kinds: 'Me muffer not in, you', was the regular cry of a neighbouring child, while Callaghan's brother preferred his standard response of 'Me muther's oot, me da's oot, an' we've got nee money, so there', before closing the door.[178]

In other circumstances, the 'door' between public and private worlds for women could not be closed so effectively, as the impact of public authority reverberated and was experienced by women within their own households. Jack Common's narrative provides one such example of when the divisions between transactions inside and outside the home dissolved in what was, for his mother, a painful process. Common's mother was arrested one day for

---

[173] Mitchell, *Proceedings in the mayor's chamber*, 14, 23, 29, 32, 40, 43, 51, 104, 109, 113.
[174] Captain Nicholls, reported in *NDG*, 1886, 226.
[175] McCord, *North east England*, 172.
[176] Ross, 'Hungry children', 185.
[177] Common, *Kiddar's luck*, 117.
[178] Thomas Callaghan, *Lang way to the panshop*, Rothbury 1987, 11.

drunkenness after she left a pub in which she had had two drinks. Watchful police, in the zealous execution of their duties, displayed a too-ready suspicion of a woman who was seen in the the vicinity of a pub. The woman's disability, which resulted in a severe limp, was mistaken for a drunken lurch by an officer, who took her to the local police station despite her attempts to explain. She was not drunk, Common recalled, but 'lame, tired, and fatally flustered'. His mother was then taken home, and 'her husband gave her a thrashing and forced her to sign the pledge. . . . I held that whatever she did was forgivable, and what my father and the police did was not.'[179] The continuum of authority over his mother described by Common emphasises again the constant interaction between the private and public spheres as sites for the regulation of working-class femininity.

Given the ready assumptions of authorities, observers and other working-class people about women's character based upon their occupation of particular spaces and the automatic association of disorderly behaviour with those spaces, any divisions of identity between the 'rough' and 'respectable' for poor women in Newcastle were sometimes only tenuously maintained. The rough/respectable dichotomy was certainly prevalent, however, in contemporary language, and its meanings were generated from within working-class culture as well as from outside it.[180] Drunkenness in particular was cited to mark off the 'rough' from the 'respectable', and concern evinced by contemporary reformers reached almost hysterical pitch by the end of the nineteenth century. It was at this time that liquor consumption in the country reached a peak, and in Newcastle prosecutions for drunkenness far outstripped any national averages.[181] At mid century there were more than 400 pubs and beerhouses listed in Newcastle, and a sprinkling of women appeared as licensees.[182] In rural areas too the number of licensed premises caused alarm; the Salvation Army officers who first went to Wooler noted with disdain that there were no less than seven pubs in that small village.[183] The participation of women in Northumbrian pub culture was long established. References to one of the few examples of a separate cultural experience for women relate to the pubs in the area of Sandgate, for example, where traditionally women-only dances were held to celebrate occasions such as 'the breaking up of women's funds'. John Wilson recalled up to three nights' dancing being held to mark such occasions at mid century, and Boyle refers to women's 'cushion dances' held in Sandgate pubs during the same period.[184]

These women's dances may have provided some particular leisure for

---

179 Common, *Kiddar's luck*, 65.
180 Ross, 'Not the sort that would sit on the doorstep', 40.
181 Brian Bennison, 'Drunkenness in turn-of-the-century Newcastle upon Tyne', *Local Population Studies* lii (1994), 14–22 at p. 14.
182 Whellan, *History, topography, and directory*, 342–7.
183 'A Salvation Army laundry up amongst the Cheviot hills', *The Deliverer*, July 1904, 7.
184 Wilson, *Memoirs of a labour leader*, 35; Boyle, *Vestiges of old Newcastle*, 90.

women when their occupation of pubs elsewhere could prove contentious. Thomas Callaghan's grandfather was a publican in the nineteenth century, and 'did not take too kindly to the presence of women on his licensed premises; only charwomen, and those seeking to have their jugs topped up, were ever allowed in the two houses he managed'.[185] The observation of appropriately gendered spaces was not just the preserve of bourgeois reformers. While the maintenance of gender boundaries no doubt proceeded throughout the nineteenth century, it was at the end of the century in particular that alarm was evinced about women's drinking activities, and steps taken to curb the 'unfeminine' public displays of drinking and the riotous behaviour which were thought to accompany them. Bennison points out that although prosecutions for female drunkenness peaked in 1900, men were represented in a ratio of about 3:1 in the statistics for prosecution overall. He has also found that in relation to persistent offenders, women were more likely than men to be prosecuted repeatedly. The decline in prosecution of women after 1900 is attributed to a decision by authorities to 'take the worst female offenders out of circulation', sending them to the Royal Victoria Home in Brentry for compulsory rehabilitation, usually unsuccessful. Bennison's conclusion on these issues, however, that arresting women for drunkenness may have been 'part of a policy which was aimed at curbing prostitution rather than drunkenness',[186] underestimates both the specific contemporary concerns about female drunkenness which were being expressed at the time, and the tendency of authorities to elide the identities of prostitutes and drunken women anyway.

In 1893 the Newcastle Board of Guardians had expressed concern about the burden which alcoholism created upon the poor rate, and had called for special inebriate homes to be established to deal with the problem.[187] That the authorities chose to focus upon female drunks in particular was certainly in keeping with the panic expressed in some quarters that women's drinking was not only socially destabilising, but was becoming unsettlingly more and more visible – even mobile. The *Diocesan Gazette* reported in a scandalised manner the growth of women's 'trip clubs' in the city in 1899:

> The landlord of the public-house lets it be known that he is getting up an outing for the women folk – subscriptions, say 6d. a week for ten weeks. A dozen or more women join, and the club starts. . . . The day arrives, and the members start in a brake for some neighbouring town or village, provisioned with liquor for the day.

The resulting scenes, it was reported, were indescribable and 'simply disgusting'. Through this means, 'all our informants agree that the number of intoxi-

185 Callaghan, *Lang way*, 6.
186 Bennison, 'Drunkenness', 16–19.
187 Clerk to Local Government Board, London, 21 Feb. 1893, Newcastle Union correspondence, 1893–4, PRO, MH 12/9130.

cated females *visible* has increased' (my emphasis).[188] This 'disordered' femininity on wheels, a literally and metaphorically 'fluid' femininity, could be viewed easily by onlookers on the Barras Bridge as the trip clubs left Newcastle on their jaunts.

But again, while participation in these exclusively female leisure activities may be interesting for the light it sheds on women's leisure patterns and shared experience, as well as some desire to escape the usual prohibitions of gendered space generated within the working-class by people like Thomas Callaghan's publican grandfather, insistence on the existence of a separate women's culture in the working class is problematic.[189] Certainly, there were moments when women claimed space or activities as their own, and these activities may have constituted a respite from their usual responsibilities in working-class households as they faced the never-ending task of making do. For women who went on trip club outings, for example, the crossing of the Barras Bridge may have signalled a freedom from some of the immediate constraints upon women's behaviour in the neighbourhood, but returning at night the bridge was crossed again and marked the resumption of more entrenched patterns and expectations of behaviour, and the localised scrutiny which accompanied them. Specifically women-centred activity often occurred in snatched space, snatched time, and existed within a broader cultural framework of assumptions within the working class about the contours of 'appropriate' femininity, where separate activities or women's behaviour at times generated tension.

The mother of Jack Common associated with what her husband called 'the Ma gang', for example, and her position within the 'gang' as explored in his narrative, often appears as both temporally and spatially distinct from her other roles in the household and community. Within the 'gang', too, there were internal formulations of 'respectability' which were noted, as well as an appreciation of how the group was perceived from without: 'it became established by reputation around the circle that they might have had a bad name with some folks . . . but we never, oh never neglect our bairns'. That an observer could see that one's children 'were all well looked after . . . was one of a repertoire of compliments which one Ma always paid to another'.[190] Common himself, with considerable condescension, observed as curious the extensive circle of ragged women in the neighbourhood who were engaged in this 'culture of the Mas', concluding that they seemed to be constantly engaged in 'running errands of misery' as they assisted one another (often, he believed, as a cover for secret drinking). The women's sense of separateness was also underscored by the evaporation of the 'Mas' at any time that

---

188 *NDG*, Oct. 1899, 150.
189 For an early discussion of the concept see DuBois and others, 'Politics and culture in women's history', 26–64.
190 Common, *Kiddar's luck*, 117.

Common's father was about: 'they fled the moment he appeared'.[191] It is clear from the account of the 'Mas' that Common overlooked the functions of mutual assistance which the group provided – caring for children, temporary loans and so on – as well as the companionship of drinking and gossip. Some years earlier the investigator in the mid-century *Inquiry into the condition of the poor* remarked in similar fashion about the poor's 'inability' to converse on any matter 'beyond the local gossip of the day',[192] yet it was just this type of shared local knowledge which could be critical in determining the success of women's strategies in managing their economic resources.[193] In fact, the distinction between survival strategies and leisure activities for women seems in many respects a spurious one, since it was in the realm of these close and friendly contacts that the bonds of reciprocity and trust were forged which were called upon in times of need.

The women's neighbourhood networks operated in ways which transgressed order in temporal terms as well. They disrupted neat boundaries between leisure and work, between private and public spaces, and in so doing were shaped and were responsive to time-frames other than those cultivated through the time-disciplines of the 'progressive' nineteenth-century industrial world. While middle-class women's appearance on the streets *en route* to shops or meetings was linked to clear, well-defined and well-timed purposes which reflected their own busy roles within a timetable of orderly family life, the apparently aimless socialising within working-class women's networks on the streets and on doorsteps where women disrupted routines to run 'errands of misery' if they arose, displayed a different use of time. Certainly women like Common's mother still had their days and nights organised around the lives and needs of working husbands and children. But this further, separate dimension of loosely scheduled and flexible 'women's time' in which leisure and the exchange of gossip was combined with assisting others as need arose – during certain phases of life or intermittent crises, such as childbirth or the death of a spouse – were more reminiscent of pre-industrial time-cultures than of the ideal routinised order of Victorian everyday life.[194]

The critical importance of neighbourhood and local networks was often exemplified by women's increased economic and social vulnerability when they moved outside them. As discussed in the previous chapter, there was recognition of kin and neighbourhood support on the part of relief authorities in some cases, while there was ample evidence of women who moved in search of work, or to a new area of residence, becoming stranded and then destitute when they could not depend upon the face-to-face relations of

---

191 Ibid.
192 *Inquiry into the condition of the poor*, 1st ser., letter iv, 29.
193 Ross, 'Not the sort that would sit on the doorstep', 52.
194 On the distinction between industrial and pre-industrial time see E. P. Thompson, 'Time, work-discipline and industrial capitalism', *Past and Present* xxxviii (1967), 56–97. For a discussion of concepts of 'women's time' as disruptive see J. Kristeva, 'Women's time', in Toril Moi (ed.), *The Kristeva reader*, Oxford 1986, 187–213.

social, economic and moral support they had perhaps enjoyed elsewhere. And the importance of such support was not confined to the city. One of four women in a gang of fourteen which had travelled a very long distance from Peterhead in Scotland for the Northumbrian harvest complained to Henley in 1867 that away from her own neighbourhood, she was forced to share sleeping quarters with male gang members in a way which 'wouldna be allowed . . . in Scotland', and which obviously transgressed her own sense of propriety: it was an arrangement which would make her own community 'look very sair upon [the women] when they came back if they knew all about it'. She told Henley that all the profits of their harvest work had been spent on alcohol by the men, and that she did not know how some of them would get home.[195]

That women's participation in neighbourhood groups sometimes created tensions in households like Jack Common's suggests that working-class culture was differently experienced and understood by men and women. In relation to other matters as well, it was the private space of the household and family which was the site for discord, and the cultural regulation of gendered behaviour. While public authorities expressed deep concern about women drinking, for example, it was Callaghan's grandfather himself who attempted to enforce a non-drinking, non-smoking regime upon his wife, although he partook in both activities. In that case his determination was unsuccessful, and he separated from his wife as a result.[196] Cookson relates how gender roles were rigidly maintained in the realm of domestic duties. Men were described as 'nappy washers' or 'Jessies' if they helped in the home, no matter how urgent the circumstances: 'Both me granda and me uncle Jack would have let the clothes go rotten on their backs before they would have washed them. . . . Man's rightful standing in his house was a thing to be guarded, to be fought for.'[197]

Whether women's transactions of gender and the negotiation of their gendered identity in Northumberland in the nineteenth century occurred in public or in private spaces, even the chronologically scattered and vastly different sources which are available attest to the continuous elaboration of both processes. Certainly in the context of charities and 'rescue' agencies in the city, and in the countryside as well, these processes were overt, and the subject of continuous scrutiny and assessment. The charitable projects of 're-making' working-class femininity were present in various forms throughout the century, shifting from an emphasis upon containment and separation to an emphasis upon transformation, and then, towards the close of the century, towards 'scientific' and systematic management of both poverty and personal identity through the spread of case work. The evidence about

195 *Women's employment in agriculture*, 1867 Report, appendix c, unnamed witness, 240.
196 Callaghan, *Lang way*, 6.
197 Cookson, *Our Kate*, 25. See also Common, *Kiddar's luck*, 80.

individual women's lives frequently underscores their relative powerlessness and material dependence, and the extent to which the meanings of their economic circumstances were refracted through the lens of femininity. None the less, in these contexts the theme of both resistance to prescribed regimes of femininity, and the subversion of the intended purposes of relief provision, appear consistently and illustrate the resourcefulness of the women involved. While women were subject to the reforming zeal of philanthropists, 'soul-savers' and others, their transformative missions were at times quite clearly themselves transformed by poor women in ways to better serve their own needs and priorities.

Within working-class culture, transactions and negotiations of gender may have shifted at times to a differently textured landscape which yielded alternative meanings and gendered behaviour, but certainly did not cease. Nor can easy, distinct boundaries be drawn between sites where the discourse of bourgeois reform predominated, and those where working-class discourses of 'respectability' and 'roughness' came into play: certainly by the end of the century, the movement of observers and authorities within predominantly working-class spaces – visiting, patrolling, advising, investigating and simply arriving uninvited – saw slum areas in particular and women within them become the object of different, but related, regulatory impulses. Further, while the available sources provide little sense of that illusion of 'complet-eness' provided in the copious charitable texts, that women operated, some-times secretly, sometimes openly and in company with other women, to secure livelihoods for themselves and survival for their families in a dazzling variety of ways, establishes the relevance for the north-east of many of the conclusions reached by historians such as Ellen Ross in other regions.

Above all, both within working-class culture and outside it, the genera-tion of particular discourses about poor women and the construction of their social and economic identities was pervasive. In charitable homes and private households, as much as at work, in the streets, and in the poor relief office, being poor and being female conditioned both material conditions for the women, and cultural understandings for both the women themselves and those with whom they came in contact. While the countryside perhaps remained freer of the intensive inspection and regulation witnessed in the city, it too yielded dominant discourses about the meanings of poverty and women's identity, which were at times distinct, but at times linked the country and the city materially and culturally. It was within and through these various and sometimes contradictory discourses that 'appropriate' femi-ninity was defined and 'disorderly' femininity constructed in opposition to it; both coalesced in the broad but shifting framework of constraints and oppor-tunities within which women operated in Northumberland over the century. If the poles of experience and meanings attached to the poor in nineteenth-century Northumberland could be represented by the alternative 'mon-uments' of progress and poverty discussed earlier – Common's bed, and Stephenson's statue – many indeed, like Common, lived life closer to the shadowy figures he describes, under the 'minus signs' of want and 'making-do', than to the monument of the region's glittering prosperity and solid future. And for women, that experience, and those shifting meanings, were conditioned distinctively by their gender.

Conclusion

Reading the future

When essayist Harriet Martineau wrote her book on paupers in 1833, she relied on two assertions which, for her at least, were iron-clad. First, in setting out the circumstances of poverty and its relief in society, she did so on 'unquestionable authority', that of the Poor Law Commissioners. Second, whatever the abuses, vice and ignorance she would expose through her work, she assured her readers that they could take comfort in knowing that 'all social systems [are] remediable'.[1] In some ways, Martineau exemplified a central belief in the nineteenth century: that gathering and acting upon knowledge in a rational manner was the way to achieve progress. The twin forces of knowledge and progress would ensure that, in the future, the worst features of the present would not be replayed.

In nineteenth-century Northumberland, discussions of the shape of society drew constantly upon these linked notions of knowledge and progress. They informed the context within which both the material circumstances and cultural meanings of women's work and women's poverty were elaborated. Increasingly, 'knowledge' about working-class women became the domain of a range of experts – reformers, charity workers, poor law guardians, investigative journalists and parliamentary commissioners. These experts were not necessarily in agreement about how to address the various problems they 'discovered' among poor working-class women, nor did they agree on a definition of these problems. However, the knowledge they produced contributed to a collective sense of unease about the shape of contemporary working-class femininity. Poverty and work, when imagined by middle-class experts and linked to women, tied into deeper Victorian concerns about feminine identity. There was, as Christina Crosby has remarked, a 'ceaseless asking of the woman question',[2] and although that question was often posed in relation to middle-class women and their roles and duties, the problems constructed around working-class women's lives and experiences were no less plentiful. And, in their distance from bourgeois life, working-class women came to be seen as both fascinating and troublesome figures in this process of investigation.

In some respects, the scrutiny and discussion of working-class women, which clearly did not involve any close consultation with women themselves

---

[1] Harriet Martineau, *Poor laws and paupers illustrated*, London 1833, preface.
[2] Christina Crosby, *The ends of history: Victorians and 'the woman question'*, New York 1991, 3.

in Northumberland, was part of the trend towards the 'typification' of social identities in Victorian society, as traced by Tolson. He argues that, from mid century in particular, the impetus to develop 'strategies for social intervention' relied more and more upon locating typical 'signs which [could] be read to support cultural generalisations', rather than seeking to locate 'the representative witness'.[3] Such generalisations can be seen, for example, in the operation of the poor law. Its objectifying categories, against which poor women were measured before they might be offered or refused relief, provided generalisations whose application to the social problem of poverty organised disorder into order. These general categories promised – though did not necessarily deliver – a more orderly social life, in which poverty would be a manageable problem; they also promised to make orderly the process by which people were publicly identified and treated as poor. In this process, at least in theory, the identity of the poor was to be non-negotiable: in practice poor women by their agency upset these categories and engaged in continuous negotiations to gain official relief on terms a little closer to their own.

Throughout the century, the growing divisions in industrial capitalism between the spheres demarcated as public and private brought increased emphasis upon public 'displays of self' which enabled others 'to judge inner sincerity and moral worth'.[4] The visibility of the public self allowed middle-class observers in Northumberland to make quick and 'obvious' judgements of social failure in their scrutiny of the working class. Their conclusions were sometimes damning and, in their view, augured ill for the project of securing the north's pre-eminence as a socially and economically progressive region. Sections of the working class such as the poor were seen by some observers as blights, which hindered and afflicted the course of social progress through allegedly perpetual indulgence in behaviour – intemperance, improvidence, ignorance – which was the obverse of progressive ideals.

A sense of 'making progress' proceeded in part by mapping current limits, to identify that which must be overcome to secure further progress. This delimitation took many forms. Frontiers of progress were imagined geographically, for example, in relation to the 'unconquered' parts of Africa. Closer to home, the frontiers were imagined within certain parts of cities like London, traversed by Mayhew and others in the search for knowledge, and constructed as no less remote than areas of 'darkest' Africa despite its physical location within the very centre of Victorian culture. There were also the imagined boundaries between the orderly urban spaces of central Newcastle, and the dangerous streets of Sandgate. At times, indeed, discourses of progress in one area served as metaphors for progress and civilisation (or lack of them) in other situations. The bondaging system was cast as a form of

---

3   Tolson, 'Social surveillance and subjectification', 114.
4   Lauren Langman, 'Neon cages: shopping for subjectivity', in R. Shields (ed.), *Lifestyle shopping: the subject of consumption*, London 1992, 40–82 at p. 44.

internal slavery for example; a Salvation Army officer contrasted the plight of slum-dwellers, and the children who starved in Newcastle, with the grandeur of 'the Empire on which the sun never sets', a heritage of which England's dead children would never be conscious.[5]

Without the construction of 'others' – unknown African geographies, the hidden 'perversions' within working-class cultures – there was no way of establishing just how far progress had come, and how far it still had to go: only by pushing beyond the boundaries might the extent of disorder be known and, by incorporating it within known society, made regular. The rhetoric of progress throughout the century then, was constantly reinvigorated as previous boundaries and limits dissolved and new ones were installed, to maintain the order achieved thus far.

How did a preoccupation with progress play itself out in the particular circumstances of women's work and poverty in Northumberland? The relationship of women to narratives of progress exposes the gendered nature of visions of progress themselves. Christina Crosby has written astutely of the ways in which women figured in, and were (necessarily) excluded from, Victorian conceptions of 'history'. She argues persuasively that the construction of women as passive and ahistorical was a critical discursive manoeuvre to maintain the integrity of historical explanation, to secure a stable, active identity for middle-class men, and to contribute thereby to the achievement of middle-class hegemony. The whole process, Crosby argues, was fundamentally dependent upon sexual politics and understandings of gender identity which fixed 'woman' as essential, and beyond 'history'.[6] In measuring the relevance of her insights for the specific history of working women and poor women in the north-east, I would insist on a perhaps obvious, but none the less important extension of her idea. If 'woman' was necessarily excluded from history, but had to be accommodated in very particular ways alongside 'history' to maintain that historical conception, the same discursive logic operated within Victorian understandings of progress. A vision of progess, the writing of the 'history of the future' in Victorian England, often positioned 'woman' outside that vision, thereby legitimating the need for social reform and, at the same time, further contributing to the process of male identity formation by providing an 'other' against whose dependence and passivity male agency and independence might be established. While women were perceived as critical in creating the conditions for progress through proper guardianship of home, husband and children, the logic of progress ultimately relied upon an assertion of women's unchanging and essentially private identity, an identity which lay beyond history, and therefore beyond progress.

The exclusion of women from public work and the ideal of their subsumption as dependants within patriarchal family structures were consistent with this gendered conception of Victorian progress, and brought clear material

---

[5] *The County Monthly* (1901), 151, cited in McCord, 'Making of modern Newcastle', 342.
[6] Crosby, *Ends of history*, 2–3.

consequences. Women's formal exclusion from industry and the pressures towards their exclusion from agriculture occurred alongside appeals to progress and Britain's civilising mission at home. The maintenance of the region's reputation, its industrial and economic pre-eminence, so much a mark of its 'progress', was built upon images of local prosperity and the independence of its population which were deployed in ways which obscured the situation of working-class women. The limits of contemporary definition meant that poor independent women seeking relief confronted a system in which female independence could not be accommodated without undermining the broader vision of progress inhering in gendered notions of independence – an independence forged around the figure of the male breadwinner. The poor law, that centre-piece of legislative intervention in nineteenth-century poverty, revealed this contradiction most clearly.

Yet what of the individual experiences of working-class women, for whom the prescriptive middle-class roles of the keeper of family and household may have appeared as a distant discursive shadow? The material conditions of working-class women saw them engage in numerous 'other' roles in Victorian narratives of progress. They were independent workers; single mothers; poor women seeking relief for their families; young women away from family influence; or women who transgressed boundaries of ideal feminine behaviour by becoming prostitutes. These experiences, born of particular historical economic and social conditions, became portentous signifiers of disorder when translated into the cultural 'knowledges' of the middle class. And these signs of disorder and the failure to make progress exercised the minds of those middle-class observers who, because of personal desire or social status, were the vocal guardians of English society's well-being. Hence, where women failed to fulfil the most 'natural' and 'fundamental' roles preordained by their gender, the resulting alarm was palpable and often urgently expressed.

Women's material circumstances were read through a moral lens which ensured that purely economic interpretations were overwhelmed by constructions about disordering female sexuality, both in broader social life and in the specific sites of workplace, workhouse and public streets. This perception of disorder took many different turns in the regional context of the north, exemplified by the overwhelming emphasis upon the figure of the prostitute, but also illustrated by reference to other women, suggesting that all working-class women were part of a continuum of disorder which stretched from prostitutes, through women in the leadworks and labouring in the countryside, to poor women in general. In turn, by the end of the century, concern about the nature of 'perverted' femininity coalesced most obviously around the figure of the working-class mother, as the rhetoric of generational progress began to hold sway. Just as Ross has found for London, in Northumberland by the 1870s 'mothers were "discovered" by social thinkers',[7] and the links made between the welfare of families, and the moral and social welfare

---

7   Ellen Ross, *Love and toil: motherhood in outcast London 1870–1918*, New York 1993, 5.

of the community, were expressed in a more sustained manner than at any other time throughout the period.[8]

Many of the experiences and situations of working-class women were, therefore, constructed against a set of ideals about femininity and motherhood. These ideals, which implied restraint and the maintenance of limits, were counterposed against middle-class presumptions of working-class feminine excess, especially in interpretations of women's sexuality, but also in their public behaviour and economic habits. And it was working-class femininity, uncontrolled by the 'civilised' prescriptions of the middle class, which threatened the order so highly valued in the Victorian bourgeois imagination.

Working-class femininity was shaped and performed, in the context of both work and poverty, at the intersection of material conditions and cultural meanings. However, the women were never passive participants in the processes of forging working-class feminine identity. While middle-class conceptions of progress may have manifested themselves as a drive to fix female identity, the variety of material conditions and the individual responses of women illustrated that idealised visions of how women should behave and what their priorities should be, were subject to constant processes of negotiation. Of course, negotiations of femininity transcended relationships between working-class women and middle-class observers and reformers as well. Classifications of respectable feminine behaviour, the observation of gendered spaces, the construction of women's identity, also occurred within working-class culture. In many situations, differences in power and status between the working women and poor women in the region, and those who sought to order or even 'reform' their lives, at times appeared to leave little room for manoeuvre. Yet none the less, there appear consistent threads of resistance and subtle subversion within the sources, as women made use of a repertoire of survival strategies which more closely accorded with their own economic needs and cultural priorities.

Reading the past

In her short story written in 1985, science fiction writer Zoë Fairbairns creates a dystopia in which 'disorderly' women from history have been transformed into frozen relics. Released from a state of suspended animation sometime in the future, the story's female protagonist, herself a woman from a bygone age who has been thawed, encounters Mr Constable. He is a researcher employed by the department responsible for the collection and preservation of these female 'objects' from the past. She is astonished and bemused by what appear to her as Constable's at times ludicrous attempts to

[8] On the rise of maternalism in the period, and its relationship to politics see Anna Davin, 'Imperialism and motherhood', *History Workshop* v (1978), 9–65.

fashion a simple and complete historical story of the women from the official documents and odd material fragments in his possession. She admonishes him: 'We were never all the same, Mr. Constable. You have to understand that, even if it does spoil your research.' Her laughter and immediate physical presence unnerve the collector, and, escaping from him, she is pleased to locate and enter the archival repository where the women 'relics' of the past are held in freezer cabinets:

> As I descend the steps, though, my optimism takes on an edge of unease.
> The air is very cold. . . . The lids of the cabinets are down, and the switches locked to FREEZE.
> With effort I can raise the lids but I cannot throw the switches. The women have been violently flung back into cold storage. Their postures of struggle are frozen in blocks of ice.
> For a long time I am immobilised by despair. . . . To pass the time I start to talk to myself. . . . My words seem to arouse strong emotions inside the deep freeze cabinets, because with growls and roars and gushes of water the ice breaks and the women sit up as one and shout with incredulous laughter. . . .[9]

And so, in this story at least, the conversations in cold rooms begin again.

But have they ever ended? The task of conceptualising past experience through the refracting prisms of the present can situate the historian in a position similar to that occupied by Mr Constable. Unable to grasp 'the raw facts of the past', the focal points we adopt inevitably determine the questions which we ask about the past and its meanings. In our answers, we occlude the many differences between women. We may hedge and qualify our findings, but create a text none the less which is far neater and more logical than raw life.

It is rare enough in history for laughter ever to be recorded. For some women in nineteenth-century Northumberland, there was perhaps little enough laughter. The sources, and certainly those relating to poor and working women, point us more insistently to stories of want, destitution and woe; evidence of botched abortions and infanticide; medical inquests on aged women who died in the streets; and encounters with twelve-year-old prostitutes. There are times when there seems little evidence to contradict Hobbes's earlier vision of life as 'nasty, brutish, and short', although the odd chink of light appears to disrupt the dreary formula: the famous music hall performer, Vesta Tilley, appears at Gateshead workhouse;[10] a photographer captures an image of children enthralled by an organ-grinder; Munby makes a brief remark about a woman laughing (at him, or with him?). Yet, in general, where women are represented or more rarely where they speak, it is within texts which are constructed from the outset around motifs of corruption,

---

9   Zöe Fairbairns, 'Relics', in Jen Green and Sarah Lefanu (eds), *Despatches from the frontiers of the female mind*, London 1985, 175–89 at pp. 187–9.
10 Vesta Tilley performed there in 1894: Manders, *History of Gateshead*, 229.

meanness or disorder. This evidence for the most part is 'all we have of them'.[11] Interspersed with this material is the occasional history of individual success, exceptions where women 'escaped' to better circumstances.[12] But whether in Wooler or Newcastle, the avenues of 'escape' from processes of gendered identity constructions and representation and the social relations which were constituted through them were few and temporary.

Accounts of specific historical events often convey a firm sense of completion. When in 1908 Lord George Hamilton had all but finished his duties to the 1905 Royal Commission on the Poor Laws, for example, and had drafted a section of work on the treatment of poor unmarried mothers, he wrote in anticipation of an ending to Helen Bosanquet: 'I am shouting hurrah like a schoolboy.'[13] In the area of gendered identity formations in the past, both for poor women and others, an historical and theoretical view which posits the constant fluidity and shifting definitions of femininity presents no obvious point of completion. The unmarried mothers about whom Lord Hamilton wrote were always negotiating their identity and negotiating the terms of their economic and cultural existence. Whether for this group, or for other working-class and poor women in different circumstances, historians can unravel the ways in which feminine identity was constructed and experienced, and avoid the uncritical replication of contemporary categories only through critical readings of contemporary texts. Significantly, such an approach provides glimpses of those times when women's agency was evident, as they negotiated and transgressed prescribed boundaries of behaviour for working-class women. Reading women's applications for poor relief; assessing the obvious omissions from the 1834 Poor Law Report; scrutinising labels of individual 'failure' in the context of charitable institutions; and re-examining contemporary invocations of custom and 'natural' difference in the histories of women's employment: all these examples show that critical reading, reading against the grain of sources, reveals female agency, as well as the complex interweavings of gender conceptions in the contemporary imagination.

And considering the ways in which gender identity was elaborated in the past, we are inevitably confronted with broader problems about the meanings of gender in other periods. Ellen Ross has observed that examining past constructions of motherhood 'permits us to be sharper observers of the fissures and fantasies in our own contemporary versions'.[14] The same

[11] Adrienne Rich, 'Natural resources', *The dream of a common language*, in J. Swindells, *Victorian writing and working women*, Cambridge 1985, 116.

[12] For example, Eleanor Dixon left Wooler for New South Wales in 1869 with her mother, with assistance from the Guardians. Her 'success', if such it can be called, was that Eleanor eventually married Henry Parkes and became 'first lady' of the colony: Collier and Stewart, *Wooler and Glendale*, 44.

[13] Lord George Hamilton to Helen Bosanquet, 17 Sept. 1908, Bosanquet papers, NU Archives, trunk iii/1, letter 53.

[14] Ross, *Love and toil*, 4.

observation holds for an exploration of the other facets of the processes by which gendered identities are forged. My consideration of women, their circumstances, and the meanings constructed around them in the Victorian north-east, through study of both language and material conditions, is then a part of that ongoing political engagement with the subject in the present – and inevitably, reflected upon with an eye to different (and, I hope, warmer) 'conversations' in the future.

Bibliography

Unpublished primary sources

Cambridge, Trinity College, Wren Library
A. J. Munby manuscript diary, vol. xxi, 1863

Durham University Archives
121/9 papers of Earl Grey
234/8 Newcastle and Gateshead Poor Children's Holiday Association and Rescue Agency, annual report 1901

London, British Library
MS Bell 11621.i.2

London, Greater London Record Office
A/FWA/C/F7/1 Provincial Charity Organisation Society files, Sunderland

London, Public Record Office, Chancery Lane
ASSI 45/64 depositions, Northumberland
ASSI 45/65 depositions, Northumberland

London, Public Record Office, Kew
MH 12/3096 Gateshead Union correspondence, 1887–92
MH 12/3201 South Shields Union correspondence, 1834–40
MH 12/8964 Bellingham Union correspondence, 1836–40
MH 12/9002 Castle Ward Union correspondence, 1836–41
MH 12/9020 Glendale Union correspondence, 1834–45
MH 12/9022 Glendale Union correspondence, 1853–61
MH 12/9023 Glendale Union correspondence, 1862–71
MH 12/9096 Newcastle Union correspondence, 1834–40
MH 12/9098 Newcastle Union correspondence, 1851–2
MH 12/9099 Newcastle Union correspondence, 1853–4
MH 12/9129 Newcastle Union correspondence, June–Dec. 1892
MH 12/9130 Newcastle Union correspondence, 1893–4
MH 12/9144 Rothbury Union correspondence, 1836–41
MH 12/9145 Rothbury Union correspondence, 1834–45

London, Salvation Army Archives (International Heritage Centre, Kings Cross)
Girls' statement books (country), Newcastle Salvation Army Rescue Home
Rebecca Jarrett manuscript autobiography
Women's social and rescue work, report 1904

225

Newcastle, Central Library, Local History Collection
L334.7 Women's Friendly Societies

Newcastle, Tyne and Wear Archives Service
213/173 letters of Elizabeth Spence Watson
T241/1–4 applications for parochial relief, parish of All Saints
359/1 Poor Law Guardians' minute books
359/300–1 Poor Law Inspectors' returns
359/341 removal orders, Newcastle Union
359/342 removal orders, Newcastle Union
359/358 Newcastle upon Tyne Borough Pauper Lunatic Asylum, medical certificates
359/371 Newcastle upon Tyne Borough Pauper Lunatic Asylum, reports
L361/30227 Newcastle Relief Fund
490/46–145 Newcastle upon Tyne Borough Pauper Lunatic Asylum, orders for the reception of pauper patients
584 Brandling Place Home for Penitent Women, records
586/1 Asylum for Female Penitents, annual reports
595/72–4 General Soup Kitchen, minute books
672/197 Lying-In Hospital and Outdoor Charity for Poor Married Women, minute book
1512 Lead Industry records
1547/10 Newcastle Dispensary, account
1547/10 Institution for the Cure and Prevention of Contagious Fever in Newcastle and Gateshead, report

Newcastle University Archives
Bosanquet papers

Northumberland County Record Office
452/D8/13 Bamborough [sic] Castle Dispensary, case book, 1881–5
452/D8/25 Bamburgh Castle School, list of boarders, 1874
851 diary and notebook of farming practices by an apprentice, Lilburn Grange Farm, 1842
958/22 census enumerators' returns, Carham Parish, Glendale, 1871
2114/5 letter from the bailiff of the duke of Northumberland to Thomas Robson, 17 Dec. 1808
3435 Diocesan Society for the Protection of Women and Children, minute book, 1885–97
MF 23 census enumerators' returns, Carham parish, Glendale, 1851
NC 12/4 Newcastle upon Tyne Constabulary, register of beer houses
NC 12/25, 2180 Alnwick House of Correction, journal and order book
NL/6/5 Newcastle-upon-Tyne Police-Aided Association for the Clothing of Destitute Children, annual report
ZS1/72 Middleton Hall [Simpson] MSS, labour agreements
EP86/124 Workhouse Visitors' Book, St Nicholas's parish

Reading University Archives
NORTHUM 1 farm account books and agreements
NORTHUM 2 farm account books and agreements

Official documents and publications (in date order)

Debates of the House of Commons, 3rd ser. xxii–xxiii, 1834

Report from the commissioners for inquiry into the administration and practical operation of the poor laws, PP 1834 [44] xxvii

Reports from the Select Committee on the Poor Law Amendment Act, 1838 [1837–38 (220)] xviii, pt I, sixteenth report

Report of commissioners on the employment of women and children in agriculture, PP 1843 [510] xii

Report of the commissioners for inquiring into the state of large towns and populous districts, second report 1845 [610] xvii

Reports of the Inspectors of Factories for the half-year ending 31 October, 1848, 1849 [1017], xvii

Census of Great Britain, 1851, 1852–3 [1691–1] lxxxviii, pt i

Census of Great Britain, 1851, 1852–3 [1691–11] lxxxviii, pt ii

Report of commissioners on children's, young person's and women's employment in agriculture, first report PP 1867–8 [4068–1] xvii

Census of England and Wales, 1871, 1873 [872] lxxi, pt i

Census of England and Wales, 1871, 1873 [c. 872] lxxii, pt ii

Census of England and Wales, 1891, 1892–3 [c.7058] cvi

Royal Commission on Labour, The Agricultural Labourer, PP 1893–4 [6894–iii] xxxv

Report from the departmental committee on the various lead industries, PP 1893–4 [c. 7239–1] xvii

Newspapers and periodicals

Alnwick Mercury
Berwick Advertiser
Charity Organisation Review
Daily Chronicle
The Deliverer
Hexham Courant
Morpeth Herald
Newcastle Chronicle
Newcastle Courant
Newcastle Diocesan Calendar
Newcastle Diocesan Gazette
Newcastle Journal
Tyne Mercury

Primary printed sources

'A day at the Tyne factories', *Penny Magazine* xiii/797 (1844), 340–2

'Agricola', 'Domestic condition of the Northumbrian peasantry', *Northumbrian Mirror* xi/12 (1840), 253–62

An affectionate address to the inhabitants of Newcastle and Gateshead on the present alarming visitation of divine providence in the fatal ravages of the spasmodic cholera, Newcastle 1832

Anderson Graham, P., *The rural exodus*, London 1892

Anon., *Harvest homes (by the authoress of Enshrined Hearts)*, printed for private distribution [Newcastle, c. 1862] (NCL)

Anon., *Inquiry into the condition of the poor in Newcastle upon Tyne*, Newcastle upon Tyne 1850

Anon., *The picture of Newcastle upon Tyne 1807*, facsimile edn, London 1969

Bede, Cuthbert [Edward Bradley], *The further adventures of Mr Verdant Green, an Oxford undergraduate*, London 1854, repr. Liverpool 1908

Blakely, Robert, *Cottage politics; or, letters on the new poor law bill*, London, n.d. [c. 1838]

'The boarding-out system', *Conference on poor law administration*, n.p. 1872 (NCL, DY 56, no. 9)

Booth, Mrs Bramwell, *A brief review of the first year's work*, n.p. 1891

Booth, Charles, *Life and labour of the people in London*, 2nd edn, London 1892

Bosanquet, Helen, 'The economics of women's work and wages', *The National Liberal Club Political and Economic Circle: Transactions* v (1907), 1–16

———— *Rich and poor*, London 1896

———— *The standard of life*, London 1906

———— *The strength of the people*, 2nd edn, London 1903

Boyle, J. R., *Vestiges of old Newcastle and Gateshead*, Newcastle upon Tyne 1890

Burdett-Coutts, Angela (ed.), *Woman's mission*, London 1893

Christie, Revd J., *Northumberland: its history, its features, and its people*, London 1904

Cobbett, William, *Rural rides*, London 1830, repr. London 1886

Davies, Emily, *Thoughts on some questions relating to women, 1860–1908*, Cambridge 1910

Dendy, Helen, 'The position of women in industry', in Bernard Bosanquet (ed.), *Aspects of the social problem*, London 1895, 63–76

Donkin, Samuel, *The agricultural labourers of Northumberland: their physical and social condition*, Newcastle 1869

———— *Observations upon the nature of parochial relief and the principles upon which the poor law amendment act is founded*, Newcastle 1837

Fynes, R., *The miners of Northumberland and Durham: a history of their social and political progress*, Blyth 1873, repr. Newcastle 1986

Gilly, Revd W. S., *The peasantry of the border: an appeal on their behalf*, Berwick upon Tweed 1841

Guide to schools, homes and refuges in England for the benefit of girls and women, London 1888

Hardy, James, *Harvest customs in Northumberland*, Newcastle 1844

Heath, Richard, *The English peasant: studies historical, local and biographic*, London 1893

Higgs, M., *Glimpses into the abyss*, London 1906

———— *How to deal with the unemployed*, London 1904

Horsley, James, *She's sumboddy's bairn*, Newcastle c. 1880 (TWAS 1074/228)

Howitt, W., *The rural life of England*, London 1838

Kebbel, T. E., *The agricultural labourer: a short summary of his position*, London 1893

Lawson, A., *The farmer's practical instructor*, Newcastle 1827

Loch, C. S., *An examination of 'General' Booth's social scheme*, London 1890

—— How to help cases of distress: a handy reference book for almoners, almsgivers and others, London 1883, facsimile edn, Plymouth 1977

Mackenzie, E., A descriptive and historical account of the town and county of Newcastle upon Tyne, including the borough of Gateshead, Newcastle 1827

Marshall, William, The review and abstract of the county reports to the board of agriculture, i, n.p. 1818, repr. Newton Abbott 1969

Martineau, Harriet, Deerbrook, London 1839, repr. London 1983

—— Poor laws and paupers illustrated, London 1833

Mill, J. S., The subjection of women, London 1869, repr. Oxford 1974

Mitchell, H. A., A report of the proceedings in the mayor's chamber, Newcastle upon Tyne, during the mayoralty of Geo. Shadforth esq., 1829–1830, Newcastle n.d.

Neville, Hastings M., A corner in the north: yesterday and today with border folk, Newcastle 1909

Newcastle-on-Tyne Society for the Organisation of Charitable Relief and Repressing Mendicity, annual report 1885, Newcastle upon Tyne 1885

Ogle Moore, Helen and Edith Hare, 'Report to the Society for the Employment of Women on the work of women in the white-lead trade at Newcastle', in J. Boucherett and H. Blackburn (eds), The condition of working women and the factory acts, London 1896, 78–83

'Our single women', North British Review xxxvi (1862), 62–87

Pashley, Robert, Pauperism and the poor laws, London 1852

Report of the Cottage Improvement Society of north Northumberland, London 1842

Rewcastle, J., Newcastle as it is: reviewed in its moral aspects, social state and sanitary condition, Newcastle 1854

Richardson, M. A., The local historian's table book, Newcastle 1846

Rowntree, B. S., Poverty: a study of town life, London 1901

Russell, Charles E., Social problems of the north, London 1913, repr. London 1980

Sherard, R., The cry of the poor, London 1901

—— 'The white slaves of England, V: the white-lead workers of Newcastle', Pearson's Magazine ii (1896), 523–30

Stallard, J. H., The female casual and her lodging, London 1866

Stuart, Revd H., Agricultural labourers as they were, are, and should be, 2nd edn, Edinburgh 1854

Thirty-fourth annual report of the Girls' Ragged and Industrial Schools, n.p. 1881 (NCL, DY 56/13)

Tomlinson, W. W., A comprehensive guide to the county of Northumberland, London 1888, repr. Newcastle upon Tyne 1985

Transactions of the National Association for the Promotion of Social Science, Newcastle upon Tyne meeting, n.p. 1870

Twining, Louisa, Recollections of workhouse visiting and management during twenty-five years, London 1880

Walker, Gladstone, Wages and pauperism: being a report as to the occupations and earnings of recipients of out-door relief and their dependants, Newcastle 1915

Whellan, W., History, topography, and directory of Newcastle upon Tyne, London 1855

White, Walter, Northumberland and the border, London 1859

Wilson, J., Memories of a labour leader, London 1910

Wythen Baxter, G. R., The book of the bastiles: or, the history of the working of the new poor law, London 1841

Secondary sources

Ashforth, David, 'Settlement and removal in urban areas: Bradford, 1834–71', in Rose, *The poor and the city*, 57–91

Bakhtin, M., *Rabelais and his world*, Cambridge, Mass. 1968

Barret-Ducrocq, Françoise, *Love in the time of Victoria: sexuality, class, and gender in Victorian London*, trans. John Howe, London 1991

Bartky, S., 'Foucault, femininity and the modernisation of patriarchal power', in I. Diamond and L. Quinby (eds), *Feminism and Foucault: reflections on resistance*, Boston 1988, 61–86

Bennett, Judith, ' "History that stands still": women's work in the European past', *Feminist Studies* xiv (1988), 269–83

Bennison, Brian, 'Drunkenness in turn-of-the-century Newcastle upon Tyne', *Local Population Studies* lii (1994), 14–22

Berg, Maxine, 'What difference did women's work make to the industrial revolution?', *History Workshop* xxxv (1993), 22–44

Blaug, M., 'The poor law report re-examined', *Journal of Economic History* xxiv (1964), 229–43

Bordo, Susan, 'Feminism, postmodernism, and gender-scepticism', in Nicholson, *Feminism/postmodernism*, 133–56

Borzello, F., A. Kuhn, J. Pack and C. Wedd, 'Living dolls and "real women" ', in A. Kuhn (ed.), *The power of the image: essays on representation and sexuality*, London 1985, 9–18

Bowlby, Rachel, *Just looking: consumer culture in Dreiser, Gissing and Zola*, New York 1985

Briggs, Asa, *Victorian cities*, 2nd edn, Harmondsworth 1968

Brodribb, Somer, *Nothing mat(t)ters: a feminist critique of postmodernism*, North Melbourne 1992

Brundage, Anthony, *The making of the new poor law*, London 1978

―――― David Eastwood and Peter Mandler, 'Debate: the making of the new poor law *redivivus*', *Past and Present* cxxvii (1990), 183–201

Butler, Judith, *Gender trouble: feminism and the subversion of identity*, London 1990

―――― 'Performative acts and gender constitution: an essay in phenomenology and feminist theory', *Theatre Journal* xl (1988), 519–31

Callaghan, Thomas, *Lang way to the panshop*, Rothbury 1987

Cass, B., 'The changing face of poverty in Australia, 1972–1982', *Australian Feminist Studies* i (1985), 67–89.

Chambers, J. D. and G. E. Mingay, *The agricultural revolution, 1750–1880*, London 1966

Checkland, S. G. and E. O. A. Checkland (eds), *The poor law report of 1834*, Harmondsworth 1974

Clark, Anna K., 'Rape or seduction?: a controversy over sexual violence in the nineteenth century', in London Feminist History Group, *The sexual dynamics of history*, London 1983, 13–27

Coats, A. W. (ed.), *Poverty in the Victorian age: debates on the issue from nineteenth-century critical journals*, II: *The English poor laws, 1834–1870*, Westmead 1973

Common, Jack, *Kiddar's luck*, London 1951, repr. Gateshead 1975

Cookson, Catherine, *Our Kate*, London 1969

Crosby, Christina, *The ends of history: Victorians and 'the woman question'*, New York 1991

Crowther, M. A., 'The later years of the workhouse', in Thane, *Origins of British social policy*, 36–55

———— *The workhouse system 1834–1929: the history of an English social institution*, London 1981

Darnton, Robert, *The great cat massacre and other episodes in French cultural history*, London 1984

Davidoff, Leonore, 'Class and gender in Victorian England', in J. L. Newton and others (eds), *Sex and class in women's history*, London 1983, 17–71

———— 'Mastered for life: servant and wife in Victorian and Edwardian England', *Journal of Social History* vii (1974), 406–28

Davin, Anna, 'Imperialism and motherhood', *History Workshop* v (1978), 9–65

de Sola Pinto, V. and A. E. Rodway (eds), *The common muse*, Harmondsworth 1965

Dex, Shirley, 'Issues of gender and employment', *Social History* xiii (1988), 141–50

Digby, A., *The poor law in nineteenth-century England and Wales*, London 1982

Drake, Barbara, *Women in trade unions*, London 1920, repr. London 1984

DuBois, E. and others, 'Politics and culture in women's history: a symposium', *Feminist Studies* vi (1980), 26–64

Duby, Georges, 'Ideologies in social history', in J. Le Goff and P. Nora (eds), *Constructing the past*, Cambridge 1985, 151–65

Duden, Barbara, *The woman beneath the skin: a doctor's patients in eighteenth-century Germany*, Cambridge, Mass. 1991

Dunbabin, J. P. D., *Rural discontent in nineteenth-century Britain*, London 1974

Fairbairns, Zöe, 'Relics', in Jen Green and Sarah Lefanu (eds), *Despatches from the frontiers of the female mind*, London 1985, 175–89

Fairbank, Jenty, *Booth's boots: social service beginnings in the Salvation Army*, London 1983

Fiske, John, *Power plays, power works*, London 1993

Foucault, Michel, *The archaeology of knowledge*, Paris 1969, trans. A. M. Sheridan-Smith, New York 1971

———— *Discipline and punish: the birth of the prison*, Paris 1975, trans. A. Sheridan, Harmondsworth 1977

———— *The history of sexuality*, Paris 1976, trans. R. Hurley, Harmondsworth 1978

———— *Power/knowledge: selected interviews and other writings, 1972–77*, ed. C. Gordon, Brighton 1980

Fraser, C. M. and K. Emsley, *Tyneside*, Newton Abbott 1973

Fraser, Nancy, 'The uses and abuses of French discourse theory for feminist politics', *boundary 2* xvii (1990), 82–101

———— and Linda Nicholson, 'Social criticism without philosophy: an encounter between feminism and postmodernism', *Theory, Culture and Society* v (1988), 373–94

Gallagher, Catherine, 'The body versus the social body in the works of Thomas Malthus and Henry Mayhew', in C. Gallagher and T. Laqueur (eds), *The making of the modern body: sexuality and society in the nineteenth century*, Berkeley 1987, 83–106

Game, A. and R. Pringle, 'Beyond gender at work: secretaries', in N. Grieve and A. Burns (eds), *Australian women: new feminist perspectives*, Melbourne 1986, 273–91

Gatens, M., 'Power, bodies and difference', in M. Barrett and A. Phillips (eds), *Destabilizing theory: contemporary feminist debates*, Cambridge 1992, 120–37

Glastonbury, Marion, 'The best kept secret: how working-class women live and what they know', *Women's Studies International Quarterly* ii (1979), 171–81

Glendinning, C. and J. Millar (eds), *Women and poverty in Britain*, Brighton 1987

Graham, Hilary, 'Women's poverty and caring', in Glendinning and Millar, *Women and poverty in Britain*, 221–40

Green, Jen and Sarah Lefanu (eds), *Despatches from the frontier of the female mind*, London 1990

Gregson, Keith, 'Poor law and organized charity: the relief of exceptional distress in north-east England, 1870–1910', in Rose, *The poor and the city*, 93–131

Grosz, Elizabeth, *Volatile bodies: towards a corporeal feminism*, St Leonards 1994

Gunew, Sneja, 'Feminist knowledge: critique and construct', in S. Gunew (ed.), *Feminist knowledge: critique and construct*, London 1990, 13–35

Hall, Catherine, 'The sweet delights of home', in M. Perrot (ed.), *A history of private life*, iv, trans. A. Goldhammer, Cambridge, Mass. 1990, 47–93

——— *White, male and middle class: explorations in feminism and history*, London 1992

Hammerton, A. James, *Cruelty and companionship: conflict in nineteenth-century married life*, London 1992

Harker, Margaret F., *Victorian and Edwardian photographs*, London 1982

Harrison, Brian, 'Class and gender in modern British labour history', *Past and Present* cxxiv (1989), 121–58

——— *Peaceable kingdom: stability and change in modern Britain*, Oxford 1982

Headlam, Cuthbert, *The three northern counties of England*, Gateshead 1939

Hennessy, R., *Materialist feminism and the politics of discourse*, New York 1993

Hennock, E. P., 'The measurement of urban poverty: from the metropolis to the nation 1880–1920', *Economic History Review* 2nd ser. xl (1987), 208–27

Henriques, Ursula, 'Bastardy and the new poor law', *Past and Present* xxxvii (1967), 103–29

Hepple, L. W., *A history of Northumberland and Newcastle upon Tyne*, Cicester 1976

Higgs, Edward, 'Women, occupations and work in the nineteenth-century censuses', *History Workshop* xxiii (1987), 59–80

Hill, Bridget, *Eighteenth-century women: an anthology*, 2nd edn, London 1987

Himmelfarb, G., *The idea of poverty: England in the early industrial age*, London 1985

Hollen Lees, Lynn, 'The survival of the unfit: welfare policies and family maintenance in nineteenth-century London', in Mandler, *Uses of charity*, 68–91

Hostettler, E., 'Gourlay Steell and the sexual division of labour', *History Workshop* iv (1977), 95–100

——— 'Women farm workers in eighteenth and nineteenth-century Northumberland', *North East Labour History* xvi (1982), 40–2

Howkins, Alun, 'Rider Haggard and rural England: an essay in literature and history', in Shaw and Chase, *Imagined past*, 81–94

Hudson, Pat, *The industrial revolution*, London 1992

John, Angela, *By the sweat of their brow: women workers at Victorian coalmines*, London 1980

Johnson, Paul, *Saving and spending: the working-class economy in Britain, 1870–1939*, Oxford 1985

Kaplan, Cora, ' "Like a housemaid's fancies": the representation of working-class women in nineteenth-century writing', in Susan Sheridan (ed.), *Grafts: feminist cultural criticism*, London–New York 1988, 55–75

Knott, John, *Popular opposition to the poor law*, London 1986

Kristeva, Julia, 'Women's time', in Toril Moi (ed.), *The Kristeva reader*, Oxford 1986, 187–213

Langman, Lauren, 'Neon cages: shopping for subjectivity', in R. Shields (ed.), *Lifestyle shopping: the subject of consumption*, London 1992, 40–82

Laqueur, Thomas, *Making sex: body and gender from the Greeks to Freud*, Cambridge, Mass.–London 1990

Levine, Philippa, 'Rough usage: prostitution, law and the social historian', in A. Wilson (ed.), *Rethinking social history*, Manchester 1991, 266–92

Lewis, Jane, *Women in England 1870–1950: sexual divisions and social change*, Brighton 1984

——— 'The working-class wife and mother and state intervention, 1870–1918', in Lewis, *Labour and love*, 99–120

——— (ed.), *Labour and love: women's experience of home and family 1850–1940*, Oxford 1986

——— and D. Piachaud, 'Women and poverty in the twentieth century', in Glendinning and Millar, *Women and poverty in Britain*, 28–52

Littlewood, Barbara and Linda Mahood, 'Prostitutes, magdalenes and wayward girls: dangerous sexualities of working-class women in Victorian Scotland', *Gender and History* iii (1991), 160–75

Long, Jane, 'Sex work and female poverty: the case of nineteenth century Newcastle upon Tyne', in P. Hetherington and P. Maddern (eds), *Sexuality and gender in history: selected essays*, Perth 1993, 144–66

Lynch, K. and G. Hack, *Site planning*, Cambridge, Mass. 1984

McCord, Norman, 'The implementation of the 1834 Poor Law Amendment Act on Tyneside', *International Review of Social History* xiv (1969), 90–108

——— 'The making of modern Newcastle', *Archaeologia Aeliana* 5th ser. ix (1981), 333–46

——— *North east England: an economic and social history*, London 1979

——— 'The poor law and philanthropy', in Derek Fraser (ed.), *The new poor law in the nineteenth century*, London 1976, 87–110

——— 'Ratepayers and social policy', in Thane, *Origins of British social policy*, 21–35

——— and D. J. Rowe, 'Industrialisation and urban growth in north-east England', *International Review of Social History* xxii (1977), 30–64

McDonogh, G., 'The geography of emptiness', in R. Rotenberg and G. McDonogh (eds), *The cultural meaning of urban space*, Westport, Conn. 1993, 3–15

McHoul, A. and W. Grace, *A Foucault primer: discourse, power and the subject*, Carlton 1993

McKibbin, R. I., 'Social class and social observation in Edwardian England', *Transactions of the Royal Historical Society* 5th ser. xxviii (1978), 175–99

McNay, L., *Foucault and feminism: power, gender and the self*, Cambridge 1992

Malcolmson, Patricia, 'Laundresses and the laundry trade in Victorian England', *Victorian Studies* xxiv (1980–1), 439–62

Manders, F. W. D., *A history of Gateshead*, Gateshead 1973

Mandler, Peter, 'The making of the new poor law *redivivus*', *Past and Present* cvii (1987), 131–57

———— 'Poverty and charity: an introduction', in Mandler, *Uses of charity*, 1–37

———— (ed.), *The uses of charity: the poor on relief in the nineteenth-century metropolis*, Philadelphia 1990

Mayne, A., *The imagined slum: newspaper representation in three cities 1870–1914*, Leicester 1993

Mitchell, B. R. and P. Deane, *Abstract of British historical statistics*, Cambridge 1962

Mulligan, Lotte and Judith Richards, 'A "radical" problem: the poor and the English reformers in the mid-seventeenth century', *Journal of British Studies* xxix (1990), 118–46

Nicholson, Linda (ed.), *Feminism/postmodernism*, New York 1990

Oren, Laura, 'The welfare of women in laboring families: England, 1860–1950', in M. Hartmann and L. W. Banner (eds), *Clio's consciousness raised*, New York 1974, 226–44

Pinchbeck, Ivy, *Women workers and the industrial revolution 1750–1850*, London 1930, repr. London 1969

Poovey, Mary, 'Domesticity and class formation: Chadwick's 1842 *Sanitary Report*', in David Simpson (ed.), *Subject to history: ideology, class, gender*, Ithaca 1991, 65–83

———— *Uneven developments: the ideological work of gender in mid-Victorian England*, Chicago 1988

Prochaska, F., *Women and philanthropy in nineteenth-century England*, Oxford 1980

'Rambler' [Revd A. S. Wardroper], *Rambles in Northumberland*, Newcastle 1924

Reed, M., 'The peasantry of nineteenth-century England: a neglected class?', *History Workshop* xviii (1984), 53–76

Rendall, Jane, *The origins of modern feminism: women in Britain, France and the United States, 1780–1860*, London 1985

Ridley, N., *Northumberland then and now*, London 1978

Robbins, Keith, *Nineteenth-century Britain: England Scotland, and Wales: the making of a nation*, Oxford 1989

Roberts, Elizabeth, *A woman's place: an oral history of working-class women, 1890–1940*, Oxford 1986

———— 'Women's strategies, 1890–1940', in Lewis, *Labour and love*, 223–47

Roberts, Michael, 'Sickles and scythes: women's work and men's work at harvest time', *History Workshop* vii (1979), 3–28

Rose, Michael, *The relief of poverty, 1834–1914*, 2nd edn, Basingstoke 1986

———— (ed.), *The poor and the city: the English poor law in its urban context, 1834–1914*, New York 1985

Rose, Sonya, *Limited livelihoods: gender and class in nineteenth-century England*, London 1992

Rosler, Martha, *3 works*, Halifax 1981

Ross, Ellen, 'Hungry children: housewives and London charity, 1870–1918', in Mandler, *Uses of charity*, 161–96

—— *Love and toil: motherhood in outcast London 1870–1918*, New York 1993

—— ' "Not the sort that would sit on the doorstep": respectability in pre-World War I London neighbourhoods', *International Labor and Working Class History* xxvii (1985), 39–59

Rowe, D. J., *Lead manufacturing in Britain: a history*, London 1983

Rushton, P., 'The poor law, the parish, and the community in north-east England, 1600–1800', *Northern History* xxv (1989), 135–52

Samuel, Raphael, 'Soft-focus nostalgia', *New Statesman*, 27 May 1983, special supplement

Scott, A. M., 'Women's working dress on the farms of the east borders', *Costume* x (1977), 41–8

Scott, Hilda, *Working your way to the bottom: the feminization of poverty*, London 1984

Scott, Joan W., 'The evidence of experience', *Critical Inquiry* xvii (1991), 773–97

—— 'Gender: a useful category of historical analysis', *American Historical Review* xci (1986), 1059–75

—— 'On language, gender and working-class history', *International Labor and Working-Class History* xxxi (1987), 1–13

—— 'The woman worker', in G. Fraisse and M. Perrott (eds), *A history of women in the west: emerging feminism from revolution to world war*, iv, Cambridge, Mass. 1993, 399–426

Sebestyen, A., 'Two women from two worlds', *Spare Rib*, June 1985, 21–4

Shaw, C. and M. Chase (eds), *The imagined past: history and nostalgia*, Manchester 1989

Shires, Linda, 'Afterword: ideology and the subject as agent', in Linda Shires (ed.), *Rewriting the Victorians: theory, history and the politics of gender*, London–New York 1992, 184–90

Shuttleworth, Sally, 'Female circulation: medical discourse and popular advertising in the mid-Victorian era', in Mary Jacobus, Evelyn Fox Keller and Sally Shuttleworth (eds), *Body/politics: women and the discourses of science*, London 1990, 47–68

Smart, Carol, 'Disruptive bodies and unruly sex: the regulation of reproduction and sexuality in the nineteenth century', in Carol Smart (ed.), *Regulating womanhood: historical essays on marriage, motherhood and sexuality*, London 1992, 7–32

Snell, K., *Annals of the labouring poor: social change and agrarian England, 1600–1900*, Cambridge 1985

Sontag, Susan, *On photography*, New York 1977

Spain, Daphne, *Gendered spaces*, Chapel Hill, NC 1992

Stedman Jones, Gareth, *Outcast London*, Oxford 1971

Street, Paul, 'Painting deepest England: the late landscapes of John Linnell and the uses of nostalgia', in Shaw and Chase, *Imagined past*, 68–80

Swindells, J., *Victorian writing and working women*, Cambridge 1985

Taylor, L., 'The days of the bondager', *Scotsman*, 5 July 1978, 8

—— 'To be a farmer's girl: bondagers of border counties', *Country Life*, Oct. 1978, 1110–12

Tebbutt, M., *Making ends meet: pawnbroking and working-class credit*, Leicester 1983

Thane, P., *The foundations of the welfare state*, London 1982

———— 'Women and the poor law in Victorian and Edwardian England', *History Workshop* vi (1978), 29–51

———— (ed.), *The origins of British social policy*, London 1978

Thompson, E. P., 'Time, work-discipline and industrial capitalism', *Past and Present* xxxviii (1967), 56–97

———— and Eileen Yeo (eds), *The unknown Mayhew*, Harmondsworth 1973

Tickner, Lisa, *The spectacle of women: imagery of the suffrage campaign 1907–1914*, London 1987

Tilly, Louise, 'Gender, women's history and social history', and replies, *Social Science History* xiii (1989), 439–77

Tolson, Andrew, 'Social surveillance and subjectification: the emergence of "subculture" in the work of Henry Mayhew', *Cultural Studies* iv (1990), 113–27

Tong, Rosemarie, *Feminist thought: a comprehensive introduction*, 2nd edn, London 1992

Townsend, P., 'Measuring poverty', *British Journal of Sociology* v (1954), 130–7

———— *Poverty in the United Kingdom*, Harmondsworth 1979

Treble, J. H., *Urban poverty in Britain 1830–1914*, London 1979

Varikas, E., 'Gender, experience and subjectivity: the Tilly–Scott disagreement', *New Left Review* ccxi (1995), 89–101

Vicinus, Martha, ' "Helpless and unfriended": nineteenth-century domestic melodrama', *New Literary History* xiii (1981), 127–43

———— *Independent women: work and community for single women, 1850–1920*, London 1985

Vorspan, Rachel, 'Vagrancy and the new poor law in late-Victorian and Edwardian England', *English Historical Review* xcii (1977), 59–81

Walby, S., *Patriarchy at work: patriarchal and capitalist relations of production*, Minneapolis 1986

Walkowitz, Judith, *City of dreadful delight: narratives of sexual danger in late-Victorian London*, Chicago 1992

Walton, John, 'Poverty and lunacy: some thoughts on directions for future research', *Society for the Social History of Medicine* xxviii (1986), 64–7

Webb, S. and B. Webb, *English poor law history, II: The last hundred years*, London 1929

Weeks, Jeffrey, *Sex, politics and society: the regulation of sexuality since 1800*, London 1981

Wells, R. A. E., 'The development of the English rural proletariat and social protest, 1700–1850', *Journal of Peasant Studies* vi/2 (1979), 115–39

Wilson, Elizabeth, *The sphinx in the city*, London 1991

Unpublished sources

Thomson, D., 'Welfare in the past: a family or community responsibility?', unpubl. paper, 5th AMBHA Conference, Nov. 1987

Index

Abraham, May, 70–3
agricultural economy, 81, 84, 101–2
agricultural labour, 82–3, 102; day labour near towns, 82; division of labour, 101–3; government reports, 100–4, 105–7; mechanisation, 101–2; mobility of, 96–8. *See also* bondagers, bondaging system, cottars, flitting, hinds, hiring days
All Saints' parish, 122; poverty relief work, 121, 122–3, 128–9, 131, 158
Alnwick, 86, 89, 113, 203
appearances, 54–5, 166, 176–7. *See also* bondagers
Armstrong, Lady, 53, 175
Armstrong, Lord, 195
Aspin family, 141–2
Asylum for Female Penitents, 54, 172, 173–4
authority of historical records, *see* records

ballads, 199–200, 206
Baumgarten, Dr, 65, 66, 68–9, 71
Bellingham workhouse, 152
Blakey, Robert, 140–2
bondagers, 15, 79, 84–5; domestic skills, 96; dress, 82, 91–2, 110; in literature, 81–2, 102–3; morality, 92–3, 96, 98–9, 104; photograph, 30; poverty, 107, 112, 113–14; work, 90, 91, 95, 107
bondaging system, 81, 90, 217–18; compulsory hiring, 111; decline of, 102–3, 104–5, 109, 111; linked to slavery, 79–80, 111; origins, 83–6; pay system, 82. *See also* agricultural labour, flitting, hinds, hiring days
Booth, Florence, 182, 191
Booth, William, 181–2, 183, 193
Bosanquet, Charles, 159, 193, 194
Bosanquet, Helen, 139, 166, 170, 205
bourgeoisie, *see* middle class

Brandling Home, 53–4, 174–5, 182; outcomes for women, 177, 192
building labourers, 39, 57

carriers, 40, 123, 130
Castle Ward Union, 147–8
Chadwick, Edwin, 136, 142, 145
charitable relief, 162, 172, 178, 181; records, 14, 40; rescue and training, 53–4, 169–70
Charity Organisation Society, 112, 113, 181, 194; case work with households, 195–6, 197; co-operation with Poor Law agencies, 194–5; discourse of suspicion, 196–7; reporting to donors, 195; screening of applicants, 193, 195, 196, 197; wives excluded, 194, 197
charity workers: attitudes, 169–70, 172, 178, 183–4, 187; employed, 175–6; volunteer, 167, 168–9
children, poor, 31; in workhouses, 159; in charitable schools, 160
cholera, 49–50. *See also* infectious diseases
clothing, *see* appearances
coal mining, 15, 38–9
Cobbett, William, 86, 100
Common, Jack, 164–5, 206, 208; mother, 208–9, 211–12
contagious diseases, *see* infectious diseases
Cookson, Catherine, 165, 202, 204, 206, 213
Cookson & Co., 73
COS, *see* Charitable Organisation Society
Cottage Improvement Society, 93, 104
cottars, 83, 94, 146. *See also* agricultural labour
Crosby, Christina, 216, 218
Crowther, M. A., 141, 157–9
Culley brothers, 81

Davidoff, Leonore, 20, 111

237